KISSING THROUGH GLASS

KISSING THROUGH GLASS

THE INVISIBLE SHIELD BETWEEN AMERICANS AND ISRAELIS

JOYCE R. STARR

CB
CONTEMPORARY
BOOKS
CHICAGO

Library of Congress Cataloging-in-Publication Data

Starr, Joyce.
    Kissing through glass : the invisible shield between Americans
and Israelis / Joyce R. Starr.
      p.   cm.
    ISBN 0-8092-4379-2 (cloth) : $21.95
    1. United States—Relations—Israel.   2. Israel—Relations—
United States.   I. Title.
E183.8.8.I7S73   1990
303.48'27305694—dc20   90-39866
                                         CIP

Published by Contemporary Books, Inc.
180 North Michigan Avenue, Chicago, Illinois 60601
Manufactured in the United States of America
International Standard Book Number: 0-8092-4379-2

To my parents, Rachel and Reuben Starr, for believing so profoundly in the heart and in the mind

CONTENTS

KISSING THROUGH GLASS

PREFACE

THIS BOOK WAS BORN IN POLITICAL FRUSTRATION AND
ended in compassion for two peoples, two countries, two cultures: Americans and Israelis. The initial proposal for *Kissing Through Glass* sprouted from my mind about six months
after the Palestinian uprising against Israel erupted on December 9, 1987. The Israeli government response to this
intifada was the harshest episode in my increasing frustra-
tions with Israeli policy and with a people I thought I knew so
well.

Why, I kept asking myself, can't the Israelis behave "like
us"? How can it be that Americans and Israelis are so much
alike and yet so different? While I felt driven to understand,
it hardly occurred to me at the time that Israelis might find
Americans just as unfathomable.

In the days of yore, bodies of water, not paved roads,
served as the byways between cultures. This book is not
intended as a concrete answer but as a stream of possibilities,
with many minor tributaries. Hundreds of Americans and
Israelis generously opened their hearts and minds to help
speed the learning process.

I have attempted to present the reader with the human

dimensions of the American-Israeli relationship from the point of view of the average citizen in both countries, American and Israeli Jews, government negotiators, businesspeople, political leaders, journalists, and even a poet or two.

As it turned out—and one can never be certain just where the mind will take us—I did not write a book about Middle East policy or the Israeli-Palestinian conflict. Although I did spend many months interviewing West Bank and Gaza residents, these encounters and my reflections are yet another book. I present the reader here with a story of a romance, a rare moment in history when the strongest power in the world embraced one of the smallest, and the tale of their affair in emotional terms, as they slowly develop toward an uncertain but common future.

Washington, D.C.
May 1990

ACKNOWLEDGMENTS

TWO PEOPLE, AN AMERICAN AND AN ISRAELI, SHEP-herded this book. Writer and editorial consultant Frank W. Martin gave unsparingly of his time and counsel, educating me in the intricacies of the writing process. Architect and Renaissance man Zalman Enav tirelessly challenged me to deeper levels of cultural awareness and sensitivity.

I am also deeply appreciative of my friends Elynne Chaplik Aleskow and Ralph Katrosh for reading and cheering the manuscript to its conclusion, to Contemporary Books editor Bernard Shir-Cliff for his editorial improvements throughout the book's many phases, and to agent Robert Eringer and publisher Harvey Plotnick for believing in this work. Oswald Ratteray and Shelly Thorman contributed their invaluable transcribing talents. My gratitude to the Joseph Meyerhoff Fund for its support.

I extend special appreciation to my research associate, Steven Dinero, for his assistance in making sense of thousands of pages of transcripts and for his calm readiness to undertake any task along the way.

And to all the Americans and Israelis, named and unnamed, who agreed to be interviewed: no doubt the book is yours as much as mine.

INTRODUCTION

THE UNITED STATES AND ISRAEL ARE INTERTWINED IN a relationship unique in the annals of history. Never before have two nations been so intimately wedded by romantic emotions, or so mutually obsessed in a marathon dance of courtship rather than conflict.

Yet the astonishing fact is that Americans and Israelis who know each other through direct, intensive contact—not through fantasy or film—are stirred by feelings of both love and fury, admiration and envy. Like two lovers forever fated to be kissing through glass, Americans and Israelis are so often denied the full warmth of intimacy by a cool, almost invisible, barrier.

The human dimensions of this alliance, the emotions that both underlie and transcend national priorities, tell a story hidden by years of guilt, giving, guts, and glory. How do the two lovers perceive and describe each other in the safe recesses of their minds and hearts? To the best of my knowledge, this tale has never been told.

After more than forty years of extraordinary involvement on every level of society, Americans and Israelis often remain as distant in knowledge, understanding, and mentality as we are in terms of the ocean and miles that separate us. Yes, the library shelves are thick with works emphasizing our common religious and philosophical roots. And no doubt Israelis and Americans share an overriding sense of destiny as the chosen people. For, in truth, most Americans in their heart of hearts also see their country as the chosen nation.

Even though many themes unite us—the Judeo-Christian ethos, the commitment to democratic values, the history as a land of immigrants, the political and strategic partnership—the people of our two nations have not succeeded in recognizing, let alone bridging, significant cultural gaps. These cultural differences shape the most important arenas of interaction between the United States and Israel: government negotiations, business negotiations, and negotiations between Jewish Americans and Jewish Israelis.

Despite the tremendous public and media exposure of Americans to Israel, and Israelis to the United States, each society's awareness of the other's daily life, customs, and pressures is typically superficial—even among those who should be most knowledgeable. Indeed, of all the Americans and Israelis interviewed for this book, not one expressed the confident belief that his or her world is deeply understood by more than a handful of individuals on the other side.

Yet, surprisingly, politics and ideology differ only slightly. Much more significant and overriding are the two societies' vastly differing approaches to friendship, civility, foreigners, and fate.

PART I

THE HUMAN DIMENSIONS OF THE AMERICAN-ISRAELI RELATIONSHIP

This is my first trip to the United States. Americans are very polite, but trying to relate to them is like kissing through glass.

—David Grossman,
Israeli author of *The Yellow Wind*

1
FOREIGNERS AND FATE

THE MOST FUNDAMENTAL GAP BETWEEN AMERICANS and Israelis at the deepest emotional level is the difference in outlook on life: innate optimism confronting innate pessimism.

Haven't the Israelis been doing the impossible since the founding of the state, winning all the "unwinnable" wars, counting miracles in their calculations and having the arithmetic come out right? Yet the truth is, Israelis as a people have never been deeply optimistic. They have only been deeply daring.

A *Time* magazine headline describing the Israeli raid into Entebbe, Uganda, on July 4, 1976, to free more than one hundred Israeli citizens highjacked aboard an Air France plane read, "We Do the Impossible." *Life* magazine captured the American image of Israelis for decades to come with its June 1967 cover photo of a strong, handsome Israeli soldier swimming in the Suez Canal, his gun held high. This man symbolized Israel's survival, its triumph in the Six-Day War, a conflict that could have as easily been lost as won. Israel's fate hung in the balance. Israel's feat of victory over awesome odds has been the enduring image for Americans ever since.

The Israeli David versus the Philistine Goliath became an integral episode in the American memory of world history.

But as Chaim Potok points out in *The Wanderings*, even the source of the metaphor is suspect. For it may not have been David, but more likely was Elhanan, a forgotten figure in Jewish history, who actually confronted and killed the giant.

The image of the invincible Israeli is a myth, fostered by the outside world, both friends and enemies, and reinforced by an Israeli leadership that easily grasped the advantage in being perceived as larger than life. But concealed behind the bravado, every Israeli knows the truth of his or her existence: an overriding sense of insecurity and fear, and a tendency never to take things at face value but to try to look beyond facades to determine what threats may lurk ahead. Israeli Prime Minister Levi Eshkol told his advisers in the glowing aftermath of the June 1967 Six-Day War, "When you deal with the Americans, you must act like Samson and look like a nebbish [a timid, meek, or ineffectual person]"—which translates into, "Let the Americans see you as a victorious underdog, constantly facing threats, but able to overcome with just a little bit of outside help from true friends."

The threats were real, and the State of Israel perfected its case for national insecurity into a higher art form while maintaining the "can do" image that can also be so deceptive.

The Israeli experience is based in the Jewish experience—several thousand years of persecution culminating in the Holocaust of the Second World War. But it is foremost an extension of that experience and the inability over more than forty years to find lasting accommodation in the region. Among Israelis, this failure has engendered pessimism beyond any emotion that Americans, including American Jews, can identify with.

To the contrary, American Jews need, indeed long for, Israelis to appear optimistic and invincible, because that is a myth that gives American Jews ultimate protection within their American universe.

It is quintessentially American to be optimistic. The American ethos is most deeply rooted in the belief that life will progress in a relatively smooth, orderly way, if only one follows the rules. When fate deals an unkind hand, we somehow feel responsible, as if it were our fault: "Where did we go wrong?" Americans don't expect to be victimized by life, and certainly not by foreigners.

Israelis start from the opposite emotional premise. They assume that major events, especially those dependent on foreign players, are going to turn out badly. Faced with a positive outcome, when their worst fears are not in fact realized, Israelis are surprised, even shocked.

American Jews, in that regard, are much closer to the American than the Israeli mentality: optimists by culture.

Sam Lewis was Ambassador to Israel from 1979 to 1985 and participated from the outset in the Camp David process. His involvement with Israel was so extensive and familiar that on his departure the Israeli Knesset conferred on him Israeli citizenship for life. Lewis is now president of the United States Institute for Peace in Washington, D.C.

Sitting in a high-backed, ambassadorial leather chair with his ever-present cigar, he pondered the special ironies of Israeli pessimism. "We, as a society and as a people, are self-confident and optimistic," he observed. "We assume that if you work hard enough at something and if you are smart, you will succeed, eventually overcoming your obstacles."

Israeli pessimism, Lewis noted, is tempered by a transcendental belief in the miracle of Jewish history. "Despite the fact that the world is against Jews, particularly Israel, and that the Arabs will never accept them, and that somebody will always betray them—despite that, somehow there is destiny working through the history of the Jewish people," he said. "Periodically, a miracle occurs, and they overcome all of these extraordinary obstacles."

Israelis stubbornly persevere, despite their pessimistic judgment of what the outcome is likely to be. "Some of the most profoundly pessimistic, world-weary, sophisticated, and cynical Israelis are extraordinarily polite and pleasant to deal with—smooth, unlike most Israelis," Lewis added. "Even those who have grown up in a different cultural tradition, who come from Western societies, still tend to have this profound pessimism if they are living in Israel and [have] committed themselves to Israel as their life."

In the early years of the state, the Israelis clearly had a great faith that if Zion were reestablished, if the land were settled with hard work, the swamps were drained, the people reunited, a new society, a better society, would emerge. Part of the pessimism almost omnipresent in Israel today is disappointment and disillusionment with that vision of the founders—that vision having been thwarted is exposed as an illusion.

"I remember one day attending a concert of the Israeli Philharmonic Orchestra in Tel Aviv," recalled Dalia Shehori, the Washington bureau chief of *Al Hamishmar*, a left-of-center paper. "It was a very special performance. Suddenly it came to my mind that the philharmonic orchestra is one of the few things left from the Zionist dream that the state sanctions, takes pride in, and lets you feel that it is good. The Philharmonic is not damaged. It is not spoiled. It makes beautiful music."

It is almost impossible for Israelis to talk about their country without becoming emotional. Their views are always, in Shehori's words, "in comparison to what you expect, what you want, what you believe, and the current situation."

The United States has not suffered war within the country since the Civil War. With the exception of Pearl Harbor, we have been spared the national trauma of invasion or the continuous threat of assault by foreign forces. This feeling of geographic security leads to immense misunderstandings with Israel, which has been in a continuous state of war since 1948. Israelis describe their fears, according to Shehori, as "something which is always behind our brain, the fact that we are never secure, while the Americans can absorb almost everything."

Ze'ev Schiff is the unofficial dean of Israeli defense corre-
spondents, and a senior writer for the intellectually bent
newspaper *Ha'Aretz*. Schiff's gentle manner and soft voice
belie the intensity of his feelings, the acuity of his thoughts.
Countless American "Middle East experts" rely on his insights and guidance into the labyrinth of Israeli politics, and
he is the unnamed source of their informed pronouncements.

"What Americans define as a tactical or minor mistake,
for Israel could be a crucial strategic, survival mistake. It
brings us to a situation where we are a nervous democracy,
and sometimes Americans don't understand the pressures,"
Schiff said.

"We are not sure what the future will be. For you, it is
absolutely clear-cut, but I am not absolutely certain what will
happen with my children in the Israeli, Middle Eastern environment. The fact that we are a nation in uniform changes
completely our perspective on many things."

From kindergarten on, Israelis are schooled in the message, "No one gives a damn about us." American students are
spoon-fed world wars, which they usually confuse, while Israelis are given an educational diet replete with centuries of
Jewish pogroms and massacres. The Israeli schoolchild mem-
orizes the stories of the Bible and repeatedly visits the ancient
places, whereas two hundred years of American history are
often considered too remote and complex for U.S. children to
digest.

An Israeli father was shocked to find his eight-year-old
daughter instructed by her teacher to role-play the same 1938
skirmish between Jews and Arabs in prestate Palestine that
he was forced to master in grade school. By comparison, a
1989 Gallup Organization survey found that a fourth of U.S.
college seniors mistakenly believed that Columbus landed in
the Western Hemisphere after 1500, and a significant percentage couldn't answer basic questions that the Immigration
and Naturalization Service administers to prospective U.S.
citizens.

"Remember the nature of our society," Schiff explained.
"We have a high percentage of people who are first- and

second-generation survivors of the Holocaust. It explains much of our nervousness. Secondly, we tend not to trust others, and we have a good reason. If we are more paranoid, it is because of the Holocaust and the wars against the Jews over the centuries."

By all rational measures, Israel should have been able to convince the Arab world by now that the Israeli nation is here to stay, that it is better to make peace and to get on with the business of living. Yet, with the exception of Egypt, no Arab country has been willing to accept Israel as a part of its permanent neighborhood.

Quite apart from Arab claims and assertions, few Israelis believe today that their isolation will ever end. Peaceful coexistence with West Bank and Gaza Palestinians is at best imagined as a distant hope. The majority of Israelis, including those in the peace camp, feel they are immersed in an unending struggle for acceptance. Political speeches aside, most believe there is practically no prospect, at least in their lifetime, of resolving the conflict.

At the same time, dreams of a society that would be recognized and admired around the world as a culminating achievement of the Jewish people have not been fulfilled. Instead of being seen as "a light unto the nations," Israel is seen too often as an oppressor, a violent country, or a military nation.

"I think that produces disappointment and pessimism as well," said Sam Lewis. "It does not make an Israeli any less convinced that he is going to stay, to stick it out, and that this is the one place in the world where Jews can be assured of being Jews. But it does lead to a fundamental sense of pessimism."

In the United States, with its all-volunteer army, the common view at the upper strata of society is that there will always be someone willing to defend the country. Facing an uphill fight to fill its ranks with qualified young people, the army, navy, and marine corps have largely been recruiting men and women from the lower ranks of their high school classes.

But almost every Israeli family (except certain Israeli Arab and Ultra-Orthodox religious groups) has at least one member, including daughters, performing compulsory army service or the approximately forty-five days of reserve duty that are also required. In 1989, because of the *intifada*, the period was increased to sixty days. Reserve duty for men continues until the age of fifty-five.

Consequently, it would be difficult to find a family that has not suffered the loss or injury of a spouse, parent, or child during one of the nation's numerous wars. This feeling of interconnectedness was vividly demonstrated in 1985 at, of all places, the Hilton Hotel beauty shop in Tel Aviv.

I have been a customer of this shop during visits to Israel primarily because of Sima, a smiling, gregarious woman now in her late forties. In addition to her self-taught proficiency in cutting curly hair, Sima radiates a warmth that captivates her clients. Her ready words of welcome, "*Mottek sheli, mottek sheli* [my sweet one, my sweet one]," along with hugs and kisses, give the feeling that a candle was lit in her soul the minute she saw you.

One Sunday a lovely young woman was sitting in Sima's chair, dressed in a flowing white bridal gown, while Sima piled striking black curls atop her head. "Who is the lucky man?" I asked Sima, when my turn came.

"Oh, *mottek sheli*, it is a sad but beautiful story. The person she is marrying is the boy with no face." I knew exactly who she was referring to: a young man in his early twenties, most of whose body had been burned in a tank explosion during the Lebanon war.

Years earlier he had been in the Hilton lobby, engaged in earnest conversation with Simcha, the self-anointed protector and patron of sorrowfully wounded soldiers. It was hard to miss the boy, as he had a paper bag over his head, with holes for his eyes, nose, mouth, and ears.

Simcha threw regular parties for these lost soldiers, often bribing young women to attend. It was at one of these parties that the couple met, he with his skin grafts, she a young woman of beauty without and within.

As I left the Hilton that Sunday, the wedding guests

began to arrive. What I had imagined to be a small, very private affair was a festive happening attended by a cast of one thousand, including almost every minister in the Israeli cabinet. The country had turned out to honor the lovers.

Israel is essentially a one-issue country; existence is that issue. When Israelis tell you that a change in the consumer price index means that Israel's existence is less secure, Americans think it's ludicrous. But in the Israeli mind, the domino effect is irrefutable: if we do this, X is going to happen, which in turn means Israel will be weakened, and, bingo, we're finished, we're back on the boats.

This obsession leads to an extraordinary level of Israeli involvement in national events. Americans beyond the Washington Beltway may be involved in the news of their community or city, but rarely in national politics. National policy has become almost the exclusive purview of a self-selected group of elites, who claim to represent what the average American thinks or wants.

In Israel, by contrast, the smallest child is aware of and involved in the life of the nation. Every hour on the hour, Israelis turn on their radios for the latest news bulletin—and nearly every hour the news changes.

Yet, from the Israeli perspective, the United States is a mature political system, while their nation is still evolving. "We are just in the first stages, if not the first stage, of developing our own structure and political framework," noted Schiff.

"In the United States, democracy and all the social systems are so clear and solid. But despite the forty years of Israel's democracy, I am not absolutely sure that the future is so rosy from this point of view," he emphasized with obvious regret.

Zohar Carthy, a savvy Israeli activist, held senior posts in the Ministry of Labor and Social Welfare and was executive director of Beautiful Israel, a public organization dedicated to educating and encouraging industry and schools to beautify the country. She maintains that people in Israel are still not used to being part of a state. Throughout Jewish history, the non-Jew was always the ruler.

"So we created a structure where the citizens are almost entirely dependent on the government and the government bureaucracy. We haven't prepared our citizens to stand on their rights," Carthy pointed out.

"The proof of the pudding is that we dedicated the last school year as the 'year of democracy.' Israel needed a special program to educate its students about the structure of government in a democracy, but our people don't translate that to daily life."

Workers' strikes take place almost daily in Israel, but social protests concerning nonwork-related policies—consumerism, feminism, civil libertarianism—are rare. Sunk in bureaucracy for more than forty years, schooled to believe that the security of the state is the highest priority, prepared for army life where conformity is the goal, Israelis seldom think it is possible to move mountains when those mountains are part of the state apparatus.

American protests are as much a part of the political landscape as party conventions, buttons, and balloons. Yet American boredom and alienation from national politics are reflected in abysmal voter turnouts.

The reverse is true in Israel, with perhaps the highest voter turnout record in the world, where psychotherapists try to convince overstressed Israelis to reduce their compulsive need for the hourly news fix. "People take so much to heart what is going on in the country," an Israeli emphasized. "If something occurs, it is as if it happens to me personally."

"What do you see when you take a look at the elections in the United States?" asked Yossi Gal, the good-natured, highly competent press spokesman at the Israeli embassy in Washington. Gal's son was almost ten at the time, and his school class had been told to write position papers about the presidential candidates.

"They had a discussion yesterday, and the teacher asked my son, 'What did you learn from this class? Was it a good idea to go through this exercise?'

"His reaction was, 'Of course, I learned a lot. I think that I will vote for Bush because of Willie Horton, the black man who raped a white woman,' which for me was really a manifestation of how shallow and how at times intellectually insulting this campaign is," Gal frankly stated.

"What is the American presidential campaign all about? Are they talking about the real issues? They talk about flags, about Horton, and about the pollution in Boston Harbor. You see a low turnout, and it drags on and on."

Most Israelis feel that while their society is still in formation, Americans have it all. "They have everything they need, everything they want. Nobody is threatening their security," Gal insisted.

"There are no economic threats to their future. So they can afford not to vote. They can afford not to take part in the process. They are too lazy. Just because there are two stages—you have to register, and then you have to vote—50 percent don't vote. I don't know what it says about America.

"I do know what it says about Israelis: a wide level of Israeli involvement in matters of state. This is certainly positive. But there is a negative aspect to it, which stems from our national character. We all consider ourselves experts in everything and believe we should have a say in every issue."

2
"DALLAS," McDONALD'S, AND COCOA

WHAT DO ISRAELIS TYPICALLY THINK OF AMERICANS? Do they see us as a hardworking people, strong, resilient—the way we see ourselves?

"Resilient?" asked J.R., a senior Israeli intelligence officer. "Do you think most Israelis think in such terms as 'resilience'"?

What terms do they think in?

"I'm not sure it's fair for me to represent them, but I believe the majority have only a very vague notion of America. They perceive America to be powerful, rich, occasionally spoiled. [Israelis] are being exposed through television. They watch more American television than U.K. television. They watch 'Dallas.' Imagine for yourself watching 'Dallas' religiously for three years. That is their perception of America."

"Dynasty" and "Dallas" were two of the most successful series in the history of Israeli television. Israeli intellectuals would be offended if accused of watching the program. But for several years on Saturday night, "Dallas" was the talk of the town, and on Sunday, the talk of the town was "Dynasty."

"The truth is that what Bobby was doing to what's-her-name, that girl from the pornographic movies, Pam, and to

J.R., to a large extent was replacing the real U.S.," another Israeli observed. "Particularly for Israelis who are not privileged to travel or to read English as a second language, 'Dynasty' *is* America. What do you see in 'Dynasty'? What do you see in 'Dallas'? You see beautiful houses, beautiful cars, beautiful ladies."

The image of America for most Israelis, with the exception of those who have spent some time in the United States or lived here, is wealth, an easy economic life. Says an Israeli government official, America is associated with "a tremendously big house, having a swimming pool, buying whatever you want. Green is the color of America, green money."

The average Israeli knows very little about Hispanics, about blacks, about the homeless, and about education in the United States. They see only the facade of America, including the glimmer and gloss of the American Jewish community.

On a hot August day in 1987, I was having lunch in Tel Aviv with a wealthy, well-traveled Israeli woman in her early forties, actively involved in projects to create bridges of understanding with American Jews. When I mentioned the poverty facing so many elderly Jewish Americans, particularly in Florida, where a large portion of Jewish elderly now reside, the woman was incredulous. "What do you mean?" she asked in complete sincerity, "I thought all the Jews living in Florida were rich."

A year later, I related the conversation to a young rising star in the Israeli Ministry of Foreign Affairs, who had just returned from one of many trips to the United States. Instead of laughing wryly, he responded with a confused, questioning expression. "Are you saying that there are poor Jews in America? I didn't know that. Why doesn't the Jewish community take care of them?"

The heart of Americana that we so take for granted— football, baseball, apple pie, and Chevrolet—is lost on Israelis in Jerusalem or Tel Aviv. "There are probably more Israelis who got up this morning at 4:00 A.M. to watch the final game of the National Basketball Association series by satellite than in any other country in the world," said Ido Dissenchik, the

fortysomething editor of *Ma'ariv*, one of Israel's largest-cir-
culation newspapers.

"You see three hours of the greatest basketball—and
probably most Israelis were happy that Detroit won over Los
Angeles, because Detroit has been an underdog for so long.
But they don't understand, it's impossible to understand, the
culture around the game," Dissenchik went on.

"For most Israelis, American basketball is like a circus
because these guys are so incredible. It's a great show. But it
has nothing to do with understanding the culture behind it.

"The only game Israelis don't like is baseball, which is an
American family affair. You go to the stands and buy a hot
dog, you get ketchup on your slacks, the kids are with you,
and you sit for four hours in the sun."

Americans like to believe that we're entrepreneurs by
birthright. Israelis familiar with Americans admire their
professional counterparts as knowledgeable high achievers.
They also frequently describe them as robotic and square.

Israelis often use words like *naive, law-abiding,* and
inflexible to characterize American colleagues and culture—
while portraying the Israeli way as more astute, clever, and
innately innovative. The patriotic Israeli stands ready to
serve his or her country under any circumstance by bending
the rules and regulations to achieve the maximum and quick-
est result.

Bruce Kashdan, a born and bred blue-eyed Yankee, has
worked for the Israeli Ministry of Foreign Affairs for over a
decade. In the first days of the Lebanon War of 1982, the
Foreign Ministry sent Bruce to Beirut to serve as liaison to
the Lebanese, although nobody was certain exactly what that
meant.

Unfortunately for Bruce, the ministry also ordered him
to take his car, since there was no other way to get him to his
destination. About a week later, Bruce barely made it back to
Jerusalem, with one side of his car demolished by a Katusha
rocket.

When he requested that the Foreign Ministry's finance

office pay for the repairs, the debate went something like this:

"How do we know you went to Beirut with an undamaged car?"

"Are you crazy? You sent me and my car to Beirut, and now you refuse to pay?"

After much haggling, the finance officer conceded. "OK, we'll pay for repairs, but with depreciation. After all, since you went to Beirut, the half of your car that wasn't damaged has gone down in value."

Several more weeks passed, and Bruce returned again from Beirut, this time to get reimbursement for all the money he had paid out of his own pocket. The finance officer was adamant: Bruce must have receipts.

Again, Bruce spoke in simple Hebrew and in straightforward Israeli fashion: "Are you crazy? Do you think I can get receipts in a war zone? Do you want me to have them written on pieces of shrapnel?"

The finance officer wouldn't budge. "No receipts, no money."

Desperate for cash, Bruce solved the problem innovatively. The following week, he sent the finance officer a bag full of garbage, and on the back of every can and carton wrote the purpose of each expense. "Finally he pleaded with me to stop sending the garbage, and I received my money."

Living in a maddeningly bureaucratic and stiflingly antiquated socialist system, Israelis find that circumventing rules is often the only way to survive, let alone prevail. Fifty-nine signatures of local and national officials, for example, are required to obtain a permit to build a house. "If each official took three days to sign, that would already amount to half a year," an Israeli contractor complained, "but unfortunately they are never that kind."

Israel is a country of "charming lawlessness," pitted against the pressures of conformity. Some Americans, for example, do cheat on their income tax, but most of us believe that it's essentially dishonest to deceive the authorities and that we have a social responsibility to comply. In Israel, by contrast, "if you pay honestly in taxes, you're a friar [a fool].

Because nobody does it," said Joanne Yaron, a successful Israeli businesswoman. "Because it's Byzantine. It's so foreign to anything American. The income tax, for instance, is really very complicated. I don't only mean high, I also mean complicated. You're guilty before you're innocent."

According to Yaron, everyone is a crook in the eyes of the Israeli income tax authorities. "You have to prove you're not cheating. So if you write down everything honestly, they won't believe you," she said. (Having recently experienced my first IRS audit, I can see certain similarities.)

"They're sure you're cheating, and they'll drive you to your death trying to find out where you cheated. And if they discover at the end that you didn't cheat, the income tax guy will probably get ill."

Israelis also take pride in their high-risk, macho driving. "The car is the Israeli castle," said Jacob Levy, president of the Israeli Gallup Poll, "while the idea that we don't give the right of way is a basic principle in Israeli thinking."

Furthermore, he pointed out, Israelis cannot keep proper driving distance "because someone will always cut in ahead of you, and you end up driving backwards."

What is the difference between the Israeli and the American? An Israeli embassy official gives the following example: If an American is driving his car on a highway, and there is a problem with the engine, he will stop in the middle of the highway and put on his blinkers.

"People will be very nice and bypass to the left, bypass to the right. He will create such a tremendous backlog, so many cars will be gridlocked for hours, but people won't honk, people won't yell. In an orderly fashion, they will be late for the office.

"If it was in Israel, [the other drivers] would simply get out of their cars, four or five of them, take the stalled car, put it to the side, and nobody would be late for work.

"This is very primitive, of course," the embassy official acknowledged. "But I believe that it does say something. By and large, Americans are still considered to be naive. Not stupid. But naive in the way they try to apply their standards to the rest of the world."

Dalia Shehori, sitting in her rented Washington high-rise apartment decorated with efficient, Swedish-style furniture, reflected on the similarities in the Israeli approach to "education, war, and McDonald's":

"In Israel, you know, we have a crisis mentality. When I was a pupil in primary school, we never studied for the sake of learning, but for the sake of succeeding in the exams. So for the whole year we did very little, and then two or three days before the exams, we made an effort just to pass and keep going.

"There is a connection between my own conduct, and others' as well, and the pattern of the way Israeli society is functioning. From war to war, we don't do anything. We are making laws, and this is not working, and that is not functioning.

"Then one day we have a war, and in the war you see we have heroes, we have people who know what to do, they are inventive, they find things out of the air. This is a country of improvisation. We are at our best when we have to improvise. This is the absolute opposite of America."

"America in this respect reminds me more of the Germans," Shehori noted. "When they have the pattern of thought, and they know what they have to do, then everything is OK. The moment you present them with something that they were not programmed to do, they are appalled.

"At McDonald's, ask the girl at the counter to give you something revolutionary—I might say, 'Do you have fresh pepper?'—and she would just stare at me. She wouldn't know what I am talking about, because it is simply not in the patterns she is used to.

"Americans are like computers. There is no room for improvisation. It seems sometimes that the American people are really trying to go against human nature, confining themselves to one small, narrow tunnel, instead of trying to open their eyes and look at the world.

"But a big society can only be handled by rules. Otherwise, it would be chaos. Everyone has to know his place. If you want to get served, you have to be patient, to stand in line, to confine yourself to the things that are on the menu."

Ido Dissenchik spent several years in the United States, covering the crucial period of the Camp David accords. Dissenchik has deep appreciation for the United States, and many American friends, yet characterizes Americans as conformists, as people hesitant to act outside prescribed boundaries.

"America is a very square society in the sense that there are rigid rules and crazy margins. If you go into a bank in America for an ordinary transaction, it will be done like this [snapping his fingers].

"But if you want to do something a little more complicated that they have never heard before, it will take you three hours to get to the right person to make the decision.

"In Israel it's just the opposite. You want to do a regular transaction in a bank, you wait three hours. You want to do the unbelievable thing of moving $2 million to Antarctica, just sign the paper, and there it is. Israel is a country of improvisation. So you have a problem of two societies not understanding each other."

Benny Bloch is an Israeli engineer and a systems integrator who worked with the U.S. Army Corps of Engineers in Turkey in the early 1960s. Since that time, he has had extensive contacts with the American corporate world, including running his own company in the West.

Bloch claims to have driven through at least half of the United States. He is also involved in planning the Voice of America transmitter station in Israel. Over dinner at the Highland Hotel during one of his visits to Washington, lazy fans, classical music, and an otherwise empty dining room gave the feeling that the discussion should have been about high-level affairs of state.

Instead, Bloch recounted his original impression of Americans in the mid-1960s, observing that they seemed "well organized, high technology, and they knew what they were doing." This impression later disintegrated.

He first visited the United States in the mid-1970s, bringing his wife and two younger children on a vacation. "It was a different America than what I envisioned at the time I worked with Americans on the U.S. Army bases."

Bloch described his experience in terms of cocoa and highway chaos: "In Turkey, for instance, I was a member of the NCO mess, the airmen's mess, the officer's mess, et cetera. So I mingled with them, joining their group on stag nights, when they started going haywire, drinking beer, and so on. They brought nude shows from Istanbul. I went over to have dinner with the colonel, knew his family, and so on.

"When I came over here, it was different from what I saw in that little America in Turkey. I am not talking about New York. New York is not America. But I went on a trip in New England. The first shock I had was that at five past ten, you cannot get cocoa in McDonald's, because they only serve breakfast between seven and ten. I just wasn't accustomed to it.

"The youngest of my two children, a girl, is really spoiled. She said, 'Daddy, I want cocoa.' I told the waitress, 'Bring me a cocoa.' She answered, 'It's five past ten. Look at the sign.'

"That was terrible. From then on, I never went into McDonald's anymore. It was stressful. I had a bad feeling about it.

"It's the herd syndrome—as in 'Read the sign, and obey the rules.' In America, people are like a herd of sheep. I am criticizing America. I will go back and criticize Israel later on.

"In the American system, you have one guy at the top, an executive, and he makes the rules. I am talking about any organization, including the government. The system works because the herd is willing to abide by the rules until the last dot.

"If you want to overrun America, you don't have to shoot a soul. You just have to change the signs on the highways and shut off the electricity. It would be chaos. People will just run around in circles, because the system is so rigid."

Amnon Cohen, an Israeli political scientist from Hebrew University, told the following story: "I spent a week in New

Jersey, lecturing. One evening I went out for dinner to a place named the Sizzler with an Israeli friend who lived [in New Jersey] for several years. The Sizzler had a huge salad bar.

"I said to my friend, 'Here is a bright idea we should apply in Israel.'

"He answered, 'No way. The salad bar will never work in Israel. If you have a salad bar in the states, everyone comes up and takes a plate. They fill the salad bowl, sit down, eat it, pay the cashier, and that's it. Israelis would bring two or three friends, all of their children, pay for one person, and send the kids to take some more salad because it's "free." If that restaurant was in Israel, the owner would have gone bankrupt.'

"In America, this is part of the game. You abide by the rules of the game, whether or not there is a policeman. You see the difference? Where the Americans are naive, we Israelis are clever. That's it. Over the centuries, the Jews were always the underdogs. They didn't have money, they didn't have rights, they didn't have anything. So the only way to survive was to look around for the shortcut, and maybe even outdo the others."

Yael Dayan, noted author, political activist, and daughter of the late Moshe Dayan, like so many of her intellectual compatriots, described Americans as a parochial people and Israelis as more sophisticated, adaptable, worldly. "Israelis are totally cosmopolitan," she emphasized.

"The ties that bind us to America—democracy, basic human rights, a system of equality and human welfare—are admired and shared by so many countries. Your system is one of the greatest things that happened to the human race," she said.

"But I still regard America as an isolated country. The role of the world leader doesn't come naturally to the people. America never made an effort to integrate with other cultures. Americans speak and read only English and don't do well in strange places. That's why they need McDonald's and Kentucky Fried Chicken in every part of the world."

From the Israeli side of the glass, it's often the American

who looks insecure, lacking in self-confidence. "Americans are a great power people without a survival kit," said Dayan. "Every day you Americans get a recipe for life that's fool-proof. When something goes wrong, the shock is tremendous, while we Israelis do not know how to handle normalcy. Give us normal conditions, and our whole life pattern would go to pieces."

In short, Israelis often criticize Americans for lacking the very qualities in which we take greatest national pride—openness to new ideas, flexibility, ingenuity—concepts firmly welded to our national identity, our image of America as we want it to be.

The conviction that one's own national group is superior to all others, more honest and sincere, may well be a universal theme in the Western world. In this sense, comparing Israeli and American attitudes perhaps demonstrates not only how we differ, but also that we are so fundamentally alike.

3
CAMELS, GLITZ, AND SKINNY TREES

How do American images of Israel merge with reality? For most, Jewish and non-Jewish, the images are inaccurate. Jonathan Kessler, tall with brown curly hair and hazel eyes and only in his early thirties, has already accompanied dozens of Jewish delegations to Israel. Development and public affairs director of the National PAC, the United States' largest pro-Israel political action committee, Kessler also spent a decade of his life working with Jewish and non-Jewish college students throughout the United States, including a seven-year stint with the American-Israel Public Affairs Committee as a political leadership development director.

He observes, "Most American Jews who haven't visited Israel think of it as a smaller and Jewish version of the United States—somewhat like Los Angeles or New York, but more overtly Jewish and essentially American. American Jews are surprised that the majority of Israelis are not religious and not enthusiastic about military service."

American Jews have a hard time believing Israelis can be as dishonest or as lazy as anyone else, that they don't spend every waking hour talking about Zionism, and that relatively few actually live in kibbutzim or work with their hands. Israel is often pictured as an underdeveloped country.

Kessler recounted a recent phone call from a fifty-year-old Jewish man thrilled about making his first trip to Israel. The fellow was especially excited to tell Kessler he had found a guide who could negotiate with Jerusalem camel drivers. Responding to my laughter at the idea of camel herds in modern Jerusalem, he added, "This guy had it in his mind that there were camel caravans in Israel, so his tour operator probably located the one camel somewhere outside of Jerusalem to keep him happy."

Yossi Nitzani, the director general of the Tel Aviv Stock Exchange, told about the time he hosted a former president of the New York Stock Exchange, a sixty-three-year-old Jew who had never visited Israel. "I looked at it as my mission to bring him to Israel—especially after he told me that his son was on a kibbutz. He was so excited. When I took him from the airport, he said, 'I can't believe this is Tel Aviv.' I get this reaction from almost every guest, Jewish or not. They expect to see a very primitive, underdeveloped country with strange people."

The image of Israel as a poor, barren country, where the citizens live in farming shacks—and, by the way, "bring your own toilet paper!"—flies in the face of exquisite shops, five-star hotels lining the main thoroughfare of Tel Aviv, and a voracious appetite for every imaginable consumer import.

It is often said that Israel is a poor country, but the people are rich. This is only partially true. Like every other aspect of life in Israel, the economy defies simple description. Israel was built on the egalitarian notion that signs of wealth should be avoided. But today the haves have a lot, as demonstrated by the gorgeous Mediterranean villas stretching from northern Tel Aviv to Caesarea. Salaries for the majority remain low—90 percent of the population lives on overdrafts—but 750,000 Israelis (almost one-fourth of the country) traveled abroad last summer, primarily to expensive destinations like the United States or Western Europe. Traveling abroad has long been implicitly encouraged by the government to enable the people to let off steam.

The government coffers are constantly bare, and every social institution in the country is an economic battleground. Israel also has among the lowest levels of productivity and worker participation of any industrialized nation. Yet, for decades, its people have had one of the highest rates of per capita savings in the world, possessing $3–$4 billion in savings in 1987 alone.

By the summer of 1987, the good life had become so good that *Ha'Aretz*'s serious political columnist, Joel Marcus, devoted a special piece to the glitz. "Truth to tell, after not having had a night on the town for a long time, I had the impression that Tel Aviv was in a state of permanent partying to which they'd forgotten to invite me," he wrote.

"Hotels, movie theaters, places of entertainment, restaurants, pubs, cafés, public gardens, traffic islands, promenades, beaches—what not? Even attendance at funerals has become a fashionable social function; we'll soon probably be seeing catered funerals too.

"Barring New York, Tel Aviv has become the liveliest of all cities this writer has ever visited. Including Paris. There's nothing you can't get in Tel Aviv stores. . . . It's only a question of price."

Marcus described this material progress as a sign of "normalization," declaring that "man cannot live on tension alone." Individual well-being, rather than calls for settling the wilderness or international peace conferences, "will determine the future" of Israel, he wrote.

Although the welfare system is sagging, development towns are crying for help, agricultural settlements are collapsing, and some senior citizens can't find a vacant bed in a hospital, most Israelis are living better than ever. Even in the face of the Palestinian conflict, religious fundamentalism, and worrisome unemployment, "the truth is . . . that the State of Israel, both physically and mentally, is at the beach, getting a good tan," penned columnist Joseph Lapid in *Ma'ariv*.

For the typical American media addict, Israel is more like the stage set of "Gunsmoke." For example, an American rabbi visiting Washington, D.C., from Maine wanted to report to his community on the progress of the peace process, which Anwar Sadat had set in motion only a few months earlier by his historic trip to Jerusalem. The atmosphere in Israel and in Washington was still euphoric at that time. Therefore, when I asked the rabbi whether he would soon be visiting Israel, his response was surprising. "Oh, no. I've never been there. I think it's too dangerous to take my children. I'd prefer to wait until they're grown."

Two years of televised *intifada*—Israeli soldiers in combat against Palestinian children and their mothers—not to mention two years of warfare in Lebanon, compounded by occasional macabre terrorist attacks, has convinced the American viewer that Israel's urban centers are constantly aflame.

Even a seasoned visitor would be surprised to see a throng of adults roller-skating in an open-air rink on the Tel Aviv beach during the worst days of the Lebanon War. How could they be enjoying themselves at such a time? Listening for the sound of war in the air, all one could hear was disco music.

There are more mundane misconceptions as well. During his four-year tenure as American Ambassador to Israel, Thomas Pickering, currently U.S. Representative to the United Nations, realized that visiting Americans—whether diplomats, businesspeople, Jewish or Christian tourists—generally weren't prepared for the level of "statism" in Israel. The role of the government in almost every aspect of public life clashed with their conception of Israel as a "free-market economy, just like the United States, only in the Middle East."

Or as Mike Gamble, a senior official at Boeing, described the government/industry web, "I thought European industry relationships were complicated until visiting Israel. But I now conclude those were simple compared to Israel, where the entropy is about as high as it could possibly get in one small space."

Ambassador Pickering—dignified, deeply knowledgeable, and outgoing—also found that Americans had a difficult time adjusting to the Israeli personality, "expecting them to be very much like us." Israeli architecture and dress initially reinforce that assumption, but after about a month or so, Americans "begin to realize that Israelis are not at all like Americans—specifically the high premium placed on frankness. Americans tend to take it personally," he explained during a conversation in an unadorned State Department office.

"Also, Americans are used to lining up and being much more orderly in a public situation. Our people sometimes misinterpreted Israeli disorder as a sign of rudeness," the ambassador added. In fact, the embassy has found the culture shock so significant that they hired a native Israeli cultural sociologist to educate new employees.

A thirty-year veteran of the Foreign Service, Pickering was recently asked by a journalist if El Salvador, where he faced a death threat from right-wing death squads, had been his toughest post. He allegedly replied, "No, there are a lot of tough places—I was in Israel . . ."

Some of the most important cultural differences that distinguish Israel from the United States are, in fact, invisible, even to the frequent visitor. Trees, for example, or the right to own land. Whenever I'm in Israel, I distinctly miss the tall, thick, rustling trees I've grown up with in the United States. Two and three thousand years ago, the land of Canaan was a haven for forests, only to be denuded by successive waves of conquerors.

Planting trees has been so central to the Zionist dream that Israel is the only country in the world where the desert area is not expanding. Still, the trees, most less than forty years old, seem thin and puny compared to America's robust wooded greenery.

The emotional importance of trees was brought home by reactions to the major forest fire in the Carmel region of northern Israel on September 20, 1989. The fires were attributed to Palestinian militants waging a campaign of arson against Israeli forests.

In a phone conversation about an early draft of my book,

an Israeli colleague blurted, "Everything you wrote is fine, but you missed such an important issue. You didn't say a thing about the trees!"

"Trees?" I couldn't understand what he was talking about. Most major American papers had not yet carried a single word on the fires, although over two weeks had passed since the devastation of over 250,000 trees. "Didn't you hear about our fire?" he asked. "It was a national tragedy, like a burial. Surely it must have been a major item in your press."

Several days later, on October 5, the *Washington Post* carried a story quoting the director of the Israel Nature Reserves Authority, who painted a picture of national mourning. A flood of 150,000 Israelis had driven from all over the country to witness the ruins of their premier pine and oak forest. According to the *Post* article, "People came by the thousands . . . from Jerusalem, the Galilee, the Golan Heights. Some of them brought picnics and had them right here in the ashes to prove a point. And a lot of people just stood and cried at what they saw."

Whereas Americans export 25 percent of privately harvested timber (60 percent of it to Japan), each tree is sacred in Israel, and the nation's trees cannot be used for building purposes. To quote the poet William Blake, "A tree is an object that moves some to tears; to others it is only a green thing that stands in the way."

We also take a vastly different view of the meaning of land. Only 7 percent of Israel is privately owned. The remainder is held by the government. Even when someone buys an apartment or house, the lease or deed is usually for ninety-nine years, based on the concept that the land should be universally shared. You can care for it for a century, but rarely own it for eternity.

Christian tourists are sensitive to the sanctity of land in Israel as a "living Bible," but most expect Israelis to be a monolithic block of biblical people. Dale McDaniels, an official at the U.S. Department of Transportation, thought the Jewish state and its people would all be the same. "I read *The*

Source by James Michener, so I had some appreciation for the values. Still, I tended to view them in one cast. I also expected the Israelis to be biblical in nature, which was much different from what I found."

Father Joseph Nangle is a Franciscan, about forty, pleasant and jocular. During an interview, he wore a sport shirt with an open collar, and a *keffiya* (an Arab headdress) was draped over his typewriter.

"I expected a monolithic, Holocaust mentality in Israel," he said. "I used to think, 'There they go again on that theme,' you know, about the Holocaust and all that. The visit increased my sensitivity. I came away thinking, 'They really have come through something incredible.' I was enormously impressed with the Forest to the Righteous Gentiles.

"But I was also impressed by the peace camp amongst Israelis, and by the women in black, who stand in front of the King David Hotel every Friday afternoon. They are the mothers of soldiers who refuse to go to the territories. Now that's real patriotism."

Dr. Milton Silva, a Milwaukee psychologist who visited Israel to study the effects of trauma on police and army officers, was particularly struck, as are so many Americans, by the significant role that Arabs play within Israeli society. "The situation is bizarre," he related. "Nurses and doctors at Hadassah Hospital are Israeli, but staff, medics, et cetera are Arab. The doctors and nurses go home at night, and the Arab attendants remain, taking care of Israeli patients who have been injured by Arabs!"

On November 16, 1989, the wife of an Israeli soldier who was killed by a Palestinian near Gaza City donated her husband's heart to a near-death Palestinian in a successful transplant operation performed at Hadassah Hospital. Summarizing the unsummarizable about life in the Jewish state, Silva concluded, "There are such ironies in Israel."

4
CIVILITY:
ARE YOU CRAZY?!

AMONG AMERICANS WHO HAVE HAD EXTENSIVE DEALINGS with Israelis, whether in government, business, or Jewish circles, the first adjectives that come to their lips are *arrogant, willful*, and sometimes *infuriating*. "Of course, there are exceptions," they add, and they usually even mention the names. But the common perception is that Israelis are impolite, brash, and basically "don't behave the way we do."

I spoke, for example, with a senior instructor at the National War College, the pinnacle of professional military education. For the past several years, he has accompanied annual delegations of his students to Israel—majors, colonels, and aspiring top brass, the cream of the crop in the services. Many will be in top-ranking policy positions in the future. He has also taught numerous visiting Israeli military students. What have his experiences with Israelis been like?

"Israelis are pleasant enough, but distant," the instructor said. "They do not socialize very much with Americans—at least they didn't here. They were pleasant, polemical, and defensive, as opposed to inquiring. That may be a function of the individual personality.

"But then I think of someone like General Mitzna in the

31

West Bank. The contacts we had with him were very open-minded—a sensitive, thoughtful man who could look at a lot of different points of view.

"But he was the exception. Most of the Israelis we dealt with seemed defensive about everything. A lot of that stems, ultimately, from the question of security and Israel's foreign policy.

"I still remember one of these characters who'd been around since 1948. He was an intelligence officer but never told us that. He stood in the background yet knew all the chiefs of staff on a first-name basis. They would say, 'Hi, Abe,' when he came in the room. He always escorted our groups. I had a lot of discussions with him.

"But I remember the last time around, we were up in northern Israel being briefed by the Northern Area commander and his staff. The discussion involved the use of cluster bombs in Lebanon.

"Our people were asking sharp questions: 'Isn't that illegal and a violation of the agreements with Israel?' I remember Abe interjecting very loudly—again, he was an escort sitting off to the side—but he pipes up and says, 'You know, I don't care. That's your problem, not ours.'

"That Israeli bluntness really ticked off everybody. The reaction was, 'Who in the hell does this guy think he is?' Here we are, friends of Israel, and this is the answer we get: It's your problem, not ours. 'We'll do what we want,' in effect. That left a lot of bruised feelings."

Lack of acceptance of Israel in the region creates a national feeling of claustrophobia. An Israeli can drive coast to coast in several hours, confronting borders that cannot be crossed. In this sense, Israel's 1979 peace treaty with Egypt was psychologically akin to the 1989 destruction of the Berlin wall for East Berliners.

Yet, for most Americans, it is difficult, if not impossible, to appreciate Israel's geographic and emotional isolation. With the exception of distant war zones like Vietnam or Lebanon, the world has generally been open to us, according respect, if not awe or adulation. Terrorist targeting of Americans on international airlines is the closest we have come to the siege mentality of Israeli life.

For Israel, geographic and psychic distance converge. Impassable borders and Israel's small size—no larger than the state of New Jersey—contribute to national tension and national aggressiveness. Americans, however, find it hard to understand how a nation that intensely dominates the headlines could be so tiny that its air space can be violated by enemy planes in a matter of minutes or even seconds. Americans generally assume that Israel is much bigger and more powerful than it actually is.

"Americans live in a country of vast expanse—no foreign borders, no alien neighbors. When you try to put Israel in perspective, it's incomprehensible for most, until they come here," said Simcha Dinitz, Israel's veteran Ambassador to Washington, comedian par excellence, television personality, and currently chairman of the executive board of governors of the Jewish Agency.

Dinitz recalled that, in one of his early conversations with Zbigniew Brzezinski in 1977, the National Security Adviser to the President asked why Israel refused to accept minor border changes proposed by the United States. "I said, 'What do you have in mind?' He answered, 'Oh, no more than twenty to twenty-five miles.' I told him, 'That will take us across the Jordan River.' Even higher echelons didn't have any idea of what we were talking about, until today."

Israelis themselves sometimes long to believe the myth of Israeli power. Doug Bloomfield, former chief lobbyist for AIPAC, the pro-Israel lobby on Capitol Hill, reflected on Israeli arrogance: "Certainly, there is no denying that it exists, but I think we have to look at the causes. You sometimes come away from Israelis thinking that there are three superpowers on this planet.

"If E.T. had stayed in the U.S. and read the *New York Times*, the *Washington Post*, or the *Christian Science Monitor*, or had watched the network news instead of riding around in bicycle baskets, when he finally returned home and they asked him, 'What is it like on earth?'—the first thing he would have said is, 'There are three superpowers. There is Israel and two others.' Sometimes Israelis think they are the center of the universe.

"At the extreme, Israeli arrogance is manifested in a way that says, 'You owe us.' But this stems from a basic insecurity. Israelis constantly need to be reassured of their legitimacy."

"Past is prologue," observes another friend of Israel, who has served "the cause" for many years. "We believe people can mutate and change very quickly. We believe the Second World War is over. But in Israel, they don't forget, so their decisions are often based on a 'screw the world' attitude that makes sense to them, but not to us."

Ironically, if you ask an Israeli, "How do you think Americans typically see you?" *arrogant* is often the first adjective that comes to his mind. My following conversation with J.R., a high-ranking Israeli intelligence officer, is a case in point.

"Most Americans I interviewed in the government sphere—the State Department, Defense Department—use certain words when they describe Israelis."

"Arrogant," J.R. replied.

"Yes, arrogant is a word that comes up frequently."

"By the way, I think it's true. It applies to most Israelis. American fairness and Israeli fairness are different."

"What is Israeli fairness?"

"Israeli fairness is 'You give me 75 percent and leave 25 percent.'"

"Do they know they do it?"

"Most of them do not. I think most of them believe that by some divine decree, they deserve to get everything."

"What is this divine decree?"

"It comes from God." He saw me laughing. "It's not funny, Joyce."

"Where does that feeling come from?"

"I don't know. I've spent a lot of time thinking about it, but I don't have an answer. It is not an inferiority complex,

certainly not. It is, I think, insecurity—perceiving an immi-
nent threat all the time. This is not misanthropy but a sort of
'we do not trust anybody' attitude.

"I'll give you a humorous example," he continued. "We
have a satiric paper in Israel which carried the headline
'Arafat commits suicide because he can't carry out his de-
sires.' The caption giving Shamir's response said, 'This is
another example of Arafat's intentions to annihilate Israel.'
You see, Joyce, even Arafat's suicide would be interpreted
here as a plot."

Benny Bloch, an Israeli businessman, readily admits that
Israelis are often rude and impolite, but he emphasizes the
"Mediterranean" influence, rather than geographic boundaries: "You bring a bunch of Israelis together with a bunch of
Americans, and the Israelis start talking Hebrew, and then
they start yelling, and then they talk at the top of their voices
because that's their way—it's the Mediterranean way. Ital-
ians will do the same."

"Americans don't like it," concurs journalist Ze'ev Schiff.
"They don't understand that this is normal for us. Americans
take it personally. Americans are much more polite, I would
say, while we are rude and have no patience. You can see this
not just when dealing with the Americans. You can see it
when some of us are waiting in a queue in a bank or waiting
for a bus. It's not because Israelis are dealing with Americans. This is the way we deal with each other, with the Egyptians, the Europeans, whoever.

"Sometimes Israelis think they are smarter, which is not
so true. We are smart but not smarter. Comparing three
million Americans and three million Israelis, as [former Israeli President Chaim] Weizmann used to say, 'We are like
the others but a little bit more'—for bad or good."

Americans object to Israeli arrogance and rudeness, but
Israelis have a countercomplaint: American aggressiveness.
Almost every Israeli I spoke with who spent time in our
country is incredulous and appalled by the level of daily
violence.

Excluding the stark violence of the *intifada* within the West Bank and Gaza, the actual number of homicides within Israel proper numbered no more than 105 for all of 1989. Though the death penalty was abolished in 1954 and the population has more than doubled in the past thirty-five years, the average number of murders per year has essentially not increased. People in some neighborhoods still leave their doors unlocked during the day, and you can freely walk the main city streets after midnight without fear.

For example, on a night in Israel in early July 1989, I joined several close friends on a dark, deserted Tel Aviv beach. There were no lights, no police. They were eager to take in the soothing solitude, and I wasn't about to admit that I thought the idea was sheer lunacy.

My Israeli friends couldn't imagine that we might be in danger, but my reflexes were purely American. Even the Road Runners Club of America warns us to write our name, phone number, and blood type on the inside of our running shoes, in case of assault or rape. I kept discreetly glancing over my shoulder, scanning the beach, listening for invisible footsteps. I was certain this was not only my last night in Israel, but possibly my last night on earth.

From the outset of the *intifada* in December 1987 through 1989, more than five hundred Palestinians were killed, including many young children, all of the deaths a tragedy by any standard. But in Washington, D.C., the "murder capital of America," there were almost five hundred murders in 1989 alone, mostly drug-related and including six stabbings outside my own apartment complex—in a neighborhood of foreign embassies surrounded by a police presence.

The United States leads the world in homicides of children. A sign of the times, New York City committed $62 million in 1990 to fight the "weapons race" in the city's high schools. Gang and drug warfare have turned sections of Los Angeles into such fierce battlegrounds that the U.S. army is now sending its doctors to L.A. hospitals to train in combat medicine. Israeli drivers top the charts in aggressive driving, but on the California highways, drivers have been known to shoot rather than shout.

American violence takes many forms. There were over 2.3 million reported cases of child abuse in 1988, for example, and over 15 percent of black children in the Washington area are born permanently brain-damaged by their mothers' use of cocaine. There are more than two hundred million guns in the United States, enough for 80 percent of the population to own at least one, and thirty thousand people die in gunfire each year.

In this respect, the sentiments of the Israeli intelligence officer, J.R., had a certain resonance: "I will tell you something about American aggressiveness. I think American aggressiveness is far more severe than Israeli aggressiveness. Israeli aggressiveness is mostly on the surface. Israelis are very fast to react, to scold you, to do many other impolite things. However, they are also quick to calm down, as soon as they have unloaded their rage.

"Take the matter of property. The Israeli does not perceive his own property to be something sacred and divine. If he sees somebody walk into his garden, this is not a major disaster. It's not a threat to his life.

"Say somebody takes a ride on his bicycle, or picks a lemon from his tree in the garden. He does not think this is the end of the world or a casus belli, whereas an American is so concerned about his property, up to the point of vicious aggressiveness.

"I will tell you two stories from my own experience. The first was back in 1976 when I was working in Washington, D.C. The embassy at that time was on Twenty-Second and R streets. You know that crummy place? It was very cozy. However, we didn't have any parking. So we were parking on the street.

"One day, the guard on the front entrance called me and told me, 'Listen, I think something bad is happening to your car.'

"I said, 'What exactly are you talking about?'

" 'An old lady is standing there and throwing huge rocks on your car.'

"I said, 'You must be kidding!'

"He said, 'You better come down before you don't have a car.'

"I went down. That was on Twenty-Second Street. What I see is a lady about eighty or eighty-five, standing on the street and throwing rocks at my car. Here's what had happened. She had a designated parking space. My car was maybe half an inch into her territory. She was so outraged that she started to throw stones at my car. 'You'll never do it again.' For me it is a metaphor.

"Another example. I was driving in the countryside in Tennessee with my family. We went to a Kentucky Fried Chicken place and bought ourselves a huge bucket of fried chicken, french fries, and cole slaw. Then we drove out into the country, and we decided—it was a beautiful day, a gorgeous day—to sit down on the grass just off the road and have a picnic. It was all wide open space. No one was around. No cars. Nothing. Just open countryside.

"We spread out a blanket and sat down. We were so happy just enjoying the peace and quietness. All of a sudden, a pickup truck comes racing up at a tremendous speed out of the field. The truck stops right in front of us, and a guy in his fifties steps out with a huge rifle, points it at us, and says, 'This is private property, you're trespassing, and you'd better move.' I told him there was no Private Property sign.

" 'I don't care,' he says. 'You'd better move out right now before I shoot.' So we moved, because I truly believe he would have shot. These are Americans. They are aggressive. Look at the way they play football.

"You know Hitler? Prior to the American entry into the war, he was concerned about American intentions, whether they were going to join the war or not.

"So what he did was to send a top psychologist to the U.S., around 1939 or 1940. As I remember, he went to Chicago and stayed there a few months. The purpose of his trip was to try to portray for Hitler what exactly is the American character. Who are those people? What are they like?

"After a few months, he presented his report to Hitler. The most striking finding was, the psychologist warned Hitler—I am not sure this is verbatim but more or less the idea—'I strongly recommend to you not to fight the Americans. I have seen them playing football, and I can tell you they are vicious and aggressive.'

"So there are two layers in the American culture. The outside layer is very polite, very cool, and very civilized. But beneath that, there is a second layer which is aggressive and can even be vicious.

"Israelis are different—aggressive on the outside, but inside most of them are pussycats. You see what is happening to young soldiers on the West Bank, how they are being traumatized, their moral struggle. This wouldn't happen to Americans.

"I watched a videotape of the 1968 Democratic Convention in Chicago. I saw what American policemen can do to American students. You would never see that in Israel. Never. They beat the hell out of them. Did you ever see it? That was awful.

"This is duplicity. You certainly cannot consider me to be a hard-liner, or hawkish in terms of Israeli politics. But at one point, when my American colleagues were admonishing me for Israeli behavior in the West Bank and Gaza, I said, 'Listen, I think this is none of anybody's business to tell the Israelis how to conduct their own internal security.' It's as simple as that."

Dissenchik's views similarly reflect what he sees as the constant violence and aggression in American society: "Israelis are violent vis-à-vis their neighbors, or vis-à-vis the people who try to hurt them. But they are not violent to each other. They may be very impolite, but there is little violence in Israel in terms of rape, murder, or extortion.

"Israelis will never, never understand this total violence in American life. It's impossible for them to comprehend the violence on every level. Business life is violent. Street life is violent. Everything is violent. So much violence in a country which has such great opportunity."

American diplomats who have served in Israel—in contrast to those who have negotiated with Israelis but never actually lived in the country—frequently take a more ironic, even sympathetic, view of the incivility of daily life. One warm, otherwise kindly, high-level foreign service officer had the first fistfight of his life in Israel, and he seemed to have fond memories of the experience.

"We had a terrific four years there, just the friendships and the closeness of the people. Everything about it was good. Even the fights in Israel. The first fistfight I had in my life was in Israel. But that's the hot-blooded nature of the society. Macho.

"I was walking home on Friday night. My kids were around eight and six at the time. I was walking with my father, maybe thirty feet behind them.

"In front of our house was a fairly wide street, two lanes on each side with traffic moving along briskly. The kids crossed the street safely. We reached the middle section, and a car stopped in the lane closest to us, and we started to go across. Another car then passed on the right, going at an enormously high speed for that street, to a point where I had to pull my father back.

"So as the car went by, I yelled in English, 'Slow down!' and I slapped the back of the car. The car stopped, skidded to a halt. My mind-set said that this is an Israeli, I have to yell at him.

"He is yelling at me, 'Why did you hit my car?' I am yelling at him, 'Why did you try to run us down?' We're yelling and yelling together. Then he punches me. So I grabbed him around the head, and I threw him down. My father jumps on top, and we're rolling around in the street. That's the only time in my life I ever had that kind of experience. You know, in Israel you always yell at drivers for doing something to you.

"My wife was also hit by an Israeli. It was a case where

he backed around the corner and hit her car. She was en route to pick up my kids at school. When they started to exchange information, she couldn't find the insurance card in her wallet.

"So this Israeli said, 'You're not moving until we get the police.' She said, 'OK. Hold my wallet. I'm just going two miles from here to get my kids from school, and I'll be back.' He put a gas can in front of the car, a jerrican, and said, 'You're not moving.'

"She turned the engine on. One of the guys reached in and turned the engine off. My wife said, 'I have to get my son. I'm leaving.' She turned it on again, and the guy came in, hit her across the mouth, pushed her aside, knocked off her glasses.

"She's not quite sure what happened next, but she slammed the door shut, drove away, and brought the police. They arrested him. It turns out the guy had a record. The guy has a record, and he's standing there demanding her insurance card instead of driving away! It was a bad mistake on his part."

The roughness of Israeli culture is a reflection of the way Israeli society works. That is, it is not directed at the outside but is rather a spillover from the anxiety and internal frictions within.

At bottom, there is a constant feeling of insecurity. Quite clearly, what separates Israelis from Americans certainly, and from the people of most other major countries, is a deep-seated sense of living on the edge of a precipice all the time and yet having to suppress that feeling, to go on about daily business and behave normally. This builds up great repressed tension between the desire to admit fears and worries, and the belief that it is not appropriate, helpful, or "masculine" to do so.

This tension spills out in sudden eruptions of rudeness. You can be standing in line in a gas station, and suddenly there will be an outbreak of shouts and terrible cursing for no apparent reason except that people explode in Israel.

In particular, they boil over in traffic, with horrible

accidents resulting from the need to let out the tension, and aggressive action by using epithets. At a closed session of the Knesset Foreign Affairs and Defense Committee in the fall of 1986, Knesset member Rafael Eitan turned to the head of the Shin Bet (Israel's internal security agency) and asked how many Israelis had been killed by terrorists in 1985 and 1986. The answers were eight and ten respectively. Micha Harish, deputy chairman of the committee, was struck by the contrast between these figures and the statistics on traffic fatalities for the same years: 400 and 493 respectively.

"The priorities of this country are upside down," said Harish. "We're doing an excellent job preventing terrorism, but [this year] we've killed almost five hundred of our own on the road. If the whole idea of defense is to save lives, then how can we say, 'OK, preventing people from dying from terrorism is fine, but we're allowed to kill ourselves on the road'?"

Since 1948 more than 30,000 Israelis have met their deaths on Israeli roads—twice the number killed on the battlefield. Equally astounding, almost 630,000 Israelis have been injured in road accidents since the founding of the state, with 80,000 suffering serious or severe injuries.

The costs to the society at large are staggering. If the present pace of accidents continues, two people in every Israeli family will be injured, and one person in every ten families will be killed. The number of children killed in auto accidents since 1967 is equivalent to almost a hundred grade school classes.

The widespread rudeness, the intensity, and the roughness that foreigners encounter in negotiating situations is the product of two basic conditions in Israeli society: a combination of suppressed tensions on the one hand, and the yet ungelled nature of Israel's ethnic identity on the other.

Business negotiations between Americans and Israelis can be smooth and successful, with billions of dollars' worth of trade to prove it. But negotiations can also run amok on cultural differences.

The Israeli, for example, who arrives at an August negotiation session in Tel Aviv wearing sandals, no tie, and a short-sleeved shirt could unknowingly offend his American counterpart, who thinks it's his corporate responsibility to swelter in a tie and suit.

Israelis typically try to provide what they define as U.S.-style hospitality (expensive restaurant, four-course meal) for newly arrived American business guests. The latter inevitably suffer through a night of jet-lagged indigestion, silently begrudging Israeli insensitivity and excess.

Both sides duly search for a common ground in communication. The Americans try to keep it on a business plane, where they're most comfortable, while the Israelis vainly try to unearth family or friendship connections. Consequently, the Israelis conclude their first evening together thinking the Americans are a cold lot, while the Americans can't understand why Israelis are so intrusive.

The Israeli workday, beginning at 8:00 A.M., competes with the nightlife, which seems to persist until sunrise. The Americans suffer from sleeplessness, while the Israelis worry that the Americans are outplanning them into the early hours of the morning. The U.S. side is typically armed with a suitcase full of slides and graphs, while the closest the Israelis come to a plan of action is arrangements to pick up their guests at the airport.

"Israelis plan?" an Israeli laughed. "I'm lucky if half my guys aren't in the reserves for fifty-odd days and the other half on vacation. Who can plan in this country? Never mind. We do fine.

"After all, we've got the technology. The Americans can't get the contract without us. Everyone knows that, right?"

Even when the witching hour finally arrives, with the clock striking deal or no deal, the Israeli is typically less nervous than the American. An Israeli employed by a large company can enjoy the game more, is less bound by ironclad schedules, and doesn't take it personally when negotiations fall apart. Rarely is his job on the line, let alone his promotion, since most major firms are still controlled by the spiderweb of government and union constraints.

"People in my division warned me that Israelis stay intransigent until the eleventh hour, fifty-ninth minute, and forty-ninth second, hoping we will blink first, and then they win the game," said an American corporate defense official. "Sometimes our people toss up their hands in total despair."

At the same time, the small-business owner or self-employed Israeli can be driven to rage, if not bankruptcy, by American legal and bureaucratic procrastination. "We know those American lawyers are going to riddle this contract with bullets the minute they get their hands on it," an Israeli complained.

Sometimes the toughest points in a negotiation are clarified, when suddenly, for no apparent reason, a war of words breaks out between two Israelis on the same team. "All hell was breaking loose," an American recalled. "The Israelis were shouting at each other, at us, at the coffee machine."

Meanwhile, the American side is agonizing over the nightmarish prospects of stalled negotiations and a return to square one. "It's midnight, and the head of the Israeli delegation asked me, 'Why don't you just give us a blank check?'" an American related. "I told him, 'I don't give anybody a blank check.' He said, 'Yes, but Israelis are different.' My guys were falling off their chairs. He was dead serious."

"I tried to explain to my American colleague that the problem between us is one of mentality," said an Israeli. "He told me, 'Fine. Why don't you just bend your mentality?'"

American indirectness versus Israeli bluntness—two different approaches to the use of language—often engenders immense mutual distrust. In many instances, the Israeli lack of facility with the nuances of English is misinterpreted as bluntness, or even as insulting. Even when we speak a common language—English—most Israelis still translate their thoughts from Hebrew, a straightforward, ancient language, not yet layered with modern subtleties of politeness.

During the summer of 1989, the Prime Minister's Adviser on Anti-Terrorism, Yigal Carmon, discussed U.S. Secretary of State James Baker's by-then famous speech before

AIPAC, in which Baker declared that the time had come for Israel to "give up its dreams of a Greater Israel." The Jewish community in America worked itself into a fury over Baker's remarks, specifically over his choice of the AIPAC platform to issue this warning.

What seemed hard to understand, however, were various press reports that Prime Minister Yitzhak Shamir had called the speech "useless." After all, *useless* is a fairly derogatory adjective, implying that not only the speech, but the man who gave it, wasn't worth very much.

Asked why Shamir had chosen such a harsh word, Carmon appeared confused. "I don't understand," he responded in sincere confusion. "Shamir was trying to be benign, to defuse the crisis. So when the Israeli press interviewed him, he said in Hebrew, 'The speech was not useful.' What was wrong with it? Why did they get so upset?"

It quickly became evident that Carmon did not understand the difference between "useless" and "not useful." Upon hearing the subtle distinction, he immediately reached for the phone to alert Yossi Ben-Aharon, the Director General of the Prime Minister's Office, who in turn placed a call to the U.S. Ambassador, William Brown, who in turn cabled Washington in a belated attempt to soften the message, if not the blow.

One American Jew who has worked in a series of high-level positions in the U.S. government and is adamantly pro-Israel concluded nevertheless that, "It would be hard for me to imagine a warm relationship between the United States and Israel. We are much more concerned with superficialities, and they with substance. I used to think substance was more important, but now I'm not sure."

Continuing on this theme, he offered the following insights: "They never phrase things with 'I think,' or 'it seems to me,' the classical WASP way of avoiding hurting the other person. Israelis don't do that.

"For example, at an academic conference, Israelis will attack with 'you are wrong,' mixing the intellectual with the personal, and that's dangerous. You are subtly destroying somebody. Americans are seen by Israelis by and large as wimps because we refuse to say things so directly—'How much do you earn?' or 'You're stupid.' Between Americans and Israelis, it's like striking a match. We keep striking and striking—we have all the tools, but we can't start the fire.

"The Defense Department hosted a group of top Israeli pilots. We watched the Thunderbirds acrobatic team, the most prestigious group in the American air force. The Israeli response was, 'Oh, yes, that's something we do on weekends.' I admire the honesty and candor of Israelis, but it can also be offensive.

"As I grow older, I'm losing patience. Maybe I'm growing more confident, and I know now they don't have all the answers. I feel tired of it, and I don't believe for a moment they can understand how Americans make decisions.

"Freud says give me a child, age five, and I'll show you a man. The Talmud says the same. It's impossible for Israelis to see there are two ways of viewing things. I realize now there is no way to get this through to them.

"On the other hand, what makes Israelis most happy is their passion for intellectual discussion, which means you have to be ready for 'you're wrong,' and all the other personal insults. Israel has the highest percentage of book purchases, meaning they read more than we do.

"We are much stronger in our ability to gather information and make much better analyses. But passionate discussions develop minds. Their national IQ must be higher. But even now, with all the time I've spent in Israel, I need American reinforcement."

Point, counterpoint from Dalia Shehori: "This is an observation from Harvard. I remember in lectures when students would talk, they would often say things that were contradictory. But not once did the teacher say, 'Look, this is right. This is wrong.' Everything was OK. If you say that now it is right, they'd respond, 'Uh-huh, there is something to what you say.'

"Once I was in a music class. It was something about

Haydn or Handel, an explanation about how many themes you can find in a certain movement. I said, spontaneously, 'Three,' and someone said, 'Two.'

"So I thought you can just count it; it is either two or three. The teacher listened, and she said, 'Well, it could be.' So I had to say something. I asked, 'Could you please say how many movements you find: two or three?'

"I tried to make her be more specific. But she wouldn't do it. It is a sort of permissiveness in thinking that becomes absurd. There is a difference between black and white, and right and wrong, and beautiful and ugly . . . beautiful and ugly, perhaps not. I confess that I don't understand it fully.

"I am not sure if it is good or bad, because I don't understand it, and I cannot play along. I cannot take part in such a game. This is a difference in mentality, I think. Israelis say what they think: 'I don't like the way you look,' 'I don't like what you just said,' 'You're wrong.' Americans will never say that. I think there is an improvement. Now Israelis try not to say, 'I think that you are wrong,' but 'I think differently.' They take the blame on themselves.

"They are also coming to understand that it is all right to say things that are really nonsense or represent total ignorance. It is OK.

"I remember going to a meeting with Israelis in Brookline, a suburb of Boston. It was a meeting of perhaps one hundred Israelis involved in shipping goods to Israel. It was like in the army: once they decided to do something, they were so efficient.

"It was really amazing to see the way that they were so well organized. There was a committee, and the committee gave reports to the members. Then they began to discuss it. So one person began the American way.

"He started with, 'I heard what you said, and it was very interesting. What I would like to point out . . .' By this stage, one of the committee members said, 'OK, if you don't want to go with us, this is a fait accompli. There is nothing you can add.'

"I thought to myself, 'I must have missed something.' I felt a little bit distant from this way of talking, this rude way of talking.

"It is so Israeli, just saying something and going right to the point, sometimes like a knife. But sometimes it is also good, because it cuts the bullshit. Here in the U.S., you are bullshitting so much.

"Also, when you are in an American group, you are encouraged to talk. When you talk, it is a sign that you participated. It is almost as if you draw your existence from the fact that you talked.

"Something like *cogito, ergo sum*. I speak, therefore I am. This is also contrary to Israeli conduct. People in the kibbutzim or what is considered the higher-level society do not jump into a conference in debate.

"It is not modest to break in. It is not modest to say, 'I am here, and I have to say—.' So people are a little bit reluctant to say what they think. They are more inclined to listen and keep silent, because it is nicer.

"It is very different in America. It took me a long time to understand that if I don't talk, it is almost equivalent to 'I do not exist.' I was not there. People will not remember that I was there because I didn't say anything."

5
FRIENDSHIP, FAMILY, AND BURGER KING

ADI EZRONI IS THIN, PRETTY, AND TEN-AND-A-HALF years old. She is the daughter of the president of Israeli Aircraft Industries International, Rami Ezroni. Adi has been living with her parents in New York for the past several years. When she heard from mutual friends that I was writing this book, Adi asked if she could phone me to give her views on the differences between Americans and Israelis. This is what she wanted to tell me:

"I was born in Israel, and I am in America right now. You feel friendship in the air in Israel. You feel peace. In New York you feel a lot of noise, a lot of craziness.

"I went to camp in America. If you do something stupid, everyone starts laughing at you for days and weeks. They keep reminding you of it. You feel very out of place, like you're not part of the right group.

"In an Israeli camp, we sing our songs and throw our hat at a certain time. I threw my hat at the wrong time, but they just went to get it for me. It was no big deal. In camp I missed all the tennis balls, and a boy said, 'It doesn't matter.'

"In the United States they make you tense. The moment I arrive in Israel, I feel that everyone is familiar; their faces are smiling at me. In America everyone tries to be fancy, confident, and young—all kinds of things that make you look important.

"My friends in Israel say it doesn't matter what you look like. It's your personality. In Israel they don't wear tons of makeup, and even if they do, you can see the friendship in their eyes. We're *sabras* [native born Israelis], but inside we're mushy; that's how we are. Israeli eyes are flowing, so understanding.

"My friends in America are different. In Israel, when you go to school the first day, everybody wants to be your friend. In America—maybe it's because I'm from Israel—everybody acts like I'm such a nerd, such a jerk.

"The first year when we flew to Israel, I couldn't say anything because I was crying for happiness to go where they understand me as an Israeli.

"Even my best friend in America makes a face when she thinks something is stupid. She puts half of her nose up, puts her eyebrows up, wrinkles her face, and goes, 'Nu? Oh, my God, you are *so* stupid.'

"You see those faces so often in America, but in Israel they don't know what it is. Parents are kind in America, but some children don't know what nice is.

"When I went to Israel the second time, I was like that, a little bragging and made a lot of those faces. And then I realized, I don't have to do that."

Israelis may envy the standard of living in the United States, but less so the standards of society. Although they admire the values we represent—democracy, human potential, freedom—Israelis are shocked by what they perceive as weak family ties, fragile human relations, and little social support.

Americans consider family and friends their two most important sources of pleasure, according to a recent study on American family values, yet a majority of the respondents gave a negative rating to American family life. (Ironically,

almost three-fourths of the same sample said they were personally very satisfied.)

"In one way, Israelis admire the values, the standard of
living of Americans," Ze'ev Schiff commented. "There are, of
course, others who despise the standard of living. I think
many Israelis know that we have certain things that you do
not have—the human relations, friends, families. It's a completely different story.

"Something happened to American society because of the
geography, the size of the country, and the fact that you can
move so easily from one place to another and change jobs.
Families were broken here to a certain extent. We don't have
this, thank God. This is something that is often discussed in
Israel.

"In America you may see your parents once a year or
twice. You know that you have grandchildren, but you only
speak with them on the phone. It is a different style of family
or relationship between friends."

You will hear many Israelis living in the United States
say, "Yes, I made my money here. I got the degree. Now it's
time to go back to my friends." Whether they actually do so is
a different question.

Part of being American, an Israeli told me, is being alien
to everything. "You change places, you change people, everything changes all the time." Many Israelis I interviewed
raised the example of McDonald's or Burger King as typify-
ing mass-culture institutions that mask the reality of American loneliness and alienation by providing an illusion of
social homogeneity.

"McDonald's or Burger King gives an American the feeling that he is American," one Israeli commented. "An American can travel all over the country and still feel at home with
his hamburger."

One Israeli shared a particularly poignant slice of
Burger King nostalgia: "I fell upon an article in the *Rolling
Stone* about a girl who was working in a Burger King. She
met her boyfriend at the Burger King. When they got mar-

ried, her boss allowed her to do the wedding at a Burger King. For two hours he closed the business because of the wedding.

"Then she became pregnant, and the celebration for the new baby was also at the Burger King. So the Burger King is a family, a place that loves you and answers all your expectations. It is a home, and people love it. This serves the function of the head of the tribe."

Americans, like Israelis, do pull together in a time of crisis. Perhaps the difference is that Israelis live under the fear, and often the reality, of continuous crisis. Commenting on the public camaraderie that poured forth after the 1989 San Francisco earthquake, syndicated columnist Ellen Goodman wrote, "For a time, this hip and civilized city has gone back to basics. Survival. Cooperation. A spirit of community. For a time, a quake, a shifting in the ground, jolted the structures that separate Americans into the self-centers of our daily lives."

Americans whose careers or avocations are intertwined with Israel probably spend more hours of their week discussing, thinking about, or acting on behalf of the Israeli state than any other single activity. Perhaps not more than sleeping or making love, but probably close to it.

Israelis, by contrast, do not ordinarily think about America or Americans. They dream of traveling to the United States, working in America, sharing in its opportunities, but they rarely feel empathetic with the stress of American life.

Israelis are generally unaware of the critical problems in the United States—the homelessness, drugs, rampant crime. As Sara Schiff, wife of Ze'ev Schiff, explained, "When you don't see it from very close, when you don't live here, and you sit in Israel—even if you hear a speech about the homeless in the United States—you have so many problems of your own, you are not aware and you don't care. But I am sure that Israelis who visit the United States or who stay here and see these phenomena must react strongly against them."

Sara Schiff is completing a doctoral thesis on the American treatment of Jewish refugees during and after World War II. She and her husband voiced amazement and horror over the poverty and vulnerability of life in America.

Although the ethos of socialism is fast eroding in Israel, the concept of national responsibility for basic health, housing, and social welfare is as firmly ingrained as the Israeli flag. The health system is in shambles, upwards of a billion dollars will be desperately required to house and train new Soviet and Ethiopian immigrants, and numerous studies indicate that Israeli Arabs have not been accorded equal social services or economic opportunities. As many as 300,000 Israelis have experimented with or are using drugs. Still, there were very few homeless Israelis until the summer of 1990 when the surge of Soviet Jewish immigrants led to a serious housing shortage.

The Partnership for the Homeless estimates that American families with children constitute almost a third of the U.S. homeless, an estimated two million people in 1989—though some experts place the figure as high as three million, close to a 20 percent increase over 1988. In most areas, single men and women constitute the bulk of the homeless, while in New York the majority are children. Twenty thousand homeless teenagers are languishing on the streets of Los Angeles alone, more than a quarter, boys and girls alike, supporting themselves through prostitution.

"To see homeless Americans lying there on a bench, on the floor, is intolerable," says Sara Schiff. "It's not that I believe that everything can be equal, and that everyone can share the same economic benefits, but the gap is so large. I hear many Americans explaining that the principle of American society is based on independence. Everyone has to take care of himself. I think that this is very wrong. I can't understand how a nation like the United States, with all its might and wealth, can allow herself things like that. It is terrible."

Even in the poorest areas in Israel, you will not find people sleeping on the streets. Almost half a million Israelis live below the poverty line, which officially includes the bottom 25 percent of the population in terms of earnings—compared to thirty-three million in the United States, or roughly 14 percent (based on a different set of calculations). But I have never heard of a case of an Israeli dying of hunger or malnutrition. If not the immediate family, then the extended family or the community at large will try to provide sustenance.

An Israeli recalled a television interview during a visit to the United States five years earlier. It made a lasting impression. "They interviewed a man in Washington who was sitting on a bench somewhere. He said that he had two sons, one living in Dallas, Texas, and the other somewhere in California. So the interviewer asked him, 'And they don't help you?' 'No, they don't care.' This, to me, is so strange."

The family net in Israel encompasses the entire nation. Because the country is small, even if a family lives in Tel Aviv and the son studies in Haifa or Jerusalem, he usually comes home every weekend. Moreover, Israel is a children's paradise. Children are encouraged to spend as much time with their friends as the free hours in the day allow, and rarely does a parent have to worry about driving or car pools.

Israeli childhood friendships typically prevail for a lifetime. This was vividly illustrated when one of Israel's most distinguished business executives phoned to cancel dinner plans because he had forgotten about his "kindergarten reunion." An American over the age of six wouldn't be caught dead with such an excuse, while for Israelis, staying in touch with childhood friends has a higher value.

Friendships made in the army, in particular—for both men and women—become part of the enduring fabric of an individual's social milieu, the ties that last for life.

"We have many friends who go back a long way," said Sara Schiff. "The interesting thing is that our children, who were born about the same time, are friends, too. For Independence Day, we have a big picnic of maybe one hundred people—a group of people who are friends for many years, and then everyone brings some others, and the children and the grandchildren.

"I would not say that everyone in Israel has this, but

people keep their friendships, their contacts with other people for many years. If we move from Tel Aviv to Jerusalem, it doesn't make such a big difference. It's a forty-minute drive between the two cities, like between Bethesda, Maryland, and Washington, D.C."

Friendship in the American vernacular also has a different set of demands. We expect our friends to be there for us emotionally—to listen to our problems, care for our psychological well-being. When Americans say, "How do you feel?" the question is emotional, not physical. Israelis are both highly emotional and emotive, but find it more difficult to express their innermost feelings. Friendship in Israeli terms is first and foremost practical: "May I borrow your car, your house, your money—and by the way, would you mind looking after my kids?"

This Israeli ethic of communal support extends even to strangers. Some years back, Jim Phillips, Deputy Director of Foreign Policy Studies at the Heritage Foundation in Washington, was backpacking alone across the United States. "I was hitchhiking," he said, "and I ran out of money in Iowa. It was raining like crazy, I was soaked, and no one would pick me up. This guy stopped and picked me up, an Israeli grad student from somewhere in Chicago. He drove two hundred miles out of his way to take me to a bus station and then gave me money to get home. Of course, I paid it back.

"Later, when I went to Israel, I saw that there's a different attitude toward hitchhikers there. Here, you don't pick people up. It's dangerous, and you're suspicious, whether you're the driver or the hitchhiker. There you get rides easily, especially if you're in uniform. People are concerned about others, not just about themselves. There's a cooperative spirit, it seems."

In the United States, we tend to come home from work exhausted, burned out. Socializing with family or friends is not high on our preferred list of escapes. Television, exercise, reading—essentially activities that we do alone or for a purpose—are more typical postwork pastimes. Israelis also come home tired. No one can explain how it is that Israelis have more time to socialize. But the fact is they generally need friends more than we do. As one Israeli described this need, "It comes from the roots.

"We don't spend every evening with friends," he continued, "but I would say that social life means a lot to most Israelis. Not everyone, of course. You can find Israelis who don't think that social life is important, but usually people spend a lot of time with their friends. They go together to movies, to the theater, or they meet together and discuss politics. It's part of life."

For Israelis, the very sense of geographic space they admire in America can also be experienced as a kind of emotional death. "The difference between us is space," an Israeli once told me. "You Americans can't live without it, and we Israelis don't know how to live with it."

The most lonely place in the world is the human heart, and loneliness can be lethal in America. The average American will move eleven times in his or her lifetime—20 percent of the American population relocated in 1989 alone. The social dislocations and stress are enormous. Israelis, by comparison, tend to cling to their home communities and to each other. Even the several hundred thousand who have emigrated to America have created their own "little Israels" abroad.

Put one hundred Israelis on a deserted beach, return an hour later, and you will probably find them congregating together in one small corner. Americans, by contrast, would instinctively establish distance and territoriality.

"Israelis don't know how to enjoy themselves when they are not surrounded by other people," offered Tamar Avidar, noted Israeli writer and editor of a leading women's magazine. "They always have to be with at least half a dozen friends wherever they go. To spend an evening by themselves, even with a good book or a good television program, it's a kind of punishment."

The roots of this feeling can be traced back to the years even before the establishment of the state, when most Israelis lived in very small settlements. "The feelings of isolation urged us to cling to each other—not to be by ourselves," Avidar explained.

"If you were living by yourself, spending your time alone, you would be considered a weird person," she added. "So therefore we socialize in such an exaggerated way. Three, four times a week we have to be with people. Going to the coffee shops, together on the beach, and talking till one or two in the morning.

"Sometimes Americans ask us, 'How do you find the strength, the will to get up in the morning?' This is the miracle of Israel. At two, three, four in the morning, the cafés are full of people. No, they are not the unemployed. Are they all Bohemian types? No. They work for the government, they work for the party, they teach in the universities, they are people from the press, and they don't sleep in the afternoon."

Israelis need to be with each other. A constant effort is made to spend time with the *hevre*—one's friendship circle. "In high school you are surrounded with people all the time," said Avidar. "Then you go to the army, and again you are surrounded with people. By then you are twenty-two. At twenty-two it's quite late to change your social habits."

If it is nearly impossible for the Israeli to get accustomed to human isolation, it is also extremely difficult for Americans to get used to the intimacy of Israeli society. In the words of an American who lived there for several years, "Israelis are nosy. Extraordinarily nosy. 'Are you married? How many children do you have? Do you have a husband? How much do you pay in rent?' "

I spoke with a group of American professionals who emigrated to Israel over the last decade. The first issue they mentioned and then immediately debated among themselves was the virtual lack of personal space in Israel.

Their opinions can be best summarized in the views of one woman, a teacher, who essentially concluded that she would prefer Israeli interference over American indifference any day: "There is a nice side to it. I discovered that people were caring about me and my daughter. We were complete strangers in this neighborhood, and people adopted us. I appreciated their nosiness.

"When I left America, I had been really sick most of that year. None of my neighbors showed any concern. Nothing. I could have died in my apartment, and no one would have known or cared.

"In Israel the contrast was so great. I couldn't sneeze in that street in Jerusalem without someone down the block or from the floor above intervening.

"It's a kind of nosiness that was also saying, 'We are all in the same boat together. We can help you. We are curious about you. We are interested. You are not a threat. Your daughter is cute.'

"In fact, they felt strong because I was in a weak position; I came with nothing. I always had questions. They became the experts, the people who knew and could give. It made them feel even better about themselves.

"They would cut down America, saying, 'You didn't have this kind of chicken soup in America.' Or 'these vegetables' or 'these tomatoes.'

"I'd say, 'Of course. That's why I'm here, because the tomatoes were so bad at home.' I prefer the overinterest in my life to the total aloofness and indifference that I encountered in the States.

"I was attacked once in California. Nobody opened their door. Not one person. I was screaming. The whole building heard. Not one door opened.

"When I walk into my apartment in Israel, my neighbor knows I am back, and she feels good. She is happy because I'm home. Everybody wants to know, 'Did you get home? Are you OK?'

"There was a hole in my street they hadn't fixed. I fell and hurt myself quite badly. All I did was give out a little peep, and everybody came rushing out of the building. The cars were all waiting to take me to the hospital. The whole neighborhood was out to help."

Israeli spontaneity is also difficult for Americans to master. Americans function on calendar time. Whether it's making an appointment to see the dentist or getting together with friends, we schedule it—often two or three weeks in advance and perhaps even further.

As one American immigrant told me, "I constantly find that people here don't want to plan in advance. If you want to socialize with Israelis, you just sort of drop in, you drop by the house. You don't need to call in advance. I am used to calling up, no matter how close the friend is, and saying, 'Can I come over?' or 'When are you free?' It drives them crazy, and it drives me crazy on the other end."

In the United States, most adults carry a calendar. Without a business or social calendar, it's difficult to function. But calendars are worthless in Israel when it comes to plans for the personal side of life.

"I can't really guard my privacy as much as I used to," an American immigrant told me. "If someone knocks on my door when I want to go to sleep, and they drove all the way from Jerusalem, I can't say, 'Excuse me, I'm tired. I have to get my rest.'

"In America, people say, 'Why don't you drop by,' but they don't mean it. God forbid you should really drop by! If you say it here, you mean it. This drives me crazy. I'm stuck between the two cultures, because my wife is an Israeli.

"We've stopped in at friends' a few times, and of course nobody was home. I'd say, 'How can you just surprise someone?' 'Oh, no. That's all the fun of it.'

"Of course, the people you're visiting see it the same way: they see it as fun. They love it. You're never interrupting anything they may be doing. Even if they're taking a nap, they get up. They'll say, 'It's OK.'"

As a colonel in the Israel Defense Forces, Ya'acov Heichal led the military delegation to Egypt in 1979 for the Camp David dialogue. He is now in charge of emergency preparedness for the Israeli government. Tall and burly, known for his generous nature and kind heart, Heichal relates a personal experience with American courtesy and aloofness that is an example of profound cultural misperceptions.

"I became friendly with an American general during his visit to Israel. I told him I was coming to the United States for a few months. He said, 'As soon as you arrive, you must stop in.' I took him at his word.

"The weekend we arrived, I piled my family into the car and drove to his house. Of course, I didn't phone. I rang the bell, he came to the door, and I could see instantly by his stunned expression that I had made a terrible mistake. I said, 'Hi, I'm here.' He said, 'Well, I'm sorry, I'm just on my way out.' "

Avidar relates a similar story concerning an unannounced visit to a prominent American Jewish couple in Washington: "They were facing a very emotional problem. I called, but a telephone call is not enough. When I phoned several days later, they were still depressed, so I decided that I'm not going to ask permission to come. I went over to their house, knocked, and then came the shock. The wife opens the door, looks at me, and says, 'How can you come here without arranging it beforehand?!' "

The smallness and closeness of Israeli society can also bring its own brand of gossip, jealousy, and competition. There is an age-old saying that "Israel eats its own." But as Avidar emphasizes, "When we are in bad times, the heart is closer. We tend to forget the frivolities of life. Everything looks so unimportant while you are in a crisis or when you hear that a catastrophe happened.

"This nation is at its best when we're in big trouble. And that's true of individuals too. If a war breaks out tomorrow, I will forget that my so-called friends talked ill about me, gossiped about me."

Israeli business and government officials frequently talk of their appreciation for the polite American demeanor. Many Israelis find that cooperative dealings with Americans are soothed by this approach. Rami Ezroni notes that working with Americans puts him at ease, which makes business dealings all the more pleasant.

"Americans are straightforward, especially in big companies," he told me. "Working with the president of McDonnell Douglas or the chairman of Northrop, if you say that in two weeks' time you will be in Los Angeles and would like to meet them, the secretary will answer you beautifully.

"You tell her who you are, the subject, and she will immediately phone back to tell you that Mr. So-and-so will be able to see you. He is now on a trip, but she will let him know. Everything is very easy."

Yet Israelis are oftentimes taken aback by what they perceive as the superficiality of daily encounters in the United States—particularly the "Have a nice day" refrain, which suggests a caring that isn't there. Drawn to the larger metropolises where American Jews and other Israelis tend to congregate—New York, Boston, Los Angeles, Miami—their impressions generally derive from big-city life. Witness an Israeli "inquiring mind":

"I have an Israeli friend who lived in New York for a year. He said that he really can't stand it when people say to him, 'Have a nice day,' because he doesn't believe that it is true. It is false, and they don't mean it.

"He was thinking about this for several months. One day as he was paying for his groceries in the supermarket, the cashier said to him, 'Have a nice day.' So he said to her, 'Have a nice *zoobie*.' *Zoobie*—I don't know if it is Hebrew or Arabic—is part of the male body. She responded, 'Thank you,' or, 'You, too.' He concluded that you just can't beat the system."

"Here, everywhere—in the supermarket, in the bank, in the store—if you call someone by phone in an office, everyone is polite," said Sara Schiff. "But in Israel it's almost a national disease that people don't say, 'Thank you.'

"Maybe they think it's a way of apologizing. I earned it. Why should I say, 'Thank you'? I think it's because life is hard in Israel—really hard—and people don't have time for niceties."

Israelis often refer to Israel as "the real thing" and to the United States as the "plastic" reality. The United States exists but is somehow unreal. "It slips through your fingers," an Israeli commented, "while it seems to me that in Israel everything is really real."

Israelis often talk about the disappointment of making a lunch date in the United States. "The first time you meet this person, you have a wonderful time. He or she is so open. You feel, 'Where was this person until now?' But the next time you meet, it's as if nothing happened, and you've got to begin the relationship again from the beginning."

Many Israelis eventually conclude that upwardly mobile Americans are also highly mobile in their friendships. "Perhaps at a certain juncture in their lives, the process of making new friends becomes too taxing for Americans, too energy-consuming," concluded another Israeli. "The time comes when they are not ready to invest anymore. They try to find ways to be human, to behave in what is considered to be a friendly manner, but also not to get damaged from it.

"Therefore Americans have paragraphs of nice behavior, and everyone tries to give the utmost meaning to every human encounter. Lunch with an American is much more intensive, nicer, and more interesting than you can find anywhere else. But on the other hand, it is a compensation for not having any relationships at all.

"This person really opens himself, his heart is on the table, and then the next time when you meet him, you say, 'Hi. How are you?' and nothing happens. So there is a good side to it and also a bad side. It is so difficult to get to know people."

Avidar had the same intensely negative reaction. "The people I was meeting with were kind, well behaved with nice manners, but behind it there was an unseen wall, 'Don't touch me.' Even, I remember the expression, 'We must meet, we must see each other, we must meet for lunch.'

"And I used to take out my little diary to find out when. And then I realized that it's only an expression. 'We should meet.' It was nothing.

"Or the usual questions that everybody asks you, even in the supermarket: 'How are you today?' In the beginning, I used to give an answer. And then I understood that people are not interested.

" 'How are you today?' I could have told them that I have

cancer, and they wouldn't listen. It was just an expression, instead of saying, 'Hello.' And this was the real shock for me."

J.R. pointed out that, in his professional circle of American acquaintances, there is a barrier to friendship that Israelis cannot penetrate, but it's masked by "superficial intimacy": "Some of the Americans I met were very ready to share even their most intimate problems, things I wouldn't expect to hear even from good Israeli friends, like 'My daughter is swinging around' or 'My wife had a terrible religious experience'—all these very intimate details which I would never, *never* share, not only with a gentile, but with many good friends.

"This is deceiving, because you think at first that they are very open and ready to accept you into their sacred place. But this is not the case. It's all *façon de parler*. It is simply a way to communicate with other people."

"I take a ride on an airplane," said a well-known Israeli businessman. "I sit by an American girl, and she will tell me things that I wouldn't hear from my wife. I'm talking about personal things, about certain infections or something similar.

"They will tell you *everything*. An Israeli girl, you would have to cut her to pieces before she opened her mouth and said such things.

"An American girl can tell you—and I'm not joking— 'I'm very worried now.' You don't even have to ask her, 'Why are you worried?'—so she is worried; why should I get into her business?—and she will tell you, 'I think that I have a late period.' In an airplane, you are only flying three, four, five hours. It wouldn't even come to my mind to ask such questions."

Washington is the hardest city for an Israeli to understand culturally or to feel at ease in. On the one hand, those who come on state-related visits or work assignments are energized by the political adrenaline of Washington. They also appreciate and emulate the professionalism of their counterparts.

At the same time, Israelis are often repelled by the coldness of human relations in our city. The human milieu for most official meetings with Israelis—meetings with Americans, especially those in the ranks of the diplomatic corps, who believe it is their professional responsibility to remain cool and detached—can be antithetical to their basic nature and visceral reactions.

Comments from several Israeli diplomats exemplify the typical Israeli reaction to human interaction in the nation's capital.

"Washingtonians are vicious. They are bad people, no question about it," said J.R. "Are they even more aggressive than Israelis? No. Israelis are awful. But they aren't vicious; they are warm people. There is a distinction. You can be vicious and warm. The Arabs are vicious, but they are warm people."

"First of all, we have to make a few distinctions. If you're talking about people in rural America, they are the nicest people on earth," a high-ranking political counselor pointed out. "I am not talking about the Ku Klux Klan, because I have never met them, but about the shopkeeper or the restaurant owner in Wyoming or down in Utah, even in Salt Lake City. They are nice people, eager to help, and very open.

"You can go into a small restaurant or bar, stop and chat, just as you could in Israel, but not in Washington. In Washington, everyone says, 'How are you today?' but nobody means it."

One Israeli diplomat was especially affected by the *Challenger* disaster: "I immediately phoned various officials and nonofficials, to tell them how terrible I felt, to let them know I shared their pain. Do I remember similar calls from Americans? I don't think so. This is very typical of Washington. If I have to characterize relationships in Washington, it would be the lack of warmth.

"You can sit in a city like this and know hundreds of people, receive hundreds of invitations, go to their homes, but never get to the real heart of the people. This is a very cold city, with very cold people," he said.

"I can have a sharp disagreement with an American

journalist or an official, but it is detached from any emotions. Completely. Maybe they don't have the primitive need that we Israelis experience, to feel embraced. Americans may be better off without these emotions.

"It was quite natural and normal to live in Washington for five years without knowing your next-door neighbor. In Israel, if you don't know your next-door neighbor, you are a terrible psychiatric case—it doesn't happen. You can look at it from this crazy primitive need of the Israeli to be loved, held close, hugged, and embraced, while Americans are cold fish. But, of course, there are exceptions."

A diplomat described Washington as "the coldest place in the world. It's sometimes even a sexless city. There is no erotic tension. There is less erotic tension between people than in any other city in the world. Tel Aviv is terribly high-tensed with eroticism. But this is the only place in the world where for three years I didn't get any ugly invitations. And not because I became so sexless. After all, I am a married woman.

"I believe it is because people are so calculating, so career-minded. There is an inner drive that works mainly to bring them to higher places in their career, whereas I couldn't help them so much.

"I had quite a minor job at the embassy. Maybe this is one of the reasons that I didn't get any nasty offers. But people in Washington are talking, eating, drinking, and sleeping politics all day.

"I used to imagine even that if I had gone to bed with somebody, at the conclusion, he'd just say, 'Thank you.' He would stay polite and official right till the end. And he wouldn't let himself go."

PART II

THE OFFICIAL MINUET: U.S. GOVERNMENT NEGOTIATIONS WITH ISRAEL

Israelis are very warm and open people in general. It does come across. People we met were extremely outgoing. It struck me that the Israeli Knesset resembles the atmosphere of an old-fashioned marketplace. People interrupt and jab at each other. There is an intellectual energy, which I think is very attractive and strikingly Israeli. I feel as "at home" in Israel as I did in Poland in a way. There is an interpersonal intensity and a boyish, buoyant quality to life in Israel. Excitability is another. In the doses I was exposed to, I liked it. Yes, I clashed with the Israelis. But I think many Israelis feel much more at home with a Polish person than with someone of German background.

—Zbigniew Brzezinski, former National
Security Council Adviser to the President

I am the last to tell you that Israelis are the greatest strategic asset—we are, rather, a pain in the assets sometimes—for the Americans, but the Americans do not give Israel $3 billion out of philanthropy. There is no philanthropy, and we don't get the money for free. There are very logical and cool considerations for it.

—Senior Israeli military official

6
THE ELEPHANT AND THE MOUSE

Is Israel a big power that looks like a small power? Or a small power that thinks it's a big power? Or a small power that acts like a big power but feels like a small power? Is the United States a big power that acts like a big power when it deals with Israel? Or is it a big power that looks like a small power? What does it feel like to be the person representing the big power that can't always act like a big power or the small power that refuses to act like a small power?

A seed of the answer is in Henry Kissinger's apple. Whenever Kissinger faced tough negotiations with the Israelis, he demanded that there be a basket of apples on the table. "When it was in Kissinger's interest, all the details of the conversation were taken down by a stenographer," Ya'acov Heichal recounted. "But when he didn't want an answer to be written, he took an apple and put it in his mouth.

"He would ask Golda Meir or Yigal Allon a question. They would answer and, in turn, ask him, 'Henry, is your answer yes or no?' Now, if he wanted the answer to be written out, he took the apple out of his mouth and said yes or no. But if he didn't want it written, he would keep the apple in his mouth and simply nod or shake his head. After six months, the Israeli government would complain to him, 'But you said yes.' Kissinger would say, 'Show me.' When they took out the stenographic notes, there was nothing on it. Then I understood what he had done. I told Golda and Allon, 'This is why he was always eating an apple.' "

For Heichal, not to mention Golda Meir, Yigal Allon, and other senior Israeli officials, Kissinger's ploy was "blackmail." How did it make them feel at the time? "He can do things like this, and it's OK, but we are not allowed to do similar tricks," said Heichal. "These are the rules of the game. We're not puppets. With a puppet you can say, 'OK, I'll pull the wire, and you will play the game.' "

"I think if there is any criticism I can make of Israelis, it's that in some cases they damaged their long-term interests, their basic interests," said a former Assistant Secretary for the Near East. "But you have to be very careful about saying that, because the one thing the Israelis cannot stand is for somebody to save them from themselves. If you move into that kind of patronizing attitude, they just go wild. It is very difficult sometimes."

Israelis, like any other people, do not like to be patronized. Kissinger once spent an hour and a half trying to convince Meir that by agreeing to his proposition, she would be acting in the best interests of Israel. Meir listened patiently but finally responded, "Don't you think, Mr. Secretary, that it is up to the Israelis to decide what is good for them, even if you are right?"

Take the word *acceptance*. If the PLO "accepted" Israel's right to exist, for example, then it would be theoretically possible for Israel to enter into negotiations with the PLO. But for Menachem Begin, as for most Israelis, that is "a lot of nonsense." Begin constantly reminded American officials, "We don't need anybody's acceptance." The primordial, ancient, tribal emotions are as much alive today as they were three thousand years ago.

The big power/small power dimension of the United States' relationship with Israel is also a constant echo in the negotiations chamber, where perceptions are easily distorted.

The American negotiator *knows* that a superpower stands behind him or her, whereas the Israeli recognizes that he or she has no real power to speak of, only personal resourcefulness. Israelis are torn daily between the conviction that their country is worthless and doesn't count, and the realization that their Prime Minister is received better in Washington than the Queen of England.

The Six-Day War created the international perception that Israel had become a regional superpower, while the Yom Kippur War brought home a different reality of vulnerability, insecurity, and isolation. The peace treaty with Egypt and the solidification of the relationship with the United States during the Reagan Administration bolstered Israel's position in Washington as a non-NATO ally of stature.

The raid into Entebbe, Uganda, the bombing of the Iraqi nuclear reactor at Osiraq, and the raids on Tunis against the PLO were actions by a nation resourceful beyond its size, acting from a "no-choice" definition of reality. Still, the common perception of Israeli strength leads to immense ambiguity: Is Israel small or great? What is achievable, and what are the limits? American officials believe that Israel should be more constrained, while Israelis fear that they make too many concessions. An Israeli diplomat pointed out, "All the Israeli politicians insist that we are not a banana republic and we stand on our rights, but when they come to the negotiations, they have their tails between their legs."

The United States has long viewed Israel as a counterpoint to Syria, Iraq, Libya, and any other Arab state that could undermine American interests in the Middle East or take actions specifically on behalf of the Soviet Union. After Israel defeated the Soviet Union's Arab surrogates in the 1973 war, its government and academic circles began to envision an enlarged role for the nation as a "bulwark" against Soviet expansion. The more precise Israeli definition was reinforced by the Reagan Administration when it signed the 1981 Memorandum of Understanding with Israel for strategic cooperation.

But the U.S.-Israeli strategic relationship in fact grew

out of a personal exchange between President Jimmy Carter
and departing Israeli Ambassador to Washington Simcha
Dinitz. In their last official meeting, the President asked
Dinitz to share his parting observations. The ambassador
responded, "Mr. President, you were great in mentioning on
every appropriate occasion the traditions that unite us. But
somehow you neglected to mention the value of Israel as a
strategic ally."

"Carter answered, 'I will do it,'" Dinitz related, "and
when my successor Eppie Evron presented his credentials,
the President mentioned for the first time the strategic importance of Israel."

Stuart Eizenstat, Domestic Policy Adviser to Carter, also
had been trying to convince the President to make such a
statement. Although pleased with Dinitz's success, Eizenstat
pointed out, "We shouldn't overemphasize Carter's endorse-
ment." He added that Jody Powell, then White House Press
Secretary, immediately attempted to downplay the importance of the President's turn of phrase. "In fact, almost all of
the credit goes to Ronald Reagan," insisted Eizenstat, a dedicated Democrat.

Paradoxically, while the Reagan years brought an expansion of Israel's global role, American officials simulta-
neously insist, "Israel has a real problem setting limits."
Meanwhile, Israelis haven't the foggiest idea what those limits should be or whether they could survive if they had them.

Americans think of "self-control" as constructive,
whereas Israelis immediately conjure up images of shackles
on their ability to fight for existence. At the same time, this
pint-sized state of fewer than four million people constantly
ends up on the front page of the international papers, and
there seems to be an Israeli angle to nearly every story about
the Middle East. The contradiction between the size of the
country and its apparent influence makes it all the more
difficult for Israelis to come to terms with American expectations.

The Israeli agenda reflects certain geographic realities.
As a small country surrounded by adversaries that have

continuously threatened its existence, Israel's attention is necessarily focused on regional mischief. As a superpower, the United States has a different set of interests in the Middle East, as in every other part of the world. Israel is only one among a multitude.

American officials are prone to argue, "We give Israel arms and money in huge amounts. Therefore they need us; therefore we can tell them what to do." The consequences of pressure, sanctions, and leverage to other nations are not very well understood in this country. Who wants to be a lion with no teeth?

The belief that we can tell other countries what to do has been challenged by the Vietnam experience, disputes with our European allies, Gorbachev's *glasnost*, the revolutionary upheavals in Eastern Europe, and our helplessness in defusing the crises of Latin America.

The bombing of Libya, the invasion of Grenada, and the Christmas 1989 Operation Just Cause against Panamanian dictator Manuel Noriega exemplify the persistence of this world view. And this view undoubtedly remains the nation's accepted wisdom (or aspiration) with respect to Israel. "It is an extreme case of 'God, they are so dependent on us, why can't we tell them what to do?' " suggested one Middle East analyst. People who have dealt with Israel over time may be more sophisticated in their approach, but there is yet the feeling that "We should be able to deliver Israel."

On the other side of the coin, it is doubtful that Israel's current leadership has ever given serious thought, let alone study, to that nation's obligations as an ally. Israel never had a dependable ally before its "love affair" with the United States. The Soviet Union was among the first to recognize Israel, but later deserted it. The French, for a time, became Israel's "best friend," but de Gaulle betrayed Israel in 1967. Since the Six-Day War, the United States has emerged as Israel's single ally, but with no detailed discussion or understandings of what that alliance should entail (or preclude), beyond certain quid pro quos related to defense.

"If you are going to be a good ally and the alliance matters to you, you don't go getting the United States involved in funny business that ends up creating major problems," a U.S. official told me. But Israelis don't generally perceive it that way. "Americans believe that because they support us, they must get everything from us, easily," an Israeli commented. "It's not easy. As we say, 'That's life, baby.' Each government official has to represent his own government's interests to maximize its profits."

Israelis know this attitude upsets American officials. "Yes," said a former Israeli official, "sometimes Americans feel they give the basic elements of support to Israel, and help us reach the point that we can conduct negotiations. Then the Americans say, 'I taught you how to do it. Now you are going to attack me?'"

The confusion is compounded by America's persistent grudging respect for Israel's presumed ability to get things done, to behave creatively and advance its interests: "Gee, if only we could act that way." But of course the United States can't act that way, because it's a superpower.

Israeli leaders, often unwittingly, confer a special importance on individual Americans. An American journalist, Middle East expert, government official, Jewish leader—to name a few possibilities—wins instant status in Washington, or in his or her special community, the minute that person can say, "Yes, well, when I saw the Prime Minister . . . and did I mention what Rabin told me when we spent an hour and a half alone?" (The whipped cream of the story is typically that the meeting stretched on at least one-half hour beyond the intended schedule.)

Both friends and foes of Israeli policy derive substantial benefits from access to top Israelis. Critics, of course, must prove to be even more critical in order to demonstrate that they weren't swayed by the hospitality, while friends come away effervescing goodwill, grateful for the recognition. Occasionally, of course, the access accorded to friends bolsters their public standing enough that they are then free to behave like critics.

The Israeli public and even the high-level bureaucracy look upon the red carpet accorded to Americans with envy and, occasionally, anger.

"We give Americans such wide access to the higher echelons that Americans don't understand that an ordinary Israeli, even a high-level Israeli, does not have such access to the Minister of Defense, the Prime Minister, or the Minister of Foreign Affairs," said IDF spokesman Ephraim Lapid. A brigadier general who served in this role through the withdrawal from Lebanon and the first two years of the *intifada*, Lapid, earnest and tireless, has seen more "American press action" than any other spokesman in Israeli military history.

"You shouldn't confuse Israeli casualness with the deep respect in this society for our leaders as symbolic figures, as the people who make the decisions about our future," Lapid asserted. "Americans come to Israel for a few days and demand to see our leaders as their basic right. An Israeli would never dream of such a demand."

7
DID YOU SAY PICKLES?

AMERICAN NEGOTIATORS BECOME FRUSTRATED WHEN Israelis view foreign policy strictly through the prism of a regional power, showing, in the words of a senior State Department official, "disinterest in anything but their narrowly defined interests." Israelis, in turn, fail to understand why Americans can't grasp the complexity of regional issues. Consequently, Americans think Israelis are "overreaching" in regional ambitions, when Israelis believe they are acting quite sanely.

A former National Security Council Assistant who had been immersed in the fiasco of the 1982 Lebanon War complained, "The Israelis get too ambitious, chew off more than they need to, and they hurt themselves in the process." To illustrate his point, he recounted the "great case study of the Israelis killing the Lebanese over pickles" during the 1983 peace negotiations between Lebanon and Israel.

The Israelis were demanding the right to export their pickles into Lebanon. The Americans saw this demand as an "inconsequential item" that could sabotage the entire effort. "It was a classic example of not letting an opportunity pass. The art of politics for Americans is finding a compromise, finding a solution that both sides can agree to. Donald Rumsfeld's formulation: 'No one gets his first choice.' "

I asked three Israeli officials who had participated in the pickle exchange to share their views of the American criticism. All were incensed that the Americans were, according to an Israeli Commerce Ministry official, so "blind to the regional importance of pickles."

"Pickle exports may not be important to Americans. But they were important to two peoples in the Middle East," an Israeli official countered. "In the Middle East, pickles are an issue. No one outside can comprehend, for example, that the discussion of the agricultural calendar of exports between two nations involved in a forty-year state of war is what made the negotiations so exciting.

"If pickles weren't important, why did the Lebanese government agree to put [that issue] on the agenda and sign the document? I can hardly believe that anybody said that we were overreaching."

When a U.S. negotiator comes to the table with an Israeli, the American should expect that the Israeli assumes that the American is going to opt for the superficial over the complex. The Israeli is probably right. For an American to understand the multicolored, convoluted historical context and incredible emotional overtones of regional issues is nigh impossible, because the American has not lived through the experience of an Israeli. Moreover, senior American officials are preoccupied with other matters besides the Middle East. The Arab-Israeli duel is only one among many, and is frequently of secondary importance. For the Israeli, it is the first issue of life and existence.

If Israelis presume that the American understanding of the region is superficial, Americans believe Israelis will never appreciate the background or "emotional underbrush" fundamental to the United States in assessing the Arab world. Americans often complain, for example, that when Israel goes to the mat against major U.S. arms sales to Arab countries, they hurt themselves in the process, for the Arabs can purchase the weapons elsewhere without conditions. Israel, of course, views such sales as equivalent to cocking the trigger.

American diplomats find that Israelis never cease to strive toward their goals with enthusiasm, energy, and fervor. This approach has gained much for the state over the years. Yet this same attribute can also leave American negotiators dumbfounded, viewing Israeli exuberance as foolhardy or even dangerous.

Israelis are tough, demanding bargainers. When Israeli Ambassador Meir Rosenne, known for his legal tenacity, found himself on the same elevator with Henry Kissinger, he asked, "Dr. Kissinger, do you remember me?" Kissinger responded, "How could I forget you? You're the man who shortened my life."

Former U.S. Deputy Undersecretary of Defense Dov Zakheim, who did battle over the Lavi, warns that "Israelis don't play hardball, they play spitball." Probably the only ordained rabbi ever to serve in a high-level Defense policy position, Zakheim is as feisty as a boxer. "The Israelis are not averse to bullying, if that's what it takes," he said. "They are no different from other nations; there's only a difference in style. The British begin by agreeing and then making 'minor changes,' which eventually become total changes. The Japanese say *hi* [yes] and then leave you to figure it out. Israeli lifestyle is fast-lane. If something can be resolved next week, let's resolve it today."

Several diplomats decried in emotional terms Israeli negotiating tactics with the Lebanese in 1983 over an Israel-Lebanon peace agreement. "The Israelis actually wanted too much, and they hurt the Lebanese," said a former Special Representative for the Middle East. "It became unbearable. The Lebanese were willing to try, but they could not talk any of their friends into going along with it, other than the Saudis and a few others. The Israelis originally wanted a full-scale peace treaty with Lebanon, which was out of the question."

His opposite number on the Israeli side calls such analysis ridiculous. This Israeli describes a tremendous shouting match between Ariel Sharon and Philip Habib, with Habib almost having a heart attack right there on the spot. "We were dealing with a Lebanese emissary. Habib thought we were trying to negotiate behind his back. But we were trying to shortcut the process.

"The Americans told us, 'Within fourteen hours of signing this agreement, we will get Syria to sign.' They were bluffing, but we had such faith that we accepted it. We were brutal and to the point. Habib was trying to get the agreement by playing by the rules. There are no rules in negotiations," said the Israeli.

Israelis contend that the Lebanese Parliament actually ratified the agreement, but that Amin Gemayel, then President of Lebanon, cowered before the Syrian bully and never signed the agreement. From the Israeli viewpoint, negotiations over this protocol pointed up significant differences in the American/Israeli negotiating strategy in a trilateral context. "One has to play angry, one has to bluff," the senior Israeli negotiator emphasized. "The Americans think this is wrong. They are crazy. It's a war. We must use every tactic we can—faking crises, disinformation. But this is not accepted by the Americans."

Israelis maneuver more deftly than American officials. There may be ten opposing opinions within the Israeli delegation on particular talks. Yet, when it comes to the bottom line, they usually present a more united front than the U.S. side.

"In Lebanon, the Israelis were more effective in manipulating the negotiations to serve their interests," admits a former National Security Council assistant. "The U.S. side was basically divided over Lebanon. The Lebanese were terribly divided over how to deal with Israel. The Israelis were absolutely united in their desire and their ability to get the most possible—which I do not begrudge them; everyone is trying to get the most they can out of a negotiation."

From the American perspective, Israel could have walked away from the May 17, 1983, negotiations with a framework that would have provided the basic principles they sought in both political and realpolitik terms. Were it not for the Israeli need to dot every i and cross every t Americans argue, the Israelis probably could have brought about the withdrawal of the Syrians from Lebanon.

"This was true not only in negotiations between Israelis and Lebanese, but between Israelis and Americans," one American negotiator insisted. "When the Israelis, putative allies of ours, would behave like adversaries—totally mistrustful, totally demanding of the extra inch—that, in the context of the type of relationship that some of us were trying to shape, undermined the good feelings that might otherwise have led to a more normal relationship."

At the opening portion of the agreement, the Israelis wanted a paragraph that essentially said Lebanon and Israel are at peace. The Lebanese, that is the Sunnis, according to an American, "simply could not swallow" the language Israel was insisting on. Finally a member of the American team came up with some artful compromise language that the Lebanese were reluctantly prepared to accept if the U.S. side could convince the Israeli team to agree.

"In any event, we took it back to Israel," the former negotiator continued. "I was sitting at the table with [Secretary of State George] Shultz, [Ambassador to Israel Sam] Lewis, and [Ambassador Philip] Habib. Across from us were Shamir, who was then the Foreign Minister, David Kimche, Moshe Arens, and the rest of their team. They were speaking in Hebrew, and they had forgotten that I understood Hebrew. Shamir was saying that certain points in the compromise language were 'not important, but I don't want to agree.' Kimche and Arens were saying, 'Listen, this is important to Shultz. We should give it to him.' They went back and forth like this for about five minutes. Finally, I leaned across the table and I said to Shamir in Hebrew, 'If it's not important, agree now, and let's get on with it.' Shamir looked at me, smiled, and said, 'I'll agree later.' "

Just in retelling the story, the American negotiator became visibly agitated. "Again," he emphasized, "here was clearly an important political point, in the context of a negotiation where the Secretary of State was involved, that had no real significance in terms of the outcome of these talks. It was not going to affect the trade relations that Israel wanted with Lebanon or the ability of Israelis to go to Lebanon. It was a philosophical issue."

Why did Shamir say, "later," especially when he knew that at least one member of the American team knew exactly what he was doing? The American side believed that Shamir feared the political repercussions inside Israel more than those without, said the American negotiator. "He knew it was important to Begin. Shamir would have to think, 'My God, what is Begin going to say to me when word gets back to him that I gave in on this? He'll find out about it from somebody else before I can get to him.'"

By the same token, Israelis are sometimes convinced that American officials exaggerate events. In one memorable incident, for example, an Israeli tank was confronted by a U.S. Marine with a gun. The marvelous thing about this story, however, is that neither side quite recalls who drove the tank and who aimed the gun.

The dispute occurred in an area under Marine control, adjacent to an area patrolled by the Israelis. When the Israeli tank moved toward the Marines, a young American soldier tried to stop the tank with a pistol. As American officials relate the episode, it exemplified "Sharon constantly over-reaching and pushing a tank to try to test the limits of the Marine lines." The young soldier was actually given a medal for bravery in confronting his Israeli ally.

Israelis obviously see the confrontation in very different terms. "I went down to hear what was going on," an Israeli told me. "It was insane. The officer claimed that we were in his territory, but he had to run down a hill and chase the tank going away from the American area. Our boys thought the whole thing was a joke. We saw it as the Americans trying to create an incident to show the Lebanese army that in fact they were neutral. It looked too contrived."

A former CIA official who considers his years spent in Israel among the best in his life and has deep Israeli friendships, also talked about overreaching. "The older brother/younger brother relationship comes from our side, not theirs," according to the CIA-nik.

"An Israeli will chide his American counterpart, 'You have the information I need. Why don't you give it to me?' I can't tell you how many times I've heard that. But when we say, 'Look, I told you all about it,' the Israeli says, 'True, so since you told me all about it, why don't you just give it to me?' When we repeat, 'I told you I can't,' the Israeli says, 'You're a louse.' The Brits wouldn't ask, they'd just steal it. The Israelis will steal it, too, but they'll ask first."

Americans and Israelis look at the same set of facts, but because of history and human events, often draw opposite conclusions. "The basic problem is that a lot of the supermacho superunpleasantness derives from fear," says a former Assistant Secretary of State for the Near East, who spent most of his professional life dealing with Israelis.

8
LEGAL GLADIATORS

TO SOME AMERICAN NEGOTIATORS, THE ISRAELI PEN-chant for legalisms is like the chilling sound of fingernails on a blackboard; to others, it's a creative challenge. "Israelis are much more legalistic than most other people we deal with, but much more American," said Richard Fairbanks, former Special Negotiator for the Middle East Peace Process. Ever cheerful and a friend to all, Fairbanks couldn't carry a grudge if it were a direct order from the President. Talented and confident, Fairbanks is a winner who gives the impression that he would rather banter than enter the race.

American negotiators, trained as lawyers and accustomed to employing their forensic skills, still tend to act more like diplomats than lawyers. The U.S. approach is to concentrate first on the political solution or outcome, then ask the lawyers to protect American interests.

The Israelis begin from the opposite direction: let the lawyers draft the document, then determine whether a political bridge can be found between the two sides. The plans and drafts they circulate really reflect their legal, not their political, position. Starting from the legal language can frustrate the American penchant for rapid political solutions.

The renegotiated 1981 Memorandum of Agreement, sanctifying strategic cooperation with Israel, is a case in point. Secretary of State George Shultz concluded that the only way to convince Israel its security interests were not at stake in peace negotiations with Palestinians was to satisfy Israeli security concerns. The Israeli government had lobbied for years to reach a strategic agreement with the United States.

Many of Shultz's advisers, as well as his detractors, thought it was a bad idea, "but Shultz was determined to prevail," a close aide confided. The secretary instructed the department to draw up the document in final form, to be signed in an official ceremony by Prime Minister Shamir during his state visit to Washington in the fall of 1983.

"In walks the Israeli lawyer the morning of the signing. The thing is done up in leather-bound copy with the ribbons and seals," Shultz's aide elaborated. "The Israeli lawyer says, 'I want some changes in this document.' Shultz couldn't believe it. He says to Shamir, 'Let's sign it.' Mind you, the changes were not critical elements. I am not a biased observer; they were not critical elements. Shamir backed his lawyer and said, 'No, we want to see changes.'

"It was a month and a half later before the document was signed, but its effect on Israel would have been much greater had the political judgment of Shamir been to override his lawyer. You take that case, and there are a thousand other examples of the way in which a legalistic view at a particular moment seems to take precedence over political views."

Israeli-Egyptian negotiations over Taba—a small strip of land in the Sinai claimed by both parties—were an irritant to the post–Camp David peace process that the United States wanted to see settled directly, simply, and quickly. But what Americans deemed a flyspeck escalated into a ten-year circus, starting soon after the Camp David accords were signed in 1979 and concluding only in 1989, after both parties finally agreed to international arbitration.

The U.S. team never "really understood why it was allowed to become an object of such concern when the downside seemed so obvious," said a leading American negotiator. "We were trying to achieve a warming of the Egyptian-Israeli relationship, which every Israeli who is serving his country had to share as a goal.

"I was always amazed at the tenacity of the debate over Taba. I have asked some of those involved after it was consigned to the international arbitrators back in 1986, 'Why are you engaged in this? Is it a test of the overall relationship, probing for sincerity and readiness to accommodate on the Egyptian side? If it is, it strikes me as just the wrong way to do it and the wrong issue to do it on.'

"The answer was, 'No, it is a legal question. The facts have to be cleared up. We wish we didn't have to go to arbitration.' They would tell me outside the conference room that they were trapped in this situation, in the 'history of a joke.' It was a joke that they spent all the money and all the energy for a battle they knew in their hearts they would probably lose."

If American officials sometimes feel that Israelis can't distinguish the conceptual forest from the legal trees, Israelis are equally bemused by the "naive" American conviction that their legal principles are universally applicable. Ambassador Meir Rosenne was legal adviser to Israel's Foreign Ministry for fifteen years and special legal adviser for the Camp David accords. He reminisced recently about a relevant experience during the autonomy talks in 1980.

"Now the U.S. team had raised the issue of elections in the West Bank—does it sound familiar? And they brought a whole team of American experts on constitutional law to Israel, very innocently trying to convince us that the relationship among autonomy, Israel, and Jordan could be compared to the relationship among U.S. federal, state, and municipal law. We had to listen to long speeches about the similarities between the organs of autonomy and the specific status of Puerto Rico."

Rosenne believes emphatically that without the personal tenacity of President Jimmy Carter and the central role of the U.S. government, the peace treaty would never have been concluded. But he also relates that this momentous effort almost came undone over an eleventh-hour legal dispute between our two governments.

"We knew Egypt had defense pacts with other Arab nations committing them to join a state of war if one were declared against us," Rosenne said. "Therefore I put in a provision specifying that if there were any conflict between the parties, the treaty would prevail. Egypt was deadly opposed. Finally I went to Yale and met with Eugene Rostow. Rostow's answer was, 'If you don't have such a provision, you have not peace, but the illusion of peace.'

"Dayan called me back to Washington right away for a critical session with Carter. I explained the case. Carter said, 'Mr. Rosenne, you are wasting my time.' I replied, 'I am sorry I am wasting your time, but I cannot advise my government to sign this treaty. I showed him eight precedents, and as a final argument, I told him about my meeting with Eugene Rostow. President Carter said, 'Mr. Rosenne, go negotiate your treaty with Eugene Rostow.' This was the only time I told my government I was resigning. There was a suspension of the talks and a crisis, until the clause was finally accepted."

If the exception establishes the rule, the best example of cooperation sidestepping legal quicksand was the successful negotiations establishing the multinational force that would oversee adherence in the Sinai to the military provisions of the Camp David agreement. As usual, the United States, Israel, and Egypt were bogged down in legal minutiae.

The negotiators of the three nations were splitting hairs in the Mena House Hotel in Egypt. Finally, in exasperation, Osamma el Baz, adviser to President Anwar Sadat, took Israeli negotiator Abrasha Tamir and U.S. negotiator Mike Sterner up to his room. About five hours later, they came downstairs and said, "Throw away whatever you guys have been doing. It's fixed." The threesome had come up with a conceptual agreement and were able to plug in legal language to overcome the problems.

"Take the 1956 Sinai Disengagement Agreement, change

some of the key words, and that's what we used. So, instead of three weeks of negotiations, we finished it in twenty-five minutes," said an American participant.

Israelis use a tactic referred to as "the goats," a biblical metaphor for something that is expendable. Morris Draper, silver-haired, with a sturdy build that makes people around him feel protected, was Presidential Emissary to the Middle East, Deputy Assistant Secretary of State for Near East and South Asian Affairs, and U.S. Consul General in Jerusalem. Draper describes the Israeli ploy, but laughingly points out that it can and has been turned to the United States' advantage. He challenges the assumption that the United States remains on the defensive.

"I don't always agree with these portrayals. For one thing, all we know about Israeli behavior, negotiating styles, and so forth can be turned to our advantage. Back in 1981, for example, we were trying to reach an agreement on neutralizing southern Lebanon. So we came up with a formula that we thought Menachem Begin would accept in substance. But we also knew that in accordance with his style, he would have to change a few things.

"So we changed things beforehand. We gave him some things to nitpick at, a few 'goats.' For example, in normal diplomatic intercourse, we make an agreement, and the countries named are usually in alphabetical order. Therefore, we changed the order. We knew that Mr. Begin was a stickler for these questions, and he would insist on the changes. We did a few other things. It's a funny kind of game, but it doesn't mean that one is helpless. We can do the same thing."

Draper found it "a lot of fun to negotiate with the Israelis because they are so good, and a mutual respect develops." Diplomats are not generally in the business of outsmarting people. "Negotiating with Israelis on all kinds of subjects, minor and major," he added, "I found that you can lay out what you think is important and get the right kind of response.

"Especially with people like Abrasha Tamir, David

Kimche, Hanan Baron, and others. But it goes beyond that, too. Begin, for example, had a special sense of honor that you could count on. There were only one or two occasions when I thought that he retreated from that. Most of the time, he would make a commitment, and you could count on it."

From the Israeli perspective, there are life-sized risks involved in almost every concession. Take the 1975 commitment by the United States not to talk to the PLO unless *A*, *B*, and *C* happen. "*C* was added later," said Eli Rubenstein, Secretary of the Israeli Cabinet. "Therefore, the initial commitment was critical.

"When the Strategic Defense Initiative was launched a couple of years ago, the White House had to prove that it conformed with the Anti-Ballistic Missile Treaty with the Soviet Union. They had these little advisers in Washington sit there like prolific scholars, reviewing with a finger the whole work to show that, in fact, it did conform. And nobody was ashamed to say that they were searching for a legal opinion.

"Personally, not only am I a great supporter of the U.S.-Israeli relationship," Rubenstein declared, "but I also feel quite an affinity in terms of the mentality of work and the people I negotiate with. I don't feel a mentality gap between us. What I do feel sometimes is a history gap or a psychology gap between a big superpower with its security, with its affluence, its status, and Israel with our baggage of history, the Holocaust, and our nice neighbors so keen on peace."

He added, "Everybody has his own vital interests and will use every possible way to defend them. My experience is that when Americans negotiate something which is bilateral, affecting their own interests—financial or strategic—they will make every argument. We've experienced it so many times. I don't think a legal argument is illegal."

Ironically, Israelis find it difficult to comprehend what they define as "American sensitivity and obsession" with the law. The Iran-*contra* hearings, for example, left Israeli observers with, in the words of an Israeli embassy official, "a mixture, on the one hand, of admiration for American society—you can go through this, through so many weeks of open investigations, determined to get to the bottom of it—but then at the same time you feel sort of pity. OK, get it over with. What in the hell is this excruciating process of witnesses? What is this show?"

The Israeli reaction to American insistence on prosecuting Jonathan Pollard, as well as Israelis involved in the spy scandal, was of the same genre. "Most Israelis thought, 'OK, we were caught red-handed. We apologized. We gave back the documents. Pollard is in prison, and that's it. Let's forget about this whole thing, and let's move to the next stage,'" a senior Israeli complained, "but it doesn't really work that way in America."

Americans are even more stubborn in sticking to their legal brief, according to Hanan Baron, former Director General of the Ministry of Foreign Affairs, now vice president of the Weizmann Institute, and personally a great admirer of the American mentality. "Their margins are narrower, and we can feel it. American negotiators are hemmed in by legalities, looking over their shoulder at what other agencies are saying. They tend to be less flexible, less patient."

According to Baron, Israel models its legal behavior after the Americans: "We learned it all from the Americans. Looking back at our history, you will see that we never used a legal adviser in negotiations until we started dealing with the Americans in the mid-1970s, when we were forced to learn the American legal system.

"Yes, of course, they see us as too legalistic," he agreed, "because in the final analysis most American-Israeli negotiations, even the Arab-Israeli conflict, will find expression in a legal document, which then assumes a life of its own." Americans put forward a formula, and Israelis "pounce on it" to see if there is a loophole that a future administration could cite to "put us out on a limb."

There is a "traumatic tradition," Baron said, involving assurances of security support given to Israel by the President of the United States in 1957. When Israel tried to invoke these assurances in the weeks before the 1967 war, State

Department officials took some time to locate the "lost" and musty document that had been filed away and forgotten.

Zalman Enav, a leading Israeli architect, has been a participant in and a keen observer of the U.S.-Israeli-Arab tripartite negotiations since 1973. As a volunteer member of a series of Israeli negotiating teams, Enav contributed counsel and skills in drawing the border maps for all Arab-Israeli agreements. Thin and erect, given to pacing, with laughing eyes and a litany of humorous stories to share, Enav has a rapid-fire mind and could be easily mistaken for a youthful college professor. (When he couldn't get a good camera-lens view at the historic 1979 Camp David treaty-signing ceremony on the White House lawn, Enav agilely climbed a tree.)

From his vantage point, the problem is not that Americans are more conceptual and less legalistic than Israelis, but almost the reverse. "Our process of decision making is insufficient," he said. "And the result is that we come to negotiations with half-baked concepts and comparatively few details. Therefore, when the other party brings out the details, we have to check them. That's when we become legalistic."

If Israel comes to the table with a detailed plan, he explained, "then we do not have to fight over its legalities or fine points." While Baron and other Israelis insist they learned everything they needed to know, and more, from their American colleagues, Enav disagrees. In his view, being legalistic is not only a national trait, but one that the country should be proud of. "I don't accept that we were taught by Americans. It's a national characteristic. It makes us Jews, which I'm proud to be.

"I remember when I studied architecture at the Technion. My professor told us the story that, while at UCLA, he met a number of Israelis who studied architecture there. He asked the dean, 'How are the Israelis?' and the dean said, 'They are very good architects, but they could have been great lawyers.'

"You see? I believe it is in our nature. And by the way, I don't think it's only Israelis. I think Jews are like that. We were taught over centuries to be legalistic because we have had to fight for survival. You fight for survival on two levels basically. You fight physically or by using the mind.

"Take the Talmud, which is a legalistic book. Take all our survival efforts, in Europe, or in the Diaspora. There were always all sorts of intricate, legalistic ways to stay alive. To argue with the *paritz*—the landlord—and to argue with the local chieftain and so forth. I believe this made us interesting. I always say that Jews are like anybody else but a little more so. It means a little more emotional, a little more insecure, a little more abrasive, and a little more legalistic."

9
LIKE US

ONE OF THE ASSUMPTIONS THAT DOMINATE THE U.S.-
Israeli relationship and frustrate American diplomats end-
lessly is the belief that Israelis are "like us," so why don't they
act their part? We wouldn't behave the way they do (except
when their behavior brings honor and merit).

Most senior Israeli negotiators over the past four decades
do indeed look like the majority of American negotiators (in
that they are of Caucasian ancestry). Furthermore, most
either were born in Eastern Europe or are the children of
European parents, speak English rather well, and certainly
share the same democratic mind-set. In fact, two of Israel's
most prominent figures—former Prime Minister Golda Meir
and present Foreign Minister Moshe Arens—emigrated to
Israel from the United States in their adult years. Golda
Meir, you might say, became an American-Israeli legend.
"Golda Meir is my heroine," a young officer from Texas said,
unaware that she had passed away many years ago.

Richard Murphy, former Assistant Secretary for Near
East Affairs at the Department of State, is a senior fellow for
Middle East studies at the Council on Foreign Relations. Tall
and lanky, with a patrician demeanor, Murphy agrees that

the surface similarities often mask deep cultural differences in government negotiation techniques.

"Americans and Israelis assume that they understand each other very well because they come from the same kind of Western democratic orientation and speak English, but when it comes to the cultural nuances that each of them brings to a situation, there is a very definite difference. One is the American sense of security and largess, versus the Israeli sense of insecurity and narrow view of the world. That translates into a whole range of problems when they try to talk to each other about issues," he said.

A former U.S. Ambassador-at-Large to the Middle East is even more blunt: "Culturally, when you run into somebody like Benjamin Netanyahu [Deputy Foreign Minister, educated in the United States] or Moshe Arens [Foreign Minister, former American] or guys who speak American-accented English and know your cultural background as well as or better than you do, it is very hard to remind yourself that you are dealing with a foreign country.

"I am such a horrible linguist that I don't speak Arabic, and I don't speak Hebrew, and I don't speak Chinese or Japanese. Since I cannot talk to them in their language, they always have to talk to me in my language. You tend to empathize and listen more to people who speak English beautifully. This is just an American cultural bias."

Safe and isolated on a distant continent, the American people have a long history of relative disinterest and lack of knowledge of or involvement with the world beyond their shores—apart, that is, from how foreign events directly affect American economic interests, property, or citizens. For example, an American congressional aide recounted a story concerning a delegation of U.S. Congressmen who visited Lebanon during the 1982 war. An Israeli colonel was asked to brief the members on the forty different militias operating in Lebanon. The colonel went on for about ten minutes, when a Congressman piped up, "Look, this is very interesting, but could you just tell us who the good guys are and who are the bad guys?"

Secretary of State James Baker likes to recount one of his first campaign experiences, at the age of twenty-three, when he attempted to deliver a speech in a Texas bar. Baker lectured the patrons of the establishment that the main problem in America is ignorance and apathy. Turning to a fellow nearby, Baker asked, "Sir, what is your opinion?" The imbiber answered, "I don't know, and I don't care."

The *New York Times* began to "folksify" the foreign affairs image of its prestigious op-ed page in the summer of 1989, by inviting personalities like television star Roseanne Barr to contribute, along with "common people" from around the United States. When a deputy editor of the page was asked by Joan Lunden on "Good Morning America," "Does this mean you won't be focusing so heavily on issues like Lebanon?" she responded, "Lebanon, of course, is very interesting, but it isn't life."

In a very real sense, both Israel and the United States can rightly be described as parochial societies—obsessed for reasons of geography and history with their own view of the world and given to interpreting the international landscape from their particular vantage point. Israelis are extremely curious about distant places, and at least one-fourth of the country travels abroad every summer. (An American rabbi traveled to Nepal last year to hold a special Passover service for the hundreds of Israelis backpacking in the mountains.) But when it comes to foreign policy judgments or empathy, the guiding question is always "How does it affect Israel?"

Americans, by comparison, generally look for the quick-fix familiarity with foreign cultures, rarely probing beneath the surface. Even Americans in the highest levels of the foreign policy apparatus tend to approach the world through the eye of the American camera. "There is very little interest in the world, except insofar as it affects American interests," said a Middle East analyst, who hails from another country. "The United States approaches the world differently than any other nation.

"Americans view the world in terms of whether the people are like us or not like us, and differentiation is very limited. So Australians are 'like us,' and there has been a great honeymoon between the American and Australian governments in recent years. Similarly, Israel is regarded as 'like us.' All those values which underpin the relationship—common values like democracy, the Judeo-Christian ethic—all are very real, in terms of the substance of the assumption that Israel is like America."

But, of course, Israel is not the United States. It exists in a very different environment. One of the consequences of the *intifada* and the way in which the Americans perceive it is that Israel is becoming much less "like us" and more "like them." Israel is seen as becoming just another Middle Eastern country, which translates into, "Israel isn't quite what we thought it was: like us."

Our U.S. diplomats may be well read on Arab-Israeli politics, but they do not have a clue about what drives the Israelis or the way Israelis lead their lives. That manifests itself in a feeling often expressed by Americans in the early 1980s: "We don't like the Begin government. We should find a way to get our guys elected."

The notion that we can intervene in Israel's domestic politics—reorient things and get the good guys in on top—is classic American thinking. There is little understanding that the "good guys" we identify with have pursued policies very similar to those of the "bad guys" we are so often against. "In the early 1950s and 1960s, the Israeli Labor Party was carrying out precisely the sort of policies, including settlements, that the U.S. government was so upset about with Begin and the Likud twenty years later," said one Middle East watcher. "The policy also proved to be highly counterproductive because of a lack of understanding of the impact on Israel of such outside intervention."

The United States and Israel are speaking from different scripts. Israelis persist in presuming that we see the world the way they do because of a shared cultural background, our empathy with their past, and, most significantly, because of the political support of American Jews. At the same time,

Americans tend to believe the Israelis understand why it is
important for us to have good relations with Arabs when
clearly they do not understand.

The sale of AWACS reconnaissance jets to Saudi Arabia
in the early 1980s is a good example, according to Geoff
Kemp, National Security Assistant to President Reagan.
Savvy and smart, Kemp is the kind of laid-back guy you
picture drinking mint juleps on a Louisiana porch—only he's
British, with a slightly softened accent to prove it. Geoff came
to the United States several years ago to do foreign policy
research, stayed for life, and quickly made it to the top of the
political pyramid.

He said President Reagan had been "genuinely shocked"
that Begin would take Israel's opposition to the sale above the
White House to the Congress. "Reagan and Deaver regarded
Israeli actions as a breach of faith. The feeling was, 'We've
done all this for you, and you're thumbing your nose at us.'
But if we really understood the Israelis, we would have
known they would fight."

Even in the State Department, where the international
arena is the business of state, there is frequently an inability
to grasp the nuances of cultural differences or the particular
circumstances of another country. One former Ambassador-
at-Large to the Middle East readily admits that he had never
visited Israel before his peace-making assignment.

Our highest-echelon positions—the Secretary of State,
ambassadors, undersecretaries, deputy and assistant secretaries—are increasingly held by political appointees with
little foreign experience. Political campaign positions and
fund-raising are hardly the right stuff for building human
bridges to other nations.

Moreover, our best foreign service officers are swamped
by crisis management, and nowhere is this more true than
with Israel, the crisis-a-day country. Israel has so many
crises each week that you need a computer to keep track. But
even under normal pressures, it can take several years to
fathom the complexity of a foreign culture, and then usually
only by living there. (According to numerous unconfirmed

reports, young men and women who have lived in Israel for any period are also finding foreign and intelligence service careers in the United States harder to enter.) However, diplomatic and military personnel are typically given three-year rotation assignments, departing just at the point where their learning curve begins to shoot upward.

The exposure of our embassy officials in Tel Aviv is further clouded by regulations precluding them from visiting the West Bank without prior approval from the ambassador—which certainly,makes it difficult, for example, to take the political pulse of the eighty thousand Israeli settlers living there.

The Gaza Strip comes under the aegis of the Tel Aviv embassy, while contacts with West Bankers are under the specific domain of the American Consulate in Jerusalem. Consulate contacts, however, are primarily with Palestinians, not with Israelis, in order to clearly demonstrate that American policy is evenhanded.

One of the characteristics of Israeli diplomacy is a superabundance of perspectives, information, and viewpoints. Literally, political officers can sit in the embassy, never leave, and do all their work by phone, with incoming calls. Said a U.S. embassy official, "Something happens, and you get a call from the foreign ministry, a call from the party, and then academics call you."

The political counselor can be deluged with calls from all sides of any issue—Israelis trying to ensure that the United States is receiving the perspective they represent. If an issue is hot, and "they know that you're the person covering it in the embassy, you will get phone calls from a variety of people just to let you know, 'This is what the party thinks,' or, 'This is the way I see it.'"

During the Taba negotiations, a State Department lawyer stayed on for a few days after the sessions had ended. He wanted to see how the embassy operated, never having worked in an embassy. "So he just sat in my office and watched," said the embassy official. "It was a day where at ten o'clock in the morning, I was ready to write a cable on a particular Taba issue. Certain events had occurred, and I had received certain information. I wrote up what I had, but I left it on the screen.

"By four o'clock in the afternoon, that cable had gone through about seven mutations because two other people had called, and they had stimulated four other questions that needed to be checked with five other people, and then the two first people would call back. The whole thing had changed so much throughout the day that one's own judgment about what it meant had changed. By four o'clock, when I was ready to send this cable to Washington, some of the conclusions in the Comment paragraph, which note what we think is real, had changed dramatically from what we would have sent at 10:00 A.M."

The lawyer said that he had no appreciation of that process in Washington. "In Washington, you receive the cable; this is what it reported. It's done in fifteen minutes." The American foreign service officer in Israel is deluged with information virtually exploding through the telephone wires. The challenge is to get away from the telephone long enough to find out what's happening on the ground.

So many Israelis have studied in the United States that attending an American university, at least at the master's and doctoral levels, has become almost a rite of passage for Israel's elite. The U.S. government has not yet been compelled to negotiate with an Israeli Prime Minister or a Defense or Foreign Minister who didn't speak at least halting English. Yet discussions in the same language can also mask large differences. "The European, Judeo-Christian background has been an enormous bond. Heaven forbid we have to deal with a North African who speaks only Hebrew and who hasn't been to Berkeley," said Geoff Kemp.

Many American officials and supporters of Israel are irked by Israeli convictions that they understand the way Americans think. As one Israeli sympathizer summarized it, "Israelis tend to assume that they know what Americans are thinking or how we are reacting at any given time. That is across the board, on both sides of the political spectrum. And they are usually wrong."

The truth is that the American-Israeli dialogue is a dialogue of elites. American diplomats rarely meet the typical Israeli, for they tend to doubt that such an encounter would be useful or that they would have time. Tel Aviv embassy officers are swamped, keeping up their contacts with the familiar elite, coping with crises, and serving as a travel bureau for the hordes of official American visitors. Anyone who is "someone" must visit Israel, meet the Prime Minister, and carry a secret message to Amman.

A senior Israeli official described the elite-to-elite dialogue in stark language: "Israelis who think about it know we're in deep shit. But most Israelis do not think about the complexity of the U.S.-Israeli relations. Who cares about strategic concepts? What does it mean? I tell you, it's a very confined dialogue. Elite to elite. Nerds to nerds."

Yet our elites keep changing, while the elites who preside over Israel's destiny have remained the same, more or less, for several decades. "I was astounded to realize," an American official told me, "that Yitzhak Rabin commanded the Haganah troops that fired on Menachem Begin in 1948 when Begin defied Ben-Gurion and boarded the *Altalena*" (the Irgun ship that was attempting to bring arms into Palestine for the underground movement fighting the British). He also commanded the brigade that protected Jerusalem in the 1948 War and took part in the Rhodes negotiations that brought an armistice in 1949.

Menachem Begin, former Prime Minister and undisputed leader of the country's largest opposition party for nearly thirty years, crossed swords with both the British and Ben-Gurion in the fight for Israeli independence. Chaim Herzog, President of Israel and U.N. Ambassador during the late 1970s, was twice called upon to serve as Director of Military Intelligence during the 1950s. Yitzhak Shamir, Prime Minister of Israel, former Foreign Minister, and for a decade a senior member of the Mossad, Israel's foreign intelligence organization, led the Lehi Jewish underground movement in the late 1940s. Yitzhak Rabin, Defense Minister, was Prime Minister in the mid-1970s, and Minister of Labor and Chief of Staff during the 1967 victory.

Shimon Peres, currently Minister of Finance, is a former Prime Minister, Foreign Minister, Defense Minister, Minister of Transport and Communications, and Minister of Information. Peres was a close aide and disciple of David Ben-Gurion, was Deputy Minister of Defense during the ministry's formative years, and is known as the father of Israel's nuclear program. Peres was Director General of the Defense Ministry under Ben-Gurion, and Deputy Minister of Defense under Levi Eshkol.

Ariel Sharon, adulated as the fearless leader of the daring IDF Unit 101—Israel's first commando unit in the 1950s—was architect of Israel's crossing of the Suez Canal during the 1973 war and hailed as a national hero. He has since served as Agricultural Minister, Defense Minister responsible for launching the 1982 Lebanon War, and is currently Minister of Industry and Trade. The list goes on.

Meeting Israel's legendary, larger-than-life figures can prove awesome even for the seasoned American diplomat. Roving U.S. Ambassador Richard Fairbanks described his first exposure to Israeli leaders: "My opposite number, the chief negotiator for the Camp David autonomy talks, was Yosef Burg. He was one of the great characters of the world— a man who likes puns as much as I do but is able to tell them in seven languages, which was somewhat disconcerting to me, since I can only make myself understood in English, and barely at that.

"Old Burg was a wonderful fellow and obviously has been in every Israeli government since 1948. He was a man of many stories, great wit, and erudition. So we developed, I thought, a very nice relationship that had certain elements of father/son in it. He, of course, was head of the National Religious Party, but was also Interior Minister in charge of autonomy."

The same piano roll of government meetings can prove

exhaustingly repetitive for Israeli leaders, to the point where American officials begin to "look alike." The Prime Minister, Defense Minister, Finance Minister, and Foreign Minister of Israel spend at least a day or two out of every week briefing American officials, members of Congress, Jewish leaders, and Middle East experts. I recently calculated that this small cadre of Israeli elites must have each attended over 1,500 dinners with a cast of thousands of American VIPs during the last decade alone.

Men like Rabin, Peres, Shamir, Arens, and Sharon have held several, if not all, the top positions at one time or another. American diplomatic stars, by contrast, shine for a few years, and then—with some exceptions—congenially fade into academic think tanks, make millions in private industry, or become television commentators on American foreign policy. It can take years for a relationship between the seen-it-all Israeli and the I-can-solve-it American to take root. Then suddenly the American diplomat vanishes into a completely different life, while the Israeli leader is left to begin all over again with his new and probably inexperienced American counterpart.

10
THE HEART OF
CLARK KENT

IN THE LAST DECADE, ISRAEL HAS BOTH SHOCKED AND frustrated the U.S. government by announcing a new round of settlements in the West Bank after the signing of the Camp David accords; annexing the Golan Heights and East Jerusalem; bombing the Iraqi reactor; launching the Peace for Galilee Lebanon War; running Navy officer cum spy Jonathan Pollard; and, in July 1989, abducting a Lebanese Moslem fundamentalist cleric as a bargaining card for Israeli and American hostages held by pro-Iranian Shi'ites in Lebanon for more than three years.

The Israeli capture of Sheik Obeid, like other actions that preceded it, enmeshed the President of the United States in a diplomatic crisis that he would have preferred to avoid—yet another feat by the Israeli Supermen.

Little do most Americans realize that hidden behind Israel's Superman bravado is the Clark Kent of the Middle East—a cautious, conservative nation that approaches almost any international policy decision as a major risk.

Israelis think of themselves as loose. In personal relations, they are extremely open and flexible. But the Israeli zest for improvisation does not exactly typify their behavior at the negotiating table—the distance they will move or the imagination they will use to surmount obstacles.

Responsibility begins at the top and remains there. Israel has a gridlocked political system that leads to a gridlocked bureaucracy. The nonconformist, heroic Israelis are actually telephone-booth conformists in the government arena, especially where the "security" of the country might be even remotely at issue.

An American foreign service officer who spent three years in Tel Aviv dealt with one fellow in particular who, on a personal level, was easygoing. But professionally he made the Russians look like trapeze artists. "He was actually one of the people I knew best and liked best," said the foreign service officer, "but whenever he had to put on his workaday hat and write a letter, the things that he would say came off sounding like real diktat.

"You would say, 'Dear what's-your-name, with regard to this and that subject that we discussed on Tuesday, what do you think about this or that imaginative solution that might smooth some of the differences? Let's get beyond this and go talk about something that is a lot more important.' He would send you back something that said, 'By no means. We cannot give in. If we start giving in around the margins of the unimportant issues, pretty soon we'll be discussing the very existence of the State of Israel.'

"You laugh, but that's the way they think. That's the way they operate. So they can't even maneuver on the margins. Taba is a case in point: seven hundred yards of beach. They had to go to arbitration because their negotiation style was just basically none; sit there and say no."

This official, like so many others, is careful to point out that neither the Arabs in general, nor the Egyptians in particular, are any more "mobile" when it comes to compromise and deal making with their international partners, especially in their relationship with Israel, "where giving in on any level is seen as sort of bending over." In fact, all of the players in the Middle East are stuck in gridlocked positions. But U.S. officials keep expecting the Israelis to act less like Clark

Kent, and more like Superman, when it comes to peace negotiations, whereas the Israelis are continuously frustrated that
Americans can't understand the significance of seemingly
tangential issues.

The national ethos becomes a personal philosophy. "I
cannot imagine that any government in the world can write a
memorandum teaching its people how to respond so similarly
to every possible issue and have them actually do it," said the
embassy officer. "These people have to be representing an
ingrained communal psychology. Everything from loan programs to agricultural policies to sewage plants to engineering consultancies—and I am not exaggerating; these are all
real examples—on all those subjects, you would face the same
set of political imponderables."

According to this official, Israelis say, "If we give in on
this issue, that establishes a precedent." Even one. Just one
deviation becomes a new rule. "And they will tell you that
right away. They will say, 'Look, we see your point. Digging
this ditch or having that engineering consultant do this, on its
own merits, is no problem with us, but the principle is what
counts.' "

While Americans chastise Israelis for their political con-
servatism, Israelis accuse Americans of suffocating negotiations by their dogmatic insistence on "going by the book." In
short, Israelis see us the way we see them. For example,
consider the following two opposing perspectives on negotiations over the Voice of America transmitter station that will
soon be built in Israel.

AN AMERICAN PERSPECTIVE

"Ask somebody who knows anything about the VOA transmitter in Israel, how the Israelis dealt with that. If I had been
in a position of authority in the Israeli government, I would
have given the United States government that little piece of
desert, and I would have said, 'Any way you want to build that
thing, as long as it's not a health hazard or is going to blow up

or something, you do it.' They would have won an awful lot of goodwill.

"What they did was argue about the terms of how the land was to be ceded to the VOA. They argued about the amount of Israeli content that had to go into the contracting. They argued about everything you could imagine about building this damned thing out in the desert. OK, they are custodians of Israeli national interest, but I think they should have taken a broader view.

"Whereas, if I had been the minister, I would have said, 'Look, don't nitpick these people. We have other, more important things on the books.' They didn't have the imagination or the flexibility to say, 'We can perhaps get a little mileage over here if we just make a few concessions.'

"We weren't going to build a time-bomb factory. This was a radio transmitter. I think the record will show that we have been much more flexible than the Israelis."

AN ISRAELI PERSPECTIVE

"The Americans came to Israel absolutely convinced that the Israelis could not undertake such a project. There was a certain arrogance in their approach, which demanded that Israel will give them a piece of land, and they would do the job. This was unrealistic, and they were inflexible about it.

"We insisted on the opposite approach—that the Americans give Israel the money, and we would then build the station for American use. That's how the Americans did it in Great Britain.

"These two diametrically opposed views were the source of friction right from the start. The Israelis felt slighted about the American approach, which seemed more like the way things were done in occupied Germany after World War II. The Americans could not comprehend that other people and nations have their own hurt feelings, national interests, or different approaches.

"In the end, a joint venture was forced on both sides, like a marriage of convenience. Neither was happy about it right from the beginning, and this was evident in the negotiations.

What the Americans saw as bickering, the Israelis saw as protecting national interests, and quite rightly so.

"It was a clash of two mentalities. For instance, what Americans saw as 'the broader view,' as in 'take my viewpoint because it is the correct one,' the Israelis saw as an infringement on rights and as attempts to escape responsibilities. The Americans believed that once the site was selected, everything would fall in place. But Israel, being a superdemocratic country, had to go through the process of obtaining approvals, permits, and the goodwill of the environmentalists, even though the land had been allocated.

"The Americans stubbornly believe they are always right and God is on their side, and the Israelis feel uncertain about their rights, yet fight for the right to assert themselves. Israel was chosen for the station because of the special relationship that brings our two countries together, but like two people in the same bed, we're each pulling the blanket our own way."

11
THE UNSYSTEMATIC SYSTEM

MORE COMPLICATED FOR THE ISRAELI NEGOTIATOR THAN for the American, though it affects both, are the different political systems under which we operate. American negotiators have a relatively straight-line responsibility to the President. They must take account of congressional views, but nonetheless operate as part of an executive branch. The domestic political consequences of a negotiation are largely dealt with by other people, not by the negotiators—although, in fact, any major negotiation usually necessitates congressional, if not public, support. (The American insistence on congressional review for most high-level negotiations leaves Israelis shaking their heads: "Why can't we just get on with it?")

In Israel the cabinet system works differently. All Israeli cabinets have been coalitions (although not all have been as divided as the last one), with as many different political positions on key issues as ministers. The Israeli negotiator might have clear guidance from the Foreign Minister on a matter but is always looking over his or her shoulder at the cabinet and at political party muckety-mucks—weighing just how to handle the negotiations so as to command maximum coalition support.

The Israeli negotiator is further threatened by the leak problem—the penetration of the diplomatic world by the journalistic cad. The diplomat on the Israeli side lives with the expectation that if he or she utters a definitive statement in a negotiation or agrees to a point that has questionable cabinet support, the chances of seeing that position quoted in the newspapers via a cabinet leak, probably maliciously and inaccurately, are high.

Israeli politicians are accustomed to playing all varieties of "you scratch my back, I'll scratch yours" games with key journalists, feeding them information about cabinet secrets to win good treatment in the press for themselves and their party. Even the best negotiators are inhibited from taking risks or trying out ideas that might reflect their own views but not fixed cabinet policy.

Further compounding the problem is the need to report the results of negotiations to cabinets composed of fiercely competitive parties. As one American official summarized the puzzle, "Everything had to go to the cabinet. Therefore, you were always negotiating on several levels. You were negotiating with the negotiators. You were negotiating with the invisible media and the after-the-negotiation. And then, even if you reached agreement with the Prime Minister, he would always say, 'Well, I'm glad we reached agreement. I cannot tell you how things will turn out in the cabinet.'"

Israelis like to negotiate surrounded by a "cast of hundreds," while Americans prefer the one-on-one approach. This contrast struck Nick Veliotes, president of the Association of American Publishers and formerly a senior political officer who accompanied Kissinger in talks with Peres and Meir, among others. "After Henry and I talked privately with Golda [Meir]," recounted Veliotes, "she would try to create a consensus by filling all of the seats around the room with colonels and their assistants. It really threw Kissinger, that he would have to deal through consensus building."

The United States proudly claims a systematic decision-making process based on the work of National Security Council staff, orderly input from various agencies, and central direction from the White House. The National Security Council Adviser has at his right hand—and thus at the President's disposal—the capabilities of a substantial staff.

A similar capability does not exist in Israel, where, according to Israeli expert Yehuda Ben-Meir, "the entire decision-making process is unsystematic and incoherent." Neither the Prime Minister nor the Cabinet has a national security staff. And there is no national security coordinator of any stature or standing. As a result, input on foreign policy issues derives almost exclusively from the various agencies, such as the Defense or Foreign Ministry—which places the Prime Minster and the Cabinet at their mercy, so to speak.

"The Cabinet can discuss an issue," said Ben-Meir, "but it's not supported by any systematic staff work, independent analysis, or overview by one group who maintains an overall approach." As a consequence, the national security decision-making system is almost totally dominated by the military— which stands alone in Israel in planning and analytical capabilities. In short, the Israel Defense Forces are basically the only body that presents staff work and analyzes options on any given national security issue.

"All the others are minimal and have no input," Ben-Meir explained. "So the head of military intelligence, to a certain degree, is the national security adviser of the government. This makes no sense, if only for the reason that above him are at least two ranks to which he is subservient: the Chief of Staff, who is his direct superior, and the Minister of Defense."

Zalman Enav also stated, and informed Israelis concur, that for the last two decades, "The only place where really serious planning took place was in the Ministry of Defense. Planning is more than just a position paper. When you prepare a position paper, you have to have a department to do it: a branch, a division, a section, or a special unit. But there was never a civilian national security team providing material for the decision makers to rely on."

Since there is no national security adviser, there is also no coordination. The Prime Minister of Israel should not have to depend on the telephone to track international affairs (especially not on the *Israeli* telephone system), but this is often the best available option. The Prime Minister's staff is a "personal" team. His group consists of a Director General, a Secretary of the Cabinet, possibly both a political and an economic adviser, and a spokesperson.

Such contrasts between our two systems frequently lead to clashes and misunderstandings. American officials may be lobbying the Defense Minister when they should be courting the Foreign Minister or an entirely unrelated minister who has the power but not the position. Said a former Israeli diplomat, "Many times we are saying, 'Talk about this to the Minister of Defense, about this to the Foreign Minister, about that to the Finance Minister.'" Even when Israeli leaders rotate positions, they generally keep meeting their previous American contacts and talking about the same basic issues.

Israelis, as noted earlier, also tend to emphasize "concepts" in the early stages of negotiations, while Americans focus on the procedures and methodology involved. "The U.S. prepares paper after paper, covering all eventualities," Enav noted. "And here is a basic difference. On one hand, you have Israelis who deal with concepts, with ideas, and go all the way down immediately to the legalistic side. On the other, you have Americans who deal less with the vision, or with the concept, and more with the methodology—how to get there, what are the possibilities, eventualities, and so forth."

General Abrasha Tamir was the director of the military planning unit from its inception in the mid-1970s into the 1980s. Tamir is burly, abrupt, tough, and to the point, and even his political enemies acknowledge him to be a great strategic thinker. In Tamir's view, the Israeli weakness on the planning side is akin to an American void in creativity: "You need creative ideas as an anchor for step-by-step diplomacy, as the starting line or common ground for negotiations.

The Reagan plan had principles for starting negotiations, but not for ending them. The same was true for Taba and for Camp David.

"Americans are not creative, because they do not understand the map. They use the ideas of one party or another for the starting line. In my opinion, they never had good ideas for starting the process. The sole reason for the collapse of the autonomy negotiations for the West Bank and Gaza was the missing principles that link the transitional period with the final status."

12
AS THE WORLD TURNS

GOVERNMENT-TO-GOVERNMENT RELATIONS BETWEEN the United States and Israel are probably more "personalized" than those between any other two allied nations in the world. Israeli government officials, for example, referred publicly to a senior U.S. State Department official who opposed their position on a particular policy as a "self-hating Jew."

The Israeli press similarly carried a story that the U.S. State Department Legal Adviser "stole" precious artifacts during a visit to Israel—a leak seemingly intended to undermine his credibility in negotiating the Taba dispute. And to a group of senators who signed a letter supporting Secretary of State Shultz's peace initiative for an international conference, Prime Minister Yitzhak Shamir said "I forgive you."

Americans are more cautious with their public expressions but also more likely to nurse silent grudges. Yitzhak Rabin, as Prime Minister of Israel, was one of Jimmy Carter's first state guests in the White House. Carter, rumor has it, never quite forgave Rabin for a vintage Rabin reply. Trying to establish rapport before dinner, Carter asked his Israeli guest, "Would you like to see my young daughter Amy asleep in her bed?" Rabin answered, without any hesitation, "No."

Yet the government-to-government relationship between the United States and Israel has survived and even thrived during a four-decade roller coaster ride of loving embraces and mutual acrimony. Furthermore, "human relations" between American and Israeli officials have remained amiable during some of the tensest periods.

Former Undersecretary of Defense, Fred Ikle, soft-spoken and taciturn, took the lead in negotiating the cancellation of the billion-dollar Lavi fighter plane project with Israel, a process packed with accusations on both sides. But from Ikle's perspective, the negotiations were "highly professional." The Israelis were clear about their positions, he said. "We had our differences, but they weren't personal."

Israeli diplomats are generally held in high esteem by their American counterparts. Talking about two such "thoroughgoing professionals," Hanan Baron and David Kimche, an American official stated, "They were absolutely fabulous people, tremendously dedicated to their country, working twenty hours a day, every day. Dedicated, selfless people. Certainly, they had their own agenda. But they were professional, congenial, smart, and tough. That's not a bad combination.

"The political guys shout. The professionals you can deal with as professionals. When you were dealing with Baron, who is a quintessential professional and who was their top career guy in the foreign ministry, or people like David Kimche, you didn't have to shout. With the politician types, you did."

American-Israeli relations are conducted in vivid colors, seldom in subdued shades, and certainly never gray. There is great premium on the need to establish trusting, personal, nonofficial relationships between American and Israeli players—where possible openings and alternatives can be explored free of the danger of betrayal if they don't work out.

"In fact," said Ambassador Sam Lewis, "the *only* way you can do sensitive business is if you have personal intimacy and trust between the two." (This intimacy is harder to achieve, the higher you get on the leadership totem, where private, unattributable, brainstorming, off-the-record sessions are a vanishing art.)

The need for personal trust is probably stronger as a requirement for Israel than anywhere else in the world. Israelis, consciously and unconsciously, make an extraordinarily creative effort to incorporate into their emotional system Americans they deal with officially, to make friends of them. But they do so in a rather special way—by trying to convince them, humanly and intellectually, of the Israeli case.

Americans discover unexpectedly that two people on violently different sides of the Israeli political divide are yet close friends connected by something in their past, usually involving the army and/or a marriage between families or an affair—and that these connections are more important than even the most bitter ideological divisions. ("And there are lots of affairs in Israel, so that is a big part of the game," a U.S. diplomat noted wryly.) Ultimately, the human dimension is the key to understanding Israeli society.

One of the most revealing incidents that helped Ambassador Sam Lewis comprehend what he was getting into occurred in 1977. Menachem Begin had just been elected Prime Minister but was not yet in office. He was still in the process of putting his cabinet together. Moshe Dayan was about to become Foreign Minister. Joe Sisco, former Undersecretary of State, was visiting Israel, and because of his deep involvement with Israeli leaders in the Kissinger era, was well received whenever he returned.

Now to explain the soap opera that unfolded: Dayan had recently divorced his first wife, Ruth, and married Rachel, with whom he had been having a public affair for two decades. Moshe and Rachel Dayan gave a dinner at their home in Zahala for Joe Sisco and twelve or fifteen guests. This was the first time that Sam Lewis and his wife, Sally, met Rachel Dayan.

"Although ostensibly this was a dinner for Joe Sisco," related Lewis, "in the course of that evening, many aspects of

Israeli political and family and social life came to light. The Rabins were there. [Yitzhak] Rabin was still Prime Minister for another couple of days. The Weizmans and Pereses were there. [Moshe] Dayan's daughter Yael Dayan, and her husband, General Dov Sion, also were present.

"The evening discussion at the dinner table was dominated by [Ezer] Weizman's euphoric ribbing and exultation about the Likud victory in knocking off the Labor Party. He had been the campaign chairman for the Likud and was at the height of his euphoria in the way he was ribbing the Rabins in particular.

"I really admired the way [Yitzhak] Rabin rather stoically and with a certain amount of dignity took all this malarkey that Weizman kept throwing at him, taunting him about Labor's perfidies, how they had finally gotten what they deserved. Dayan, of course, characteristically said little, but would make a few sardonic sallies every now and then.

"I sensed that there was something else going on there that night that I couldn't quite figure out. Yael Dayan was over in the corner of the garden, very earnestly in conversation with Ezer at one point. Dov was off in another corner with Reumah Weizman. I couldn't quite get it altogether, but there was an electricity about the politics and about the human relationships, all mixed up together in one stew. We were trying to figure out what it all meant. What we later learned gave us some interesting insights into the interaction between family and ideology and politics in this society."

It turned out that this was the first time that the Weizmans had been to the Dayans' home in Zahala since Moshe had divorced Ruth. Ruth Dayan is Reumah Weizman's sister. Yael Dayan was the only one of the three children of Ruth and Moshe who had spoken to Rachel Dayan, the second wife, after the divorce. Moshe Dayan's extramarital relationship was a "national affair." Everybody in Israel knew all about it "because it had been like the Royal Family's exploits at everybody's dinner table for years." But Sam Lewis and his wife did not know anything about it.

"The tension was enormous. It was only because of Joe Sisco that the Weizmans had come that night and finally

broken the barrier with Moshe's second wife. Reumah Weizman had decided to put aside her feelings about the way
Moshe Dayan had treated her sister, Ruth, and agreed to
come because of Ezer's new responsibilities in a government—in which he and Moshe were now going to be not only
ex-brothers-in-law but also key cabinet ministers sitting together. Yael, according to Lewis, was attempting to "cool
down in the corner the emotions that would begin to boil up,
while over at the other table, Ezer is berating Rabin, and all
of this high politics is going on."

In one evening, the new U.S. Ambassador to Israel experienced all of the complexity of Israeli life, for which no one
had prepared him. (There are no State Department briefing
books about the consequences of extramarital affairs on Israel's foreign policy leadership.)

The relationship between Ezer Weizman and Moshe
Dayan also fascinated Lewis: "I saw a lot of it later on. They
were both cabinet members, and I met with each of them
individually many times. Ezer had this frustration about
Moshe. He looked up to him, admired his mind, desperately
wanted Moshe to view him as an equal, but could never make
it because Moshe really regarded Ezer as a kind of sopho-
moric kid, attractive but with a shallow mind, and therefore
paid little attention to him throughout the peace negotiations,
even when Ezer's role was quite crucial. [Ezer] was persona
grata to Sadat, as nobody else really was in the Israeli hierar-
chy. For a number of other reasons, Ezer's role was quite
important, though not as important as Moshe's or Begin's.

"Here he was, Commander of the Defense Ministry and
the biggest 'macho' in Israel, running half of the government
through the Defense Ministry, yet Moshe was still treating
him as a junior brother-in-law."

Family tales, shared war experiences, high school ro-
mances, kindergarten playmates, and extramarital affairs
might just be the missing ingredients in explaining Israeli
policy decisions about war and peace.

"Israel is the most highly politicized country I have ever
been in, including ours," declared Ambassador Richard Fair-

banks. "They take their own temperature about every ten seconds. There are polls on everything under the sun, constantly. It is such a small country that everybody has a view about everything.

"The questions facing the country are so important in terms of the survivability of the country, not your position on housing policy or welfare reform. The issues they continue to wrestle with go right to the heart of both 'What kind of country are we going to become?' and 'Are we going to be able to survive as a country and as a people?' That tends to focus one's attention.

"Israelis are under constant threat and fear of a terrorist incident or attack. They live in the center of a hostile sea, and you have that feeling when you're there. Since the *intifada* began, it must be difficult psychologically. Israelis have a feeling of aloneness and isolation. I think it wears on them psychologically.

"Does it get tiring? Oh, God, yes. Very much so. Beirut is the only place where it would be more difficult to be a citizen."

13
TWIST AND SHOUT

IN GENERAL, AMERICAN OFFICIALS ARE POLITE AND NOT
interested in confrontation. They can be frank at times, but in
a politically charged situation they are seldom prepared to
admit what's really on their mind. Israeli society, by contrast,
is zestfully confrontational, with comparatively few restraints
on private or public encounters.

Civility is not exactly one of the luminous achievements of
Israeli society. Israelis are more wont to engage in discussions in which "your arm is torn off, and your ear is bitten
off"—figuratively speaking, of course. At an Israeli political
rally, it's not extraordinary for there to be chaos over who is
going to hold the microphone, whereas in America political
events are carefully staged, times are charily allotted for
speeches, and everyone cheers at the right moment.

This difference in style produces colorful anecdotes of
communication gaps between U.S. and Israeli officials. A
constant Israeli refrain is, "When I sit with an American
government's representative, I'm sure that he is involved. I'm
sure that he cares as much about his position as I care about
mine. But he cannot understand my emotionality, and I cannot understand his being cool."

Misreadings can lead to major policy mishaps. Take, for example, a tête-à-tête breakfast between George Shultz and Yitzhak Shamir. As a backdrop, remember that when Yitzhak Shamir goes to a Likud meeting or a coalition negotiation, he prepares for the attack with his shoulders hunched up knowing that almost everyone, including the rabbis, are going to beat him over the head. A government meeting without a screaming match is no meeting at all.

But when Shamir visited the United States during a period of serious tension with his U.S. ally, Secretary of State Shultz invited him to "come by the house for breakfast." And George's caring wife cooked blueberry pancakes. You can imagine the homey scene, Shultz and Shamir congenially discussing the peace process over Aunt Jemima's finest.

Shultz took the unusual step of welcoming the Prime Minister to his private abode for morning fare in the hopes of building a "personal" relationship and thus encouraging the Prime Minister to be more "forthcoming" on the peace process, said an American observer. The result was exactly the opposite. "Shamir concluded that he didn't have to be more forthcoming, because George Shultz was so nice to him."

Some American analysts conclude that George Shultz left office "truly angry with Israel in general and Shamir in particular." But you would never guess that from any verbal exchange he had with the Israelis. No, you would have to look closely at a series of actions the secretary took at the end of his tenure—the most obvious being Shultz's decision to open the U.S. dialogue with the PLO. And by all accounts, it *was* definitely Shultz's personal decision.

When they heard about it the Israeli leadership "went ballistic." Several days later, to calm jangled Israeli nerves, members of Congress called on the secretary to issue a substantial reassurance to Israel, via a letter to Congress. Shultz did write a letter of reassurance to Israel's friends on Capitol Hill, but with the emotionally charged clause "territory for peace" in the very first paragraph—the one phrase he knew Shamir could not abide. It appears that George Shultz chose the subtle, calibrated, and constructive American diplomatic way to vent his frustration. (Why shout if you can sock it to them in a demarche?)

Israeli leaders viewed Secretary Shultz as "a guy who treated them incredibly nicely," a U.S. official commented. "They didn't hear the other message that was coming through about what he wanted them to do." In the end, the Israelis felt betrayed.

American officials find that shouting at an Israeli politician is sometimes the only course of action. A National Security Council assistant recounts, "One of the great moments was when I met Sharon. In the course of our talk, our voices were raised. I started shouting at him in Hebrew, and he didn't know what to do. He said, 'How can there be somebody in the White House who speaks Hebrew like you? You're supposed to agree with me.' I laughed, and I said, 'It's because I understand how to deal with you, so I don't have any complexes.

"My friends in Israel thought it was great that I was involved, because they said, 'You know how to deal with these guys.' Nobody cowed me in Israel. I would tell Begin that I thought he was full of it. Respectfully, of course. I would say, 'Well, I think you are wrong.' I told Sharon. I told Shamir. I told Peres. That's what Israelis say to each other. They scream at each other. You know that. You have to do it respectfully, because you are a representative of another government. Other Americans were saying, 'Oh, my God. Sharon is shouting. What are we going to do?' Shout back."

Israelis like shouting matches. The freedom to engage in a heated exchange can be a sign of friendship. "You call it shouting," Zalman Enav countered. "We think of it as raising our voices in an intense way to make a point."

One American embassy counselor said, "My closest Israeli friend's wife and my wife would leave the room sometimes because we were shouting so loudly.

"Friends tell each other, 'That's dumb,' or, 'You can't really believe that.' I would have two very different kinds of conversations, office to office, saying no within parameters.

You can set officialdom aside, call it trash. You can move from one role to the other. I can't recall shouting at or being shouted at by someone whom I didn't understand with affection."

The intensity of the debate in Israel is an unusual phenomenon for most Americans. Every Israeli is a total news junkie—not just for the morning and evening news but for the hourly fix, tuning in to Israel Radio, the BBC, Monte Carlo, or whatever is available. This high-strung quality is foreign to Americans, but they soon race to adjust.

Richard Murphy commented, "I saw it in our embassy in Israel. They are constantly on the phone, the radio is blaring, special messages are sent halfway up the hill to meet the ambassador coming down from Jerusalem because there is yet another problem that has to be handled the instant it gets on the book.

"Sam Lewis used to drive with an enormous sheaf of news tickers, tearing them off and then throwing them on the floor of the car. Pickering lived with that phone built into his ear. Always on the alert. We think of ourselves as hardworking, and we are, but we have a somewhat more relaxed attitude toward work and life. We take ourselves too seriously, as do the Israelis, but with less intensity."

Americans who have dealt with Israelis over long periods usually do develop personal relationships, and therefore most negotiations take on a certain familiarity. "If I was jumping up and down, they were doing the same. It's the way they deal with each other," said Nick Veliotes, former Assistant Secretary of State and U.S. Ambassador. Veliotes was asked by Israelis, "Your Israeli consular officers are so polite, have you thought of opening training programs for the Israeli government?" His conclusion after almost two decades of negotiations was that "Israelis don't respect you unless you stand up for your ideas."

Veliotes made history for his unfettered language during the *Achille Lauro* hijacking incident. U.S. Ambassador to Egypt at the time, he boarded the ship once the hostages-for-freedom agreement was struck, only to discover that a passenger, Leon Klinghoffer, had been killed. Immediately contacting his embassy team on the ship-to-shore open-frequency radio channel, Veliotes shouted instructions to stop the Egyptian government from allowing the terrorists to leave the country (as previously agreed) and to tell the Egyptians "to prosecute those sons of bitches."

Of Greek origin, dark and deeply emotional, Veliotes has an old-fashioned ardor and dedication that are the best testimony to ethnicity in the foreign service. He recently shared the following Sharon story:

"In early 1981, we went to Jerusalem for the first or second trip that [Alexander] Haig made regarding the Sinai withdrawal. Haig was trying to understand what to do in the peace process. In one of these rooms, we met Sharon. We had just turned him down on co-production of a Romanian tank. Sharon was explaining his theory that Israel should become an American surrogate, [carrying out activities] like bombing Pakistan.

"In May or June I learned about the plans to transport arms from Israel to Iran, which McFarland authorized. This was uppermost in Sharon's mind. We had a bitter exchange. It was in front of his captains and majors. I was seething. We went over to the Prime Minister's house. I walked over to Sharon and said, 'Don't you talk to the American Secretary of State like he's a bellboy!' A few minutes later, Sam Lewis took me aside and said that Shamir wanted to talk to me. He was thrilled that I had shouted at Sharon."

Geoff Kemp recalled the same tense exchange between Haig and Sharon, with a slight twist: "Sharon was proposing that Israel would sell military equipment with U.S. parts. He ticked off a list of countries, starting with Romania. Haig said, 'But, General, Romania is part of the Warsaw Pact.' Sharon responded, 'Oh, so what about Yugoslavia?' "

If Ariel Sharon didn't exist, the U.S. diplomatic corps would be forced to invent him—a man who infuriated, intimidated, and intrigued more U.S. officials than any single foreigner in diplomatic history, except perhaps Menachem Begin. The stories linking Ariel Sharon and shouting are legendary. None captures the flavor of such an exchange better than the following episode conveyed by a U.S. ambassador:

"Sharon was probably the most difficult man I have ever had to deal with in any circumstances. His nickname in Israel—'the bulldozer'—characterized his personality. In our first meeting with Haig in Israel, he and Haig just went at each other viciously.

"When I first went out there on my own, he spent an entire day flying me around the country in a helicopter, showing me the geography and telling me the classic story about the Golan Heights. Sharon showed me things from his helicopter that you cannot see looking at maps and reading books—a sense of the small geography of the country, the highs and the lows. Sharon, who was Defense Minister at the time, made a real effort to acquaint me with it from his point of view.

"The last individual meeting I had with him concerned the argument over where we would hold the Camp David talks. All the previous meetings of the Camp David negotiating teams had been in Herzliyya. This time, the Israeli side said they would not meet in Herzliyya, only in Jerusalem. The Egyptians said, 'We can't go to Jerusalem.'

"We went around and around about this. I talked to the Egyptians, I talked to the Israelis, I sent my team out to talk to the Egyptians and the Israelis. Our ambassadors were talking to everybody. Everybody was trying to solve this problem. Finally I figured I had a way. Substantively we were moving into the ballpark of negotiations, but procedurally this venue issue was killing us.

"Finally, because Sam Lewis was off on vacation—scuba diving in the Red Sea—the number two guy, Bill Brown, said, 'Lewis left word that in addition to dealing with Burg, you have to have a briefing with Sharon on this.' I said, 'Oh, save me!' He said, 'No, you have to have a briefing with Sharon.'

"We go off and have a meeting with Sharon at about three o'clock in the afternoon in a conference room in the

Knesset building. It is just Sharon and one of his military staff guys, Bill Brown, and me. As usual, there are ten thousand reporters and TV cameras outside.

"I sit down, and I start explaining my ideas to Sharon on how to break this impasse. He keeps fiddling around and playing with his pencil, looking at his watch. Finally, he turns to me after a few minutes and says, 'Mr. Ambassador, why do you come here and waste my time with your problems?'

"I was really strung out. I had had a long series of meetings. I had been going around the clock and not sleeping. So I turned to him, and I said, 'Listen, General.' I always called him 'General.' I never called him 'Minister.' I said, 'Listen, General, these are not *my* problems. These are *your* problems. This is the peace process you're talking about for the West Bank and Gaza, the Camp David process, Israel. The United States is here doing its best to broker these differences, and we are trying to be of aid and assistance to you and your people, as well as to the Egyptians and the other parties. This is not a problem of mine. It is a problem we are coming here to try to help you all solve.'

"Sharon responded, 'Oh, I did not mean anything by this.' Then he starts giving me this entire briefing. He pulls out a big map about the order of battle, what is going on, and where everybody is deployed. He spends about a half an hour, and he is thoughtful and kind. Sharon says, 'Thank you very much for coming. I really appreciate it. These are difficult problems, and I know you are working hard.' He lays all this soft stuff on me, and I am still steaming by the time I walk out of the meeting.

"All the reporters and TV cameras swamp me: 'Do you have any statement to make after this wonderful meeting, Ambassador?' I said, 'No,' and I slammed right past them, jumped in my car, and we drove off. I turned to Bill Brown and said, 'That's what you get when you have an amateur diplomat out here, dealing with all you professionals.' He answered, 'Are you kidding? That's the best meeting with Ariel Sharon we've ever had.'"

The Americans' understated reaction to the Pollard spy story left Israelis completely confused. "It showed us a lot about American culture and about Americans," an Israeli embassy official confided.

The news story broke on a Thursday. Jonathan Pollard, a senior analyst with Navy Intelligence, was caught about noontime. Allegations concerning his spying activities on behalf of the State of Israel hit the American press around four o'clock. The following day, Moshe Arens—then Minister Without Portfolio—arrived in Washington. He had a meeting with Secretary Shultz at four o'clock that same day. The Israeli ambassador, Meir Rosenne, was in Paris. The Deputy Chief of Mission, Eli Rubenstein, who keeps the Sabbath, couldn't attend the meeting with Shultz because of the late Friday hour. So Moshe Arens was left to confront Shultz on that terrible day, with only a few aides at hand.

"Needless to say, we were quite embarrassed by this whole thing," said one of the Israelis present. "We went there for a meeting that lasted fifty-one minutes. I took notes, of course. The first forty-nine minutes, nothing about Pollard was even mentioned. The secretary led the discussion. He was just back from Geneva, and he was telling Moshe Arens about his visits with the Soviets and all of this and all of that. Only after forty-eight or forty-nine minutes, the secretary said something like, 'I must tell you that the President and I are quite upset at what happened yesterday. We won't let it interfere with our good relationship, but we were terribly upset.'

"Then Moshe Arens said, 'I don't know anything about it. I should have known, because I was Defense Minister at the time, but I must tell you that I don't know anything about it.' To which Shultz reacted, 'The question is not whether it took place. The question right now is, how large is the network?' That was the entire exchange, which said a lot about Americans and about the tone, the message.

"The message was not less strong," the Israeli official stressed. "I expected that Shultz would open the meeting with a very sharp, 'OK, we need the whole story. We need it

now. What is it? This should not happen.' I was quite surprised to see that I was absolutely off the mark. He was
terribly upset; there is no question about that.

"I learned a lot about the way Americans react. I don't
know if it's Secretary Shultz. I think that other Americans
would have reacted the same way, in the same position. That
was one side of the story. What it said to me was that here was
a man—I don't know how much this is a Shultz story or an
American story—here is a man who even during the height of
his frustration, the height of an unpleasant experience (and it
was an unpleasant experience) knew how to treat it severely
but to put it in the right proportions.

"Then the other side of the story is that I came back to the
office. Of course, the telephone was ringing like mad. I had to
wake up quite a number of people in Israel, trying to push
them: 'Listen, the sky is falling on us. Give me some ammuni-
tion. Tell me what to say. What in the hell is this? What are
we saying? I cannot go on forever saying, 'We are checking
into this.'

"The reaction from our people in Jerusalem was, 'You
know it's the Sabbath now.' 'What do you mean, it's the Sabbath?' I said. 'Everybody is banging on our door. They want
answers. *I* want answers.' 'No, it's the Sabbath.' Then the
Sabbath finishes, you call them, and you say, 'What is it?'
They say, 'What do mean, what is it? Tomorrow there is a
Cabinet meeting. It will help a lot if you write one of your
nasty cables.' Everybody in Israel sends cables. They told me,
'If you put in your cable that this is really a situation of the
sky falling on you, maybe it will move some people.'

"I am talking about people who should know enough
about America, people who spent some time in America, but
did not experience this same sense of urgency, this sense of
importance or understanding. It really took three or four
days for them to realize the depth of the problem here and to
come out with a statement. It took them that long to understand what Israelis in the embassy were going through. And
I must admit that it worked. Had there not been this tremen-

dous pressure from the embassy, we would have probably gone for quite some time before they understood.

"I think that in terms of the gaps or misunderstandings, this was one of the best examples of Israelis misunderstanding America. It was unbridgeable. It was quite common for me, calling Jerusalem, to find reactions like, 'OK, what do they want now? We apologized. We gave them everything. We gave them the documents. What do they want now?' "

14
MENACHEM BEGIN

WHEN DESCRIBING THEIR MOST POIGNANT ENCOUNTERS with Israeli negotiators, almost all the American diplomats I interviewed related a story about Menachem Begin. Begin often aroused the ire of American officials in his dogmatic persistence. Tempers flared on many occasions. Yet, even so, Begin—who most Israelis think of as so atypical and worlds apart—seems to represent, for American diplomats who knew him, the very best of "every Israeli."

Morris Draper, former U.S. Ambassador-at-Large to the Middle East, talked about the dignity of Menachem Begin and those unexpected, private moments when the depth of his sadness came to the fore. Draper had perhaps more "human" contact with Begin than almost any other American diplomat.

"The Israelis don't really warm up to anybody unless they think he has a little bit of humanity," said Draper. "They have to sense something other than cold, rational thought. So the little touches are pretty important.

"I found Menachem Begin a fascinating person in so many ways. One of the things I found very touching was that you could have a terribly serious discussion with him, but if the conversation turned to his family or his grandchildren, he warmed up completely.

"He once asked me, in his very formal, always courtly manner, 'Tell me, my friend, do you remember the first girl you fell in love with?'

"I said, 'Yes.' Begin responded, 'All right, but do you remember the second and the third?' Begin was making a point. He told me, 'I want you to know that I fell in love with my wife Alisa when I was such and such an age. It took a few years before we were married. I have never fallen in love with a second woman.'

"Once, when Phil Habib and I were meeting with Begin in his office, the Prime Minister said, 'Last night, I went to see a Swiss film of the Holocaust. There was a scene of a little boy standing by a railroad siding, and he had a yellow star on his chest. The boy's expression has haunted me ever since.'

"Suddenly, tears started streaming down his face. Of course, never a day went by when Begin was not thinking about or being reminded of the Holocaust, the deaths in his family and among his friends. But this was a particularly dramatic moment because it lasted for about ten minutes. There was total silence. Phil and I were the only non-Israelis there. He didn't say a word. He couldn't talk. The tears just gushed.

"In another instance, Phil asked Begin, 'Mr. Prime Minister, did you ever play poker?' What he meant was, 'Who is bluffing whom?' So Begin told this story.

"He said, 'Yes. I played poker on one occasion. It was in Poland. My friends and I knew we were going to be arrested the following morning at eight o'clock. So we decided we would play cards all night. We started at ten o'clock, and we went through until 6:00 A.M. At six o'clock, I decided that I had wasted an entire evening and that I could have been studying languages. I could have reread parts of the Torah. I had completely wasted my time. I vowed at that time that never again would I waste my time playing cards.'

"Phil said to him, 'That's because you lost, Mr. Prime Minister.' Begin stopped dead, because nobody interrupted him, and then broke into laughter. Phil could get away with it. 'That's because you lost.' God, he laughed.

"Begin also gave us a lecture once on the definition of an

adulterer under Hebraic law. His point was that there are
exceptions to everything. He said, 'For example, it's not adul-
tery under Hebraic law to make love to an unmarried
woman. A married woman or a betrothed is something else.'"

Draper added, "Begin was not overbearing, but if he
cracked the whip, every Israeli obeyed. He could silence
Sharon with a glance. During a cease-fire in Lebanon, with
Israeli and Syrian troops only two hundred meters apart,
Sharon instructed the troops, 'If the occasional shot comes,
just ignore it.' Begin blew up. He said, 'We are not Christians.
We don't turn the other cheek. If one Israeli soldier is attacked
or shot at, fire back.' His point was that never again—echoes
of the Holocaust—do Jews remain passive when challenged.

"Begin felt this in the innermost depth of his being. But
you could respect him. We told the Syrians, 'Don't fool
around, because Begin is not going to accept it.'"

Howard Teicher was National Security Adviser for the
Middle East during the Lebanon War. "The most moving
moment with Begin was when they decided to withdraw from
Sinai," said Teicher. "That morning, an Israeli jeep had gone
over a land mine inside Lebanon, and a lieutenant had been
killed. Begin told us, 'I was at this boy's *bris*, and his uncle
was with me in the underground.' He was saying, 'They are
going to pay.'

"Here is where you could see the emotion in policy. Indeed, within minutes of the Israeli parliament announcing a
withdrawal, Israel was bombing targets in Lebanon. The
human side was very clear: It was revenge. Begin was seeking vengeance for the death of the nephew of his comrade-in-
arms. He was clearly moved and almost crying."

For Richard Fairbanks, who had had only limited exposure to Israeli leaders before his appointment, Menachem
Begin appeared like a character out of a biblical epic: "Begin
was, without a doubt, one of the smartest people I have met in
pure intellectual terms and also, in an odd way, one of the
easiest to deal with because you knew exactly what his beliefs
were. He never hid them. He was a man without guile.

"The positions that he staked out when he was a young
Jabotinsky follower in the 1930s were exactly the policies he

was following when he was the Prime Minister. Begin decided he was right from the start, which is difficult to deal with as a negotiator."

Zbigniew Brzezinski, who spent his childhood in Poland, was appointed National Security Adviser by President Jimmy Carter in 1977. As principal adviser to the President on the peace process, Brzezinski played a pivotal role in formulating the Camp David accords. His relationship with Prime Minister Begin—Polish academic scholar to Polish Talmudic scholar—was highly charged with feelings of admiration and aggravation.

On the eve of one of several historic meetings between Carter and Begin, the Prime Minister suddenly phoned Brzezinski and asked him to come immediately to Blair House, the guest quarters for visiting heads of state. Begin had prepared a surprise. With great flair, he issued a formal presentation of lost documents bearing on the work of Brzezinski's father, who was a Polish diplomat. Begin presented the National Security Adviser with letters written long ago by his father, but given up as lost.

"The officials of the Polish Foreign Department in Germany came largely from liberal families," Brzezinski later explained. "I recall walking with my father at the age of seven, when he suddenly charged a crowd with his cane as they shouted anti-Semitic slogans. My father would drive up to the concentration camps and demand the release of Jews.

"Begin had directed his people to find my father's letters. I was very touched. It was half an hour before Begin was about to see Carter, and he made a little speech." Press tapes were rolling, and cameras flashing.

"When I negotiated the release of a Soviet dissident, Begin immediately phoned me. 'You have done a *mitzvah* [good deed],' he said. At the time, we had a tense relationship. Yet even though I was at the forefront of these tensions, Menachem Begin called me at home to convey his personal feelings of gratitude."

PART III

AMERICAN-JEWISH/ JEWISH-ISRAELI RELATIONS

I'm president of the Jewish Community Council, active in the Young Leadership Cabinet, and I've been to Israel twelve times. My wife summarizes her feelings about Israel by saying, "I'll move to Israel when Bloomingdale's moves there."

—a New York Jew

I have visited Israel many times and probably will continue to. I crave the tremendous intellectual, spiritual, physical, cavalier existence in Israel. I love the vitality and drive, but it's still not home. America: this is home, but a home you love to leave.

—a Midwestern American Jew

Do I like it in Israel? I love it here. I live in an American neighborhood, all my friends are American, and I go to American plays. I've never been happier.

—a successful American emigrant

Of course, the Israelis realize that we're not going to make aliyah. The question is, are American Jews ever going to visit Israel? Twenty years ago, I made my first trip to Israel. I was in a small high school group, and David Ben-Gurion gave us a speech: "You have to make aliyah. You have to come. This is the end of it." The last time when I was in Israel, it was Peres and Shamir saying, "Come visit."

—an American Jewish visitor to Israel

If we didn't have to deal with the occupation, if we didn't have to deal with "who is a Jew?" if we didn't have to deal with the constant source of American governmental and community aid, a paternalistic relationship as opposed to an ally, a partnership—if we could put those away, put all that aside—what would be left is "Move here," and I would say, "No. Let's have a debate. I don't want to move here." That would be, I think, very healthy. We would be able to have the kind of relationship that we had, glorified as it may have been, a generation ago: "Come live with me. Be with me. I love you. I want you." I am talking about an ideal.

—an American who will never emigrate

15
THROUGH THE
BUS WINDOW

IN SEPTEMBER 1987 I WAS INVITED TO ADDRESS MAJOR donors of one of the largest American Jewish organizations. The meeting was held during the week of the Jewish New Year, a period calling for deep personal reflection and candor. After some soul-searching, I decided to dispense with my normal update on the Middle East conflict and to try instead to warn this distinguished group of national leaders about the emotional volcano that I sensed would soon erupt from beneath the surface of the relationship between American Jews and Israeli Jews.

In the summer of 1987, the workers of the Soltam defense plant had locked up the chairman of their parent company, KOOR, along with other officials, for forty-eight hours—holding them hostage in a conference room. Less than three weeks later, when the multibillion-dollar Lavi aircraft project was canceled, twenty thousand aircraft workers had demonstrated, vilifying Rabin, Peres, and Finance Minister Moshe Nissim as "Nazis" and "fascists" for their decision.

Religious extremism was accelerating, and the Palestinian situation was growing worse, with no hope in sight beyond the status quo. Few could imagine that a full-scale uprising would ignite by the end of the year, although the signs were clearly evident.

In the course of my speech, I called for American and Israeli Jews to engage in greater dialogue on these realities. I urged the group to reach beyond the usual round of Israeli notables like Shamir, Peres, Rabin, and Abba Eban, and to widen contacts with factory workers, students, and army recruits—the "real" Israelis—in an effort to limit, if not prevent, the enormous schisms that could result from Israel's internal tensions.

The hostess of the event became visibly furious. "My dear," she virtually seethed upon regaining the microphone, "I will have you know that we visited an Israeli factory just last year."

Upon retaking my seat at the head table, I was certain the air conditioner had been turned down by about thirty degrees, so glacial was the reception. An elderly grandmother-type finally took pity on my shock and confusion. "Darling, you must understand," she comforted. "Everything you said is true, but you never should have said it here."

Is it not remarkable that American and Israeli Jews should be so entwined in their dreams and goals, yet so shallow in their understanding of one another's culture, mentality, and daily life? As expressed in the fatherly lament-in-song about a lost soldier son, "Johnny, I hardly knew you," American and Israeli Jews are intimate family separated by differing emotions and experiences.

If the American Jewish community could appoint a queen, I've always been certain they would choose Sylvia Hassenfeld, a regal figure in the best sense of the word. A descendant of Sigmund Freud, statuesque with opal blue eyes, Sylvia inspires awe and respect.

Sylvia is chairman of the Rural Settlement Division of the Jewish Agency, and has long been a member of the Budget and Finance Committee of the Agency's board of directors. She was vice chairman of the United Israel Appeal and is the first woman president of the Joint Distribution

Committee. She is also chair of Hasbro Industries, a Fortune 500 firm.

"Sure it's a love affair," Sylvia said about the relationship between American and Israeli Jews. "It's a love/hate affair. When you're real good, I love you. When you're bad, I hate you.

"I guess most Israelis like us, but they don't understand us. They don't understand us any more than we understand them. Fifteen years ago, we all thought that we did. But we've learned from so many mistakes that we don't actually understand each other.

"We really don't communicate. We speak the same language and often don't mean the same thing. We think they're abrupt, when they don't mean to be. Or let me put it this way: they don't mean it as I think they do. We all make judgments within our own terms and think we understand, but it's not true."

In Sylvia's experience, very few American Jewish leaders have made close Israeli friends. Rather, "they just shake hands with people in the government or the army. Many of the people I know have met only government or military people. They really don't know Israelis.

"I believe we have the same goals," Sylvia commented. "We want the Israelis to be better than they are, better than we are. They also expect the impossible from us. Israelis must have instant solutions. They think if we wanted to, we could make much more happen. But nobody really speaks for the American Jewish community."

I now live in quarters thought to have been home to the august former Supreme Court Justice Louis Brandeis. Brandeis is also remembered as one of the American Jews who led the early-twentieth-century movement for the creation of a Jewish state in Palestine. In the decades preceding the creation of the state, the community of Jewish-American Zionists was small but ardent, while the American Jewish community at large felt little emotional identification with Palestine or the fate of their "Palestinian Jewish" family. Nor did the

American Jewish community rise up in protest during the
Holocaust—as the information seeped in—or against the decision by the Roosevelt Administration to severely restrict ad-
mittance to American shores for German Jewish refugees
attempting to escape the Nazi nightmare.

These are facts that American Jews born after World
War II might not know and those born decades before might
prefer to forget. But Israel's present aging leadership lived
the story, and even if they rarely utter a word about it, their
knowledge has been silently transmitted to later generations.

Rabbi Stephen Wise, the leader of the organized Jewish
establishment in the 1940s, suppressed the first verified report of German extermination plans, fearing an anti-Semitic
backlash at these "fantastic allegations." The horrors were so
immense that even the most caring could not allow themselves to believe they could possibly be true.

According to Peter Grose, author of the seminal work
Israel in the Mind of America, in the three months it took
Wise to confirm the reports, another million Jews perished.
Converted finally to the truth, the Jewish leadership in the
early 1940s did not have—or perceive that it had—the politi-
cal leverage to raise the curtain of silence of an uninterested
American press and public.

Immigration visas were kept to a trickle by a hate-filled
Foreign Service bureaucrat, supported by silent complicity
throughout the American government. And even a pathetic
boatload of German Jewish refugees who managed to buy
their way to freedom was turned away from our coast, forced
to return to sure death in German hands. There were no
American marches then.

In poignant acknowledgment of the passivity of the
American government in the face of Hitler's atrocities, President Jimmy Carter presented Prime Minister Menachem
Begin with top secret aerial photographs of Auschwitz, taken
by the American military in the early 1940s, when millions of
lives could yet have been saved by target bombing. The smallest details, including the gas chambers and ovens, were
marked and noted, according to Carter's Domestic Adviser,

Stuart Eizenstat, who participated in this emotional exchange. The photos had been classified for over forty years.

Peter Grose reminds us that information is not knowledge: "Roosevelt failed to act on the information available to him; so did many others, Jews and Gentiles alike, who might have been able to goad the President into action had they tried. The options for action open to the United States government were pitifully few. But even the possibilities scarcely came up for discussion. Roosevelt's guilt, the guilt of American Jewish leadership and of the dozens and hundreds of others in positions of responsibility, was that most of the time they failed to try."

The documentation of this shameful episode in American history has been thorough, and I will not attempt to recount it here. But it is important to understand that the American Jewish "love affair" with Israel began on a low flame.

Ambassador Max Kampelman was a young faculty member at the University of Minnesota and Bennington College in 1948. A six-year stint as legislative counsel to Hubert Humphrey turned into a lifelong relationship between the two men. A highly respected lawyer behind the scenes in the Democratic Party for decades, and a leading figure in the American Jewish community, Kampelman received a surprising request from Vice President Walter Mondale, who asked him to represent the U.S. government as ambassador and head of the U.S. delegation to the Committee for Security and Cooperation in Europe, the Helsinki talks.

His outstanding performance led President Ronald Reagan to request that Kampelman be appointed ambassador and head of the U.S. delegation to the nuclear arms talks with the Soviet Union. Thus, Max Kampelman, a Humphrey-Jackson Democrat and active Jewish figure, led the Republican negotiations that made diplomatic history with the Soviet Union.

"The dispute as to whether Jews should be Zionists ended with the Second World War," he recalled during an interview in his Washington law office. "Before the war, Reform Jewry had been hostile to the idea of a Jewish national homeland.

"I remember when I was a kid there was a strong debate. Many rabbis were against a Jewish national homeland, arguing that Jews shouldn't be concentrated in one place. There was a Council of Judaism made up of the upper strata of Jewish society, which opposed a Jewish homeland in Palestine. It disappeared with the war.

"After the Holocaust, the Zionism question also disappeared." The Jewish community rallied to Israel's side, Max explained, although "the support wasn't organized. People weren't certain what was the proper thing to do. The Jewish community had to educate people how to give money to support the Zionist cause, and how much to give. Even in the thrilling but threatening weeks following the creation of the state in 1948, Prime Minister David Ben-Gurion was compelled to send Golda Meir on an emergency mission to the United States to beseech American Jews for their financial assistance."

When Golda Meir arrived on American shores in the early winter without a coat, American Jewish leaders cautioned her that she would face difficulties in trying to arouse American Jewry. They were wrong. Her stirring words to a Chicago conference of people who served as fund-raisers for the Council of Jewish Federations (CJF)—"a cynical, sophisticated, partly hostile audience," according to Ralph Martin's biography of Meir—are by now legend: "You can't decide whether we should fight or not. We will. . . . You can only decide one thing: whether we shall be victorious in this fight."

Meir sought $30 million within three weeks. Thanks to her work and the impassioned assistance of the United Jewish Appeal's executive director Henry Montor and the "Three Musketeer" millionaires, Sam Rothberg, Julian Venezky, and Lou Boyar, money poured in. Also, individuals throughout Jewish America, like economist Robert Nathan in Washington, readily volunteered as soldiers without arms, moving guns and equipment in defiance of the Washington embargo, providing political counsel to Israel's new leadership, and advocating Israel's cause to the U.S. government.

Nevertheless, following the 1948 armistice, it was fledgling but dedicated charitable groups like the Joint Distribution Committee, Hadassah, the United Jewish Appeal (UJA), and Israel Bonds, among others, that carried the torch. The warmth of unconditional embrace by American Jewry would come almost twenty years later, in the morning light of the June 1967 war.

The 1967 war injected life into the American Jewish relationship with Israel. Israel's victory conferred enormous pride and sense of purpose. The war was a morale lifter. A vigorous identification with Israel emerged from this tremendous risk. Israel's vulnerability and victory in that fight fired not only the admiration of the world press, but the souls of American Jewry.

The percentage of funds raised by the Jewish community today is small relative to Israel's overall budget, and certainly compared to the aid from U.S. government coffers. But in the first two decades of the state's existence, American Jewish contributions undoubtedly meant the difference between life and death, and determined the quality of life of hundreds of thousands of immigrants.

"Right after the Holocaust, the American Jewish community felt very guilty," Sylvia Hassenfeld said. "Suddenly people who were not Zionists became involved, because they knew they had done so little in those days of the late thirties and early forties.

"Certainly what we have accomplished over the last fifty years could not have been realized without the enormous outpouring of money from the America Jewish community. It was an experiment in building a country. How do you integrate so many people? Nobody could say the money was not used wisely or well."

Four decades later, American Jews make pilgrimages to Israel searching for their roots, only to conclude that their roots are in the United States. The land of Israel, the very rocks and earth, the sites of biblical history, typically find more resonance among American Christians. For Christians come to Israel seeking historical places, while American Jews long to connect with the Israeli people. Many invest their savings in a once-in-a-lifetime trip, only to find that they cannot bond with their spiritual cousins.

Pulitzer Prize–winning journalist David Shipler was stationed in Israel for five years with the *New York Times*. He recently shared one of the most dramatic encounters he witnessed in Israel, which took place at an American Jewish Congress–sponsored dialogue between American and Israeli Jews: "As I came into the room, an Israeli was trying to explain his problems with American Jews. He was in the army in 1970 during the War of Attrition. There was a lot of shelling, and everyone was in foxholes. One day, when the shelling had stopped for a few hours, this Israeli suddenly saw a bright red Israeli Egged Company bus come rumbling across the desert.

"It was full of American Jews on a UJA tour. They got off the bus with their little box lunches from the King David Hotel, hugged the guys, climbed on the tanks, took pictures, and said, 'Well done, men. You're real heroes.' Then they climbed back on the bus and rode away.

"The Israeli was trying to explain to the Americans at this American Jewish Congress meeting, 'That's the problem. You always get back on the bus.'"

Tom Falik, a successful young Houston businessman, agrees that the vast majority of American Jews have experienced Israel primarily through the window of a bus: "Within my community, there are few individuals who have had an opportunity to develop real one-on-one relationships.

"Most of the people, even strong supporters of Israel, have gone there mostly on UJA, CJF, ADL [Anti-Defamation League], or other missions. They have never had the personal contacts to be able to say, 'I am going to spend two weeks in Israel and see my friends.'

"They will meet dignitaries, speakers, and communal staff. There have been some enlightened attempts to introduce home hospitality on these sorts of trips. But that's still very limited. You may send them a nice letter and thank them, but I don't think very many of those relationships continue."

The American Jewish romanticization of Israel made it relatively easy for several generations to identify with the formation of a state and the redemption of Jerusalem. There is a post-Holocaust reasoning that there must be a Jewish homeland "at least for everybody else and, God forbid, us too." None of this, however, requires in-depth knowledge of Israelis.

American Jews may talk about Israel extensively, petition on the nation's behalf, and give generously from their bank accounts, but this does not mean they "know" Israel. American Jews read voraciously about the country and are familiar with the Dead Sea, Jerusalem, and the Green Line. Yet the human perspective is all but out of reach.

In the view of an active member of the United Jewish Appeal's Young Leadership Cabinet, "People come to visit Israel with enormous expectations in terms of their dealings with Israelis, without really investing the necessary amount of time to understand Israelis. The result is that a lot of those people come back from Israel and say, 'Israelis are so rude. They are not accommodating enough to Americans who are going over there and working so hard to help them. They don't understand us.'"

American Jews would like to have more Israeli contacts, because they have so few. Jewish organizations are finding that members increasingly report, "The best part is when you took us to someone's home, when we could talk to an Israeli." Less than a third have visited Israel even once. As one American Jew wryly noted, "Most American Jews, in fact, do not know a single Israeli on the intimate level of friendship. Most American Jews haven't been to Israel. So right off the bat, if you're going to say, 'Do we as a people here all care about Israel?' obviously we don't."

Sara Tobin is an American, now residing in Canada, who moved to Israel in her late twenties and remained for seven years. Tobin met her Canadian-born husband on an Israeli ski slope. She has worked in the North American Jewish community for almost fifteen years and quickly acknowledges, "We were taught to deal with Israel on a level of romanticism, idealism, and fantasy.

"I would meet people who had been to Israel five to ten times but still weren't dealing with Israel. They were dealing with a mental image that had been built for them by Jewish organizations in the 1950s and 1960s; it was just not real.

"Having lived in Israel, I knew another Israel that was very much hands-on and three-dimensional, which they were just not encountering. On the other hand, a lot of Israelis I had contact with never really understood what the Diaspora was in its complexity, what gave birth to the Diaspora, why Jews would consider themselves as having a viable role to play in North America. There was just no common ground, there was no meeting, there was no contact.

"It is irrelevant whether we like or don't like Israelis," Tobin insisted, echoing the sentiments of almost every American Jew that I interviewed. "The point is, it's Israel that we like, we love, we care about, and want to support. That overrides all the personal considerations. The Prime Minister of Israel, in the midst of economic crisis, spent an enormous amount of money to bring all of these Jews over to show solidarity.

"He must, and others must, think there is a relationship there that is worth sustaining, that matters, yet those are the same Israeli leaders who have consistently outraged North American Jewry by their decisions. They ignore what we care about."

But for Sara Tobin and thousands of other American Jews, the ultimate quandary is "this thing called 'Israel'"—which comes first, overriding all other aspects of the relationship. "I'll tell you how I define it for myself," Tobin offered. "For me to be a Jew today means having a personal relationship with Israel. That is my bottom line, my definition of Judaism. Israel is the overriding reality in Jewish life today. It tempers, it touches, it colors every aspect of our Jewish behavior and thoughts.

"My relationship with Israelis is an extension of my relationship with Israel. But fundamentally, I have to come to terms with this historical, psychological, emotional reality of two thousand years. It's intellectual, emotional, psychological, and then it gets to the inner person or people-to-people. But it is almost like an afterthought.

"That is why I go back to the fact that the vast majority of American Jews are not going to know Israelis on a human level. A fraction of us do. We have our stereotypes about it, and we know wonderful Israelis, and we know arrogant Israelis. We know the rich Israelis, and we know poor Israelis.

"Most of the Americans who support Israel don't know any Israelis at all. So therefore, the image they draw has nothing to do with the human relationship.

"What is my connectedness? My connectedness is the concept, the mythology. Reality is secondary. It can't change my connectedness."

Ed Robin is the chairman of the North American Jewish Forum, which, together with its sister organization, the Israel Forum, was created to provide the missing bridge of understanding between the coming generation of American and Israeli Jewish leaders. The members of the two groups represent a distinct minority: those having some desire to project themselves to the other side.

The Forum process began when the Young Leadership Cabinet of the UJA first invited several young members of the Knesset to join its annual retreat in the fall of 1982. The Lebanon War, launched only a few months earlier, further crystallized awareness, said Robin, that "the current American and Israeli Jewish leadership really didn't have any personal relationships—no common language, no ability to call on one another in a serious way. And the future looked even worse."

During a conversation at the fifth Forum conference, which was held at the Moriah Hotel in Tiberias in June 1989 and was attended by several hundred Israelis and Americans, Robin said, "The war in Lebanon exposed the communication gap, deriving from the black-and-white image that Israel had among American Jews and the generally black image that American Jews had with Israelis." The Forum began as an effort to break through this traditional, institutional gridlock.

In Israel, formalized contact with Diaspora Jews had always been the domain of the political establishment, whereas American contacts with Israelis fell largely under the aegis of the Jewish fund-raising establishment. "The Forum was an earthquake," Robin said.

"The ability to relate to Israel-Diaspora issues—with all of the organizational and financial implications—was under the control of Israel's political parties, and the politicians were highly reluctant to give a portion of that up to persons who hadn't paid their partisan dues.

"I'm really referring to the Zionist organizations and the Jewish Agency, because the partisan definition of Israeli society goes far beyond the Knesset."

Political or fund-raising credentials are not necessary for Forum membership, which succeeded in tapping young people on both sides who would otherwise have had no contact, Robin explained. "We have brought together professionals, academics, journalists, lay people, and businessmen who have not been part of any activities relating to Israel or the Diaspora.

"Initially, some of the American professionals didn't feel comfortable functioning with those who didn't belong to Jewish organizations," he continued. "And some of the academics weren't well attuned to the problems.

"But what we really learned from this process was how genuinely different American Jews and Israelis are and yet, paradoxically, how much we like each other and enjoy participating in joint endeavors."

Why, after forty years of interaction, is there still so little dialogue between American and Israeli Jews? Robin suggested that the system was built with the consent of the leadership in both places for their own convenience. Israel needed emigration, as well as political and financial support, whereas American Jewry was engrossed in establishing the infrastructure of a burgeoning Jewish community in the United States.

The way to accomplish both objectives was to build a black-and-white stereotype of Israel as either an idealized society or as a society with security problems. These stereotypes, in turn, stimulated philanthropy and political action as tangible activities that volunteers could take on. Israelis grow up in a highly structured culture, with deeply inculcated obligations to their society. The United States, by contrast, is an almost purely individualistic and voluntary culture.

"American Jewry has largely been fueled by that volunteer infrastructure and by the communal organizations supported by their financial commitment, providing philanthropic dollars with very few strings attached," Robin explained. "But the premise, in my view, was incorrect. Israel, like any national entity, is gray, not black and white.

"Simply being involved in fund-raising or political action is really not fully satisfying for American Jews, because there's no essence. There's only the involvement. The premises were wrong, and therefore the results were frustrating."

Do the leaders of American Jewish institutions believe they have achieved real dialogue with Israelis? "You would probably get one answer on the record and one answer off the record," he said.

"American Jewish leaders now think they have the key to the Israeli political system because many of the leaders flew to Israel to press their position on the 'who is a Jew?' issue. In fact, they were the butt of ridicule in the Hebrew press. Yes, they had a political influence, but through confrontation, not persuasion. They also strengthened the political hand of the major parties to do just what they wanted to do anyway."

Hirsch Goodman was a star military and political reporter for the Israeli English-language daily, the *Jerusalem Post*, for over a decade. He has probably visited more cities and Jewish communities in the United States than most of his American Jewish contemporaries. In a discussion about the human dimension of the American Jewish–Israeli relationship, Goodman adamantly rejected the concept "we are one."

"You see, first of all, I have done a lot of lecturing in this country. I have been to as many as one hundred cities, maybe more, and I have discovered that there is no American Jew. People are very different in terms of their expectations of Israel and its actions, their sophistication—how much they know and how much they don't know—about the problems.

"Any conversation about the human dimension of the Israeli–American Jewish relationship is incredibly complicated because there are so many different pieces of the puzzle on both sides. Because it is so complicated, everybody tends to use slogans. I really cannot stand the slogans, especially the Israeli–Jewish American slogan that 'we are one.' We are *not* one.

"I will serve in the army. My kids go into the army next month. I pay 60 percent income tax. We live under very difficult conditions. We are not the same as a dentist living in Dallas with tennis courts, swimming pool, and a sauna. Sure, he has his worries and problems and important issues, but they differ totally from mine.

"We think of American Jews as these people who come here on missions. They arrive on a Monday and leave on a Friday. They stay at the King David Hotel and meet all the important people, and get taken about in a bus, and jerk a few heartstrings, and then they fly off again.

"It's crass. It's like an industry. I suppose it's good—it fills the hotels. They buy some of Ya'acov Hiller's statues, and they return to America. Then they have meetings, they raise money, but more and more of the money stays in the United States. Still, they need the Israeli aspect of it."

Israeli and American Jews may not be one, but they would probably react in more or less the same way if placed in similar circumstances. Israelis live in a hostile environment: the terrain is harsh, the Arab neighborhood is unfriendly, and the different tribes of Israel tend to bicker about almost everything.

Immigrants from distant enclaves, carrying on their

shoulders several thousand years of insecurity, found themselves in the land of Israel, where emotions are as extreme as the geography. And in Israel they were taught, in the words of Zalman Enav, that "whatever you were until now was wrong.

"The fact that you were a Jew in the Diaspora, in Yemen and so forth, was terrible," says Enav, the Israeli architect, who was born in Israel and served in the Palmach, the forerunner of the Israel Defense Forces. "That you were a merchant or an intellectual was terrible. We were building a new Jew in Israel. A pioneer. A farmer. This was hammered into our heads. The workers were the Israeli blue bloods.

"The worst insult to a child was to be told that his father was a businessman. A businessman was a big shame. But if you were a worker . . .

"What is a pioneer? I remember Dayan said once in the late fifties that air force pilots were also pioneers. Everybody went for his throat. What? How can you say that a pilot is a pioneer? Only kibbutzniks and moshavniks are pioneers. People from Tel Aviv were always feeling guilty for being from Tel Aviv, from the middle class. Eventually, they became defensive."

The exact opposite occurred in the United States, where what Enav deems "Jewish traits" were allowed to flourish. "Only in the last ten years or fifteen years did the truth come out," Enav said. "The truth is that we don't like manual labor. We like to be businessmen; we like to deal with the intellect.

"We always have to defend ourselves, to be on guard against our own past, our own people, and a hostile environment. Many Israelis have no roots because of it. What are roots? Roots are something you build layer upon layer, which we don't have yet.

"Take a taxi driver here and in America. In Israel, if the government puts more income tax on taxi drivers, immediately what would be their reaction? The taxi driver would say, 'I'm leaving Israel,' because he has no roots. An American will swear, but he'll never say, 'I'll leave America.'"

Enav's view of the American Jewish reality represents

the silent thoughts of many Israelis: "In America, the ideal is the WASP. It's a fact. You want to be like him. You always want to be part of the upper crust—it's human nature. You want to behave like him, to look like him. You change your name to sound like his.

"We changed our names to be Israelis, not to be Jewish. Just think about that. That's how our leadership—I don't want to say they forced—but influenced us so strongly that we all changed our names. The same is true in America. They don't want to have Jewish names, but American names.

"The result," declared Enav, "is that American Jews view us as the wild animals in the family. Right? You have a family with two brothers. One is well behaved, and the other is wild. The way they would look at him, no need to explain.

"So they look at us and say, 'They are members of our family, we have no choice, but these Israelis are the wild ones in the family. Let's not do business with them. Let's give them money to keep quiet. It will cost us less to give him a thousand dollars a month so that he will not raise hell, he will not be an animal, than to go into business with him.

"Is there a love affair between American Jews and Israelis? I don't know whether there is love. There's a bonding, yes. But not love. I'll put it this way. American Jews have a love for the country, but not for Israelis.

"You have an empty room, and Americans and Israelis walk into the room. Now what happens? First of all, immediately you feel tension in the room. The tension in the room is a result of several reasons.

"The Israelis are emotional, and they project their emotionalism even through their body language. It's not only by words. They are restless. They move around. They are nervous. They project it, there's no doubt.

"Americans project their own brand of emotionalism—coolness, aloofness, and sort of—I don't want to say the word—disdain. They keep us at arm's length. 'You stay where you are, I am one step above.' So, if we look at the room as having a floor on two levels, the American will feel that he stands on the upper level and the Israeli on the lower level. Why?

"The American will think to himself, 'I represent, or I come from, a powerful country. I have to project a certain image of the country.' And he projects this American aloofness.

"With American Jews, there are extra elements. The Israeli will think, 'You have the money. You have the power. You think you can exercise your power.' And immediately he puts himself on the defensive vis-à-vis the American before the American even realizes that the other fellow is already on the defensive. The result is a clash.

"The American will not understand why the Israeli is emotional. He will say to himself, 'This bloody bastard. Look how aggressive he is!'

"With the Jews, it's even more complicated because Israelis have a much more acute sense of inferiority vis-à-vis the American Jews than other Americans. Because he is the brother who made good. You see?

"The American Jew will feel more sensitive about the Israeli because he is both the brother who didn't do so well and yet he fulfilled the dream the American could not fulfill. The American Jew also feels insecure.

"He thinks, 'This bloody Israeli, why is he so cocksure? Because he has his own country? Because he's not ashamed of being Israeli?' Meanwhile, the Israeli is saying to himself, 'You American Jew, I am secure in my country, you are the one who feels insecure, and yet you behave toward me in such a demeaning way.' It is a game of Ping-Pong."

Motta Gur is a leader in the Labor Party, an aspirant for the Prime Ministership. Gur was the Labor Party co-chairman of the Solidarity Conference convened by Yitzhak Shamir in the spring of 1989 to alleviate growing tensions with American Jewry. He has held a long list of important posts, including his service as Defense Attaché in Washington during the Yom Kippur War.

In response to a question about how he would characterize the feelings of Israelis toward American Jews, Gur said, "I can't tell you about many Israelis, because I don't make friends very easily. So, for example, I don't have any personal

friends in the United States among the Jews. The few I had
are older, and they're not active anymore. And I don't go so
often now to the States.

"We were really very friendly because we were acting
together, working together for Israel Bonds and the UJA.
They were very attached to Israel.

"But, for me, and that's the real answer to your question,
it's almost impossible for me to feel full identification with
anybody who doesn't live here. Because I don't believe he
really understands the situation. Except of course those Jews
now who have families here, so through families they understand better.

"But I'm talking about the vast communities and most
people. Again, I don't blame them, but they do not live here all
the time and have to send their children and grandchildren to
the army, to go through these or other difficulties and emotions.

"I believe that there was a resentment many years ago. I
don't know to what extent it exists now. We have a lot of
yordim [emigrants] in the States with family ties. Our world
has become smaller. So, no, I don't think that there is a
resentment.

"But there is a distance between not having resentment
and being good friends. Even when I speak with 'peace people,' there is a limit. Unless you are here, obliged and responsible, it's not the same thing.

"Let me give an example. When we were in Washington,
we had a couple of very good friends. The Yom Kippur War
started on Shabbat. Everybody was shocked, of course. And
that evening our American Jewish friend said to my wife,
Rita, 'Really, sometimes those Israelis can be very impolite.'

"Rita asked, 'Why? What happened?' Our friend said,
'You know, at 3:00 A.M., when I am asleep, they call and wake
me because the word has gone out to start collecting money
for the war!' So you understand that the friendship stopped
immediately. And we were really good friends.

"During the Six-Day War, we had something like that in
Akron, Ohio. Israeli friends of ours were supposed to go to a

picnic. And then they received the news about the war. There was a very sharp discussion with their American friends. Some of the Americans said, 'Listen, what can we do? OK, they have a war. We plan to go to a picnic. Let's go to the picnic.'

"I was sent to the United States after the Six-Day War to be the military adviser to our mission in the U.N. I spoke a lot about Jewish unity and the Jewish people as the only friend of Israel.

"And then I received a letter from a twelve-year-old child who wrote to me from bed. He said that he was sick for quite a long time. And he watched all the TV news and listened to the radio. And he was very worried about what was going on during the three weeks that preceded the war.

"He wrote, 'Because I was in bed all the time, all the family was around me, and that's what I want to tell you. I see and I listen to you when you say that the Jews are the best friend and the only friend.

" 'But you have to know that whenever they heard all the military assessments of the American military experts, that Israel had no chance, and that if Arabs will attack Israel, it's going to be a disaster, a destruction—the only thing they did was to say, "Oy, oy, oy." I want you to know that there is a limit to what we can do. Don't mislead yourself.'

"Which, of course, is true. I mean, everybody knows it. Maybe that creates resentment; I don't believe so. But people know."

16
AMERICAN
EXPECTATIONS

THERE IS A BASIC IMBALANCE IN THE RELATIONSHIP BE-
tween Israelis and American Jews. For tens of thousands of
Jewish Americans, Israel has become so central to their lives
that dedication to "the country" has become a religion unto
itself, without religiosity. Deeply committed American Jews
spend the better part of their working and/or leisure hours
thinking about, working on behalf of, and worrying about the
State of Israel. Few Israelis spend more than a few minutes
a year worrying about the future of American Jews.

The centrality of Israel to the lives of committed American Jews is all but impossible for Israelis to fathom. Israel
has become the anchor of life, the psychological spring of
renewal, the singular rationale for feelings of self-worth for
hundreds of thousands of Jewish Americans.

Yet the anguish is ever present that one cannot find the
strength to make the final commitment: living there. This
human conflict, which becomes intensely personal, psychological, spiritual—affecting professional choices and essential
relationships with family and friends—is probably unique to
American Jewry. No other people suffer or chastise themselves so constantly in the solitude of their thoughts for a

commitment they feel certain they will probably never make.

"The single most overriding difference that I've seen is the level of intensity and commitment," said UJA leader Eric Zahler. "Many of the Israelis that I deal with lead lives of great significance within their society, and they have a personal perception that their actions have an impact and that, in fact, their actions are essential for the growth of the state, or for the growth of a joint enterprise.

"They're involved. Israelis bring a level of intensity to whatever they're doing that, by and large, American Jews don't have. We don't have the same individual feeling of significance and therefore the same individual level of responsibility in some ways."

Israelis do express a feeling of closeness, kinship, and sympathy toward the American Jew. They look upon their American family as almost essential to the well-being of Israel and to the civilized posture of Israel.

Nevertheless, said J.R., the Israeli intelligence official, "Israelis certainly don't spend their nonworking, home hours thinking about the future of American Jews. There is a real imbalance. They do not even spend their leisure thinking about the Palestinian problem.

"Do you think the guy in Omaha, Nebraska, thinks about the strategic agreement between the U.S. and the U.S.S.R.? Does he care about Gorbachev? Does he care about what is going on in Afghanistan? So why do you expect this of the Israelis?

"Listen, Israel is small, but even in a small country, you have a division between the provincial and the elite. But even our elite do not spend their time worrying about the future of American Jews or how American Jews feel."

"We are introverted," another Israeli explained. "We think we are in the center of the world. If you ask Israeli students what they know about the history of American Jewry, 90 percent of them know nothing about it."

"We want to know them. We care about them. It's the focus of our lives," said Dr. Howard Tepper, a respected New Jersey plastic surgeon. Tepper has made seventeen trips to

Israel. He keeps close count, like so many American Jews, who see each trip to Israel as a notch on their commitment belt, although "sometimes I wish I could have said I went once and stayed."

Tepper seeks out Israeli culture and artifacts, whether here or there. But as he sees it, "Israelis don't seek out things that are Jewish-American, but rather symbols of materialistic America. They use it as an adjective: 'This is America'—meaning it's the latest in technology, but there is no human component there at all.

"When Israelis think of America, they don't even consider Diaspora Jewry that much. The average Israeli does not particularly care about American Jewry. Those who get to visit as members of missions find that it's a tremendous learning experience. At that point, they may become involved, but it's a slow process."

Israel has fought more than forty years for acceptance, yet, ironically, it is now those American Jews deeply involved with Israel who long for acceptance, for validation of their importance, their contribution—but cannot find it.

A Washingtonian who is a Jewish expert on Israel and views himself as a conduit to the U.S. government expresses this mix of anger and expectation—without the slightest recognition of the meaning of his words: "I've never ever looked for thanks or expected it. But by the same token, one guy did thank me. I thought that was so strange that somebody would. He was the first Israeli who ever said thank you. They take it all for granted.

"They expect Jews to support them, but they are not terribly interested in the welfare of other Jews, foreign Jews, whether in the United States or elsewhere, as long as they remain there, wherever 'there' might be. It is unreasonable, but I don't resent it."

The simple truth is that American Jews want Israelis to love them, to admire them, and to be grateful. What they cannot appreciate is that Israelis rarely thank each other, let alone bestow honors or plaques.

Israelis have learned the importance of bestowing honors

on Americans and other foreign Jews, but this doesn't mean they feel comfortable with the process. When Israelis do offer a thank you—in Hebrew—it is almost always to the man or woman who has made an outstanding contribution to the army or the society through a lifetime of service.

Despite their heroic image, Israelis seldom use the word *hero*. Very few medals are granted by the Israel Defense Forces, and almost none above the level of major. There are only three medals in the IDF: the Yellow Medal for Heroism, the Red Medal for Bravery, and the Blue Medal of Commendation. Those who receive such recognition have performed extraordinary feats of valor.

"In America, every person with a scratch on his bottom gets the Purple Heart," an Israeli ex-soldier commented wryly. "We do not give medals to officers above the level of major, because it is assumed that the individual is doing his duty, and it is taken for granted that he is doing his utmost." Much more important than medals is the actual number of wars in which one has fought—the "Club of Five Ribbons" being the most distinguished of all.

American Jewish males involved with Israelis sometimes feel a mixture of envy and guilt when confronted with their contemporaries in the IDF, or when they think about the wars they never fought. Whenever I mention this reaction to an Israeli, the response is always the same: "I didn't know that they feel bad. Why don't they ever say so?"

"We think they are guilty," declared Yitzhak Shachak, who owns an insurance agency in Jerusalem. "They should be here and fight. But at least if they told me they felt guilty or bad about it, I would appreciate it.

"All this activity in so many Jewish organizations is to reduce their guilt, but Israelis don't understand this frenetic involvement. I just had a discussion with an American Jew from Texas. He said, 'I work for the Jewish Federation, and I feel very good. My roots are in America.'

"So I asked him, 'If your roots are in America, why are you participating in so many organizations for Israel?' His answer was that his parents were born in the U.S., he knew life there, and nothing was bothering him.

"I said, 'OK, what would make you sacrifice your life for America? Will you fight for America?' He responded, 'If I have no choice, I might fight.' "

"Israelis like to make us feel guilty for not serving in the army," said a young American Jew. "They give us the impression that we're not as much of a man, that we don't have the strength or the stamina." Status in Israeli society, at least for men, is often linked to army service and the unit served in, whereas in Jewish-American circles, a man's status derives from his role and integration in American society.

"I was in Israel for almost a year," continued the young American. "My feeling was they didn't care about me as an individual, but as a body to fill the ranks of the IDF and to expand the number of Jews in Israel. They didn't care about me as a person or whether I could adapt. It was, 'Join us so that you can be a number so that you can fill the ranks and serve.' "

Stuart Rossman, a lawyer and young Jewish activist, shared the feeling of inner turmoil that American Jews experience when they confront Israeli soldiers during fund-raising tours. Rossman was part of a delegation of about one thousand young Jewish-American men and women who went to see a tank demonstration. The tanks were attacking a hill in the northern part of the country. "You could hear their commander in his tank giving orders over the military radio. When the tanks stopped, he lifted up the hatch, and we see this eighteen-year-old with a yarmulke, never shaved. It made me feel sick," declared Rossman. "And we had five hundred American guys jumping up on the tank, stuffing shells in their pockets.

"Jewish fund-raisers stir and tear their guts, their *kishkes* so these American Jews will give big money. Then several days after they return home, they start to feel cheated. There is a hole in their heart but nothing to fill it."

American Jews face perpetual disappointment. It is only human to hope for some level of recognition or gratitude for generous contributions of money or time on behalf of Israel, but Israelis are probably the people least likely or able to meet that need.

"The work of American Jews is Sisyphean," an Israeli explained. "It's the rolling of the stone up the mountain all the time. They are trying to do their best, but they will never be rewarded properly. Never. Neither by the Americans nor by the Israelis."

Perhaps the most poignant difference between American and Israeli Jews is the constant anxiety and sadness of Israeli parents in knowing that their sons are "sacrificial lambs" in the life-and-death struggle of the Israeli state.

"In Jewish culture, the boy is the jewel of the family," said Batya Keinan, London representative of the Zionist/Socialist MAPAM political party. "The real difference is that our sons are facing death, and American Jewish sons are not. We see a young boy, and we think, 'This child may never reach adulthood.'

"Israelis are so afraid that they will lose the son that they feel joy when a girl is born, and not a boy." For centuries religious Jewish men have begun each day with a prayer that includes the words "Thank God I was not born a girl." Yet, for most Israelis, when the first child is a boy, "we know that we must have a second child. We cannot put all our eggs in one basket."

Keinan, intensely sensitive and direct, with a lionesque mane of black hair framing classical features, joined the Israeli peace camp as a personal response to the Lebanon War. A realistic idealist, she speaks directly, without embellishment, and her words are like an arrow speeding toward its target: "Think of the mothers signing the death warrant of their children."

According to Israeli law, the army can place a child in any unit. If the boy is an only child, however, or if his father was killed in a previous war, he cannot be assigned to a dangerous front unit without written parental permission. "This creates a dramatic situation," said Keinan. "The boy will say to his parents, 'Do you want me to be viewed as a sissy? Is it my fault that I am an only child?' And if he goes to a backup service unit and is killed, the mother will grieve forever."

Keinan recalled the case of the son of a Holocaust survivor. The boy forged his parents' signatures, thus enabling him to join an elite unit. On weekend visits to his family, he would exchange his combat gear for a borrowed uniform from the less dangerous unit. One day the soldier was injured in combat, losing his leg. Yet when his parents came to see him in the hospital, the son managed to hide the injury for an entire day through a combination of brave cheer and the complicity of the nurses.

"You can understand the boy, because he grew up in this military environment," Keinan explained. "The lowest and most disgusting thing you can say about someone in Israel is 'He's *galuti*,' meaning from the Diaspora and not one of us." The negative connotations of the word *galuti*—speaking Hebrew with a foreign accent, not masculine, lacking leadership—are unfathomable to most American Jews. "His parents, European survivors, were *galuti*," said Keinan, "and this boy used all his intellectual energy to kill this *galuti* nature in his heritage.

"But what is important is not the child. Think about the drama of the poor mother. She is weighing the sacrifice of her child against all the love she feels for Israel. This is a hell that no woman in the world goes through. The problem is that the choice belongs to her—in this case, the mother is like God. If she says yes to the son, perhaps he will be killed as a result of her permission. If she says no, perhaps he will not forgive her for the rest of his life."

The burden of the Israeli mother goes far beyond the question of war or cold peace. "Surely there are no mothers in the world who have the burden of the Israeli mother," declared Zohar Carthy, whose son served in the Israeli navy. The army is part of civilian life. With men serving in the reserves until the age of fifty-five, a woman may have both her son and her husband on call at the same time.

"And because our society is so family-oriented, the parents are constantly involved with their sons," added Carthy. "If the soldiers don't come home on the weekend, we go to visit them. I never baked so much in my life as when my son was in basic training. My clothes dryer was used every weekend for the sons of many of my friends. American mothers worry about drugs, alcohol, but it's not compulsory. Here, the constant worry over the life and death of our children is something we cannot avoid."

The IDF launched a campaign against smoking during the Lebanon War, and it failed completely. "I almost cried from laughter," said Keinan. "They send a nineteen-year-old boy to Lebanon to be killed any minute, and the army is afraid he'll die in thirty years. This is Israeli existence in a nutshell.

"How can our men be verbal?" Keinan continued. "At the age of nineteen or twenty, when a Western man develops his intellectual powers, our men go to the army. This is the time to be romantic, to fall in love, to give flowers and hold hands. But all our boys want is flesh and relief.

"Sometimes a nineteen-year-old is responsible for two hundred men. He doesn't trust a woman to understand what he is going through. Yet at the same time he has the biggest respect for his mother. The woman he marries is like another Jewish mother, the symbol of family, stability.

"The time when he would develop a soft feeling toward women, toward a spiritual experience and simple pleasures like walking with his girl on the beach, he comes home tired like a dog.

"We have to understand his toughness. But when we become older, Israeli women suddenly understand what they miss. I am not talking about arrogant men. Our men can be very nice, but they're not verbal."

How do American Jews think that Israelis view them? I once asked a congregation of about a hundred American Jews how many thought Israelis cared about their opinion on any given political issue. One lonely hand was raised.

"Do they like us? Not particularly," a prominent American Jew confided. "Israel's aristocracy would prefer to be European."

The relationship on which Israelis now so overwhelmingly depend is fraught with ambivalence, resentment, and sometimes contempt on both sides. "Israelis are reluctant to acknowledge this, but it is obvious," a leading U.S. Jewish figure said. "It's the mirror image of American Jewish organizations. You have the passionate Israelis who want to deal with the Palestinians but have total contempt for American Jews. There is also the contempt of right-wing Israelis toward American Jews.

"Yet there is a vital need to work the American Jewish connection. It's their lifeline. Without it, they would go berserk. Israel is a tiny society, with everyone at each other's throats. This is reflected in all the debates. Israeli critics of American Jews like Y.A. [a leading professor at an Israeli university] are a perfect example—he's over here every two months. America pays half his salary."

The Israelis encountered by Jewish-American activists are essentially on an equal intellectual or financial level. But, one Jewish fund-raiser sadly confided, the bulk of Israeli society has "no idea who we are, and there still is resentment. They don't know what we're doing."

"I think the average Israeli is ambivalent," said another. "They believe that the Diaspora is supporting them. What has changed is the realization that the American Jews aren't going to come.

"In any serious discussion with Israelis, the first issue for them is always aliyah [immigration]: 'Why are you living in the United States? If you really feel strongly about Jewish issues, why aren't you in Israel?' Most Israelis don't get very far beyond that.

"If Jews in the United States are not interested in learning about Israel, why should people in Israel bother to learn about what is going on in the United States?" Tom Falik asked.

American Jews who have had extensive contact with Israelis will begrudgingly admit that Israelis "see us as somewhat naive, superficial, and materialistic," says Dr. Tepper.

Most Israelis, especially those who have never visited the United States, are exposed only to that small segment of

American Jews who can afford to make the trip overseas. "They might see them in a hotel lobby or tour bus and never really talk to them," Tepper added. "Israelis judge American Jews by their outfits, their nail polish, their hairdos, and how loud their voices are. Those are small cultural things, but frequently they don't get past them.

"They think we have life very easy here," he continued. "I believe they are always shocked to find out how hard we work. In a sense, I think we do work much harder here than there. We may be working for different things, but our daily lives are harder and tension-filled. But do you compare that to the tension of being constantly on call for combat? Obviously, you can't. They see our lives as carefree and simplistic.

"I think they feel that American Jews give the money and Israel produces Jewish life. But the American Jewish community has made its own form of Jewish art, Jewish music, certainly its own form of Judaism and Jewish dance. We are contributing here. I don't think that they always see or appreciate that.

"Do they try? Not necessarily. We're trying, because they are important to us. But my circle of friends, who are all concerned about Israel, sometimes feel that Israelis don't really care about us."

Howard Tepper, the plastic surgeon–fund-raiser–Jewish activist, talked at length about "caring so much that it hurts." From his point of view, "Israelis see us as coming over to Israel on a vacation, on a trip, while our real life goes on in the United States. I don't think they have any concept of the central role that Israel plays in our lives. Or the conflict.

"The truth is a lot of my Israeli friends are surprised when I try to explain it. More than surprised, they are shocked. I always say, in my personal life Israel is my greatest joy and my greatest sorrow.

"[It is] my greatest joy in terms of something that I feel so strongly about and that I can learn about. It gives me a heritage, roots, et cetera. But [it is] also my greatest sorrow because I have never taken the ultimate step. It's always, 'What's happening with Israel? How is it going?'

"It's part of my own tension in American society, because I am not there, and I am not here. I usually say, 'My body is here, and my heart is there.' When I'm there, I'm a little bit more alive. There is something different about me—an added dimension.

"I don't think most Israelis understand that. Maybe they can only understand it once they leave Israel and see us in our own environment, see how much a role Israel plays in our lives in terms of our activities, our time, our homes, just in terms of buying Israeli foods or products.

"They cannot understand that I am always a little frustrated, because there are times when you say, 'They don't even feel as strongly as I do.' But it's just their country; they cannot walk around feeling this intensity. I feel intense about America, but that's a separate issue. In a sense, sometimes I feel many American Jews are more Zionistic than Israelis might be, particularly people of my age.

"Some of the Israelis that I have become closest with are older people, people I call the *vatikim*, the old-time Israelis. They are still not materialistic. There is a freshness about them.

"With Israelis who are my counterparts, educationally et cetera, I think there are fewer gaps. It has taken me a long time to find those people. So many of the gaps that I thought might have been Israeli-American were really East-West gaps or intellectual gaps or economic gaps or political gaps or religious gaps.

"In many ways, there are large segments of Israeli society that I would have a problem relating to, but I think that if you would take person for person, I could find more people in Israel who I could relate to than I could in America.

"I have probably traveled the land more in Israel than in the United States. I will do different things there. I will go hiking and camping in Israel, which I never do here.

"I grew up with very Zionistic feelings: youth groups, summer camps. Jewish art, Jewish music, Jewish dance are what motivated me. I guess because of those experiences, the idea of aliyah was formulated in my mind before I ever set foot in Israel. So, going the first time, I had a tremendous fear: What if I don't like it? Then I am left with nothing.

"On my first trip, the morning after I arrived at my cousin's, I had the feeling I had made it. Then a friend of my cousin's just dropped in by accident, on leave from the army. I guess I wanted to like him.

"Americans who have feelings for Israel want to be liked by Israelis. It is part of loving the land. You want them to like you, too. So I wanted him to like me. I wanted to be a friend.

"We ended up spending a very nice day. We left my cousin's apartment and went to the beach. He was in his khakis, and I was in my T-shirt and shorts. He took off his uniform, dropped his gun, and we went swimming. In a sense, we were contemporaries, but in another sense, our life experiences and responsibilities were so different.

"He had that one day of leave, and then he was going back. I had that one day, and then I had two or three months before school started again. I felt like a child in comparison to him. I had come here feeling that this was 'my country'—but at that moment, I felt like a guest because he was going back to defend his country, and I was just going to be a tourist.

"Men and women who are from the Zionist youth groups want to be accepted by Israelis. To this day, even the *olim*— the people who migrated to Israel—after ten or fifteen years still don't have Israeli friends. They still want to be accepted.

"I don't think it's a case of *wanting* to be in the army, certainly. I'm glad I didn't have to have that experience. It's a case of wanting the legitimate right to say, 'It's my country.' I think that's the difference that the army, at that stage of my life, would have served.

"My father always said, 'You don't have to go there. You can be in America and be a Jewish leader. You can do more good here than you can do there.' My response was always, 'That's a cop-out,' and I still believe it's a cop-out, but that's what I have done.

"From that viewpoint, I am still motivated by guilt. I am

still motivated by the feeling that I want to protect the country, that I want to make it the best country it can be. That it's important to me, and how do I do it? Now I do it from a distance. I do it by bringing people there on trips and raising money and trying to change people's attitudes. I have grown up a little bit, and I am not so concerned about every Israeli loving me.

"I think that situation has improved, perhaps because I am interacting with different types of people. Once I was there in more of a professional role, I think there was an acceptance to a certain degree. People appreciate you for your feelings and what you did.

"They aren't going to say, 'You're a hero.' But the more they're well traveled and have been to the States, the more they can at least understand my life and say, 'Don't live with your guilt. If you would like to come, we would love to have you. You happen to have been born in the United States, and now you deal with it.' You live from that viewpoint.

"The sense of guilt is not conferred by Israelis as much as it is self-initiated or self-felt by American Jews. That feeling 'We want to be loved, we want to be equal.' Absolutely. We want to be part of the process."

Israel has long been regarded by American Jews as a focus of Jewish life, culture, and religious practice, but Israel's position as *the one and only* Jewish center is increasingly disputed by American Jews. American Jews are now openly expressing the opinion that Israelis may even envy the Jewish education provided in the United States, a connection to Judaism that is more deliberate, intentional, and what they describe as "richer" than what Israeli kids have.

"I don't know why it's an 'Israeli' family," Texan Tom Falik declared. "Why isn't it just a Jewish family? 'Israeli family' indicates that I am part of 'the family' over there. Why aren't they part of my family over here?

"I consider myself a very viable member of the Jewish family. No, I am not trying to be part of their family at all. Still, I am envious in that if I can accumulate the assets at some point, I would really like to have a home in Israel and spend more time there. I am very drawn to it, but I feel no insecurity about my position or my Jewishness by being in the United States."

A young American Jew from California expressed the often heard desire to live out the final days of her life in Israel, but not her vital years: "I want to know that it's there. I want to know that, though I might be secure today, I have that haven. I want to have a condominium for retirement."

Yet increasing numbers contend that there is no need to leave the United States to live as a Jew; indeed, by residing here, one may live as Jewishly as in Israel or more so. Only one in ten Jewish Americans believe they could lead fuller Jewish lives in Israel, according to a 1988 survey conducted by Professor Steven M. Cohen on behalf of the American Jewish Committee.

Steven Dinero, an aspiring academic, attended a Shabbat dinner at the University of Illinois Hillel some years ago and struck up a conversation with a fellow about his age. After a few minutes, Steve innocently inquired, "So tell me, have you ever been to Israel?"

"Israel?" the other man said, as if it were on another planet. "Oh, never. I'm *frum* [ultrareligious]!"

Somewhat surprised, Steve asked where, if not Israel, someone as Orthodox as he would feel at home.

"I live in Muncie, New York," he answered, referring to a small Jewish haven for the Ultra-Orthodox. "Why would I want to go to Israel?"

Israelis often say that the Jews of the world are going to disappear through assimilation and intermarriage. Indeed, it is one of their deepest fears. (In 1940 only about 3 percent of American Jewish marriages involved a non-Jew; in 1988 the figure was between 17 and 37 percent, depending on the locality.) "My responsibility as an Israeli is to postpone the tragedy," said Zalman Enav. "Living in Israel is the only way to buy time."

Tom Dine is the tall, ever-smiling executive director of the American-Israel Public Affairs Committee (AIPAC), the major pro-Israel lobby in the United States, and a driven optimist. "Life is not doom and gloom," he insisted, "Life is taking your experiences and doing something with them that will enhance your position."

Dine readily admitted, however, that few American Jews will ever emigrate to Israel. "Sure, life in the U.S. is comfortable, but it's also our culture. American Jews are increasingly feeling comfortable with the fact that there are two centers.

"What you have forty years later are two distinct communities. There is still a love affair and an affair of high expectations on both sides, but culturally the two are growing apart. Consequently, the Israeli desire for American Jewry to come home makes less and less sense. Home is here."

17
ALIYAH, OR
WHERE IS HOME?

THROUGHOUT THREE THOUSAND YEARS OF HISTORY, THE
Jewish people have never excelled at staying home and playing state. The creation of Israel in 1948 marked the first real
freedom from foreign domination since the forced dispersions
from the Land of Canaan in 70 C.E. But even when much
worse fates—such as slavery and forced conversion in Spain—
befell the Jews, the dream of "next year in Jerusalem" was
hardly a siren song compelling the masses to return.

For over two hundred years, American Jewry has enjoyed freedom, prosperity, and a (relative) lack of anti-Semitism. Emigration to Israel has ebbed but never flowed. Yet
immigration is the lifeblood of the Israeli state; indeed, its
raison d'être is to serve as a gathering point for the world's
Jewish exiles.

American Jews fervently celebrate Israel's Independence
Day each year, are mystically inspired by soulful Israeli
songs (though they often can't understand the words), and
flock to classes in Israeli folk dancing at local universities.
Several million attend annual banquets sponsored by Zionist
and philanthropic organizations, throng to lectures by Abba
Eban or similar Israeli figures, and write checks to their

favorite Jewish organization (or countercause) each year.

Aliyah, however, is frequently discouraged in Jewish-American homes. Parents will encourage their children to visit Israel in any one of numerous high school or college programs. But they do so with the hope and prayer that the Zionist ideal will never strike their child. A high percentage of families who emigrate to Israel soon return, disillusioned by experiences that shatter their Zionist expectations, leaving them with memories of a culture they find so discordant with their experience of America.

"I think there are a lot of stereotypes on both sides," Sara Tobin said. "In all the years I lived in Israel, the discussions always came around to the same thing. I think Israelis in general, whatever their background, feel that the Diaspora is not justified after the creation of Israel."

In Tobin's view, "Israelis feel that every Jew who is living in America is there because life is easy, and that they really have done Israel a terrible wrong by not coming. That attitude changed a little bit after 1973 and the fact that so many Israelis themselves have left. Still, I think they feel betrayed by the Diaspora.

"I feel apologetic all the time. I lived there seven years, and I could never really win the argument. Israelis don't see any cultural value to North American Jewish life. They keep telling you that there would be no problems in Israel if 250,000 or 500,000 Americans came to Israel. Not making aliyah is a betrayal."

The concept of the rich American cousin who chooses comfort over Israel is a fixed image in the Israeli mythology. Tobin reported that she often encountered this image.

"I was working, I had a salary, and I went in to ask for a raise because the salary couldn't sustain me in a tiny little apartment as a single person. The personnel manager, who was a young, very well-educated Israeli, said to me, 'Aren't your parents sending you money from America?'

"I felt angry. I told him no and said I needed a raise and a loan because I couldn't make my payments. There are tremendous differences in understanding and in attitude."

Another American who eventually returned to the United States recounts the following story: "I remember renting a room from someone. The first time I met her she said, 'You're an American Jew? If you're not moving to Israel, I want nothing to do with you. I have no patience for you. Your cousin arranged for you to have this room, but that's it!'

"We became good friends. Three years later, the person visited me in the United States and said, 'You know what? I see for the first time what you have here. I see why this is your home. It's not for me. Jerusalem is my place. But now that I have been here and seen your family, seen how you live, I understand.'

"Now, ten years later, she is living here in California with her husband, who had tried to make aliyah as a Zionist, and their two kids."

The following story on the Jewish-American and Israeli views of aliyah was shared by Jim Roche, the former Senate aide to Scoop Jackson:

"One time I was going over to Israel for some defense meetings, and a Jewish colleague of mine on Senator Jackson's staff asked me to pick up some dirt. He wanted Israeli dirt to sprinkle on his casket when he's buried.

"The fellow was my age at the time—say, his late thirties. So I get my little bottle, and I take it with me to Israel. But the only time I remember to get the dirt happens to be when I'm at Israeli military headquarters in Tel Aviv, the Ha'Kirya.

"I turned to my military host and said, 'Listen I need five minutes. You got a spoon? He said, 'Yes.' He gave me a spoon. So I run down to the courtyard where there is a tree with dirt around it. I get down on my hands and knees, and I'm filling up my little tiny vial with dirt.

"As I'm doing this, I observe two pairs of shoes, one on either side. I look up, and here are two Israeli soldiers with their guns, staring down, saying, 'What are you doing?' I said,

'I'm collecting dirt.' 'Why would you want our dirt?' they demanded.

"I said, 'Look. It's a long story.'

" 'What's the story?' So I tell them about this guy. They start shouting, 'What's the matter with that *putz*? Why doesn't he come for his own dirt? Why doesn't he come live here? If we give up all our dirt, there won't be any dirt left. How can we grow anything if everybody comes and takes our dirt back there? He should come and live here. He should come and serve in the armed forces here.'

"The guy's pointing his Uzi at me, so I said, 'Look, I'm a nice Catholic. Leave me alone. I'm taking dirt back for this guy. He's a Democrat.' My host, an intelligence officer, finally saw this was getting out of hand, so he came over and chased them away."

In 1988, more American Jews were flown to Israel in coffins for burial than arrived as alive-and-kicking candidates for permanent residence. Over one thousand Americans were brought to Israel in 1988 for interment in the Eretz Ha'hayim Cemetery near Bet Shemesh. With requests rising for non-Orthodox burials, some cemeteries are changing their requirements to attract more American corpses.

According to Jewish folklore, a very wealthy Jewish-American woman, well known among Israelis as a "big giver," informed Israeli authorities that she would be bringing her beloved dog with her to Israel aboard the national Israeli air carrier, El Al. El Al officials assured the woman that the dog would be safe and provided her with a special box.

When the plane landed at Ben-Gurion Airport, El Al personnel discovered to their horror that the poor dog was dead. Terrified of offending the woman, they informed her that the dog was temporarily in quarantine, while sending an emergency alert to all stations around the world to rush a duplicate dog to Israel. Finally an exact replica arrived, the woman was brought to the airport, and the box was opened.

"But this is not my dog, " declared the woman.

"Madame, it has all the characteristics of your dog," argued a nervous El Al employee.

"That is impossible," the American woman responded. "My dog is dead. I was bringing him to Israel to bury him."

Since the State of Israel was created in 1948, fewer than seventy-five thousand American Jews have emigrated to Israel, and approximately 50 percent have returned to the United States. The majority of American emigrants chose life in Israel for religious reasons. And more than half of American immigrants in recent years settled in the West Bank, primarily in religious settlements. Less than a third of American Jews have ever visited Israel—and only 10 percent ever make a second trip.

"I heard the mayor of an Israeli city say there are thirty thousand illiterates in Israel," said Rabbi Ben Hirsch, the national executive director of Women's American ORT in New York City. "It set up an unbelievable conflict in me. My wife teaches literacy to the lowest-class kids in Far Rockaway."

Jews had 99 percent literacy in the Middle Ages, while the rest of the world had 1 percent, he remarked, "and here we are with thirty thousand illiterate Israelis. It burned a hole in my soul, the fact that we Jews don't go to Israel, we who have unbelievable skills."

Hirsch has spent decades of his professional life working on behalf of Israel, including senior posts with the United Jewish Appeal and the David Ben-Gurion Centennial Committee of the USA. A happening in his own right—emoting, citing, joking, philosophizing—Hirsch nevertheless declared that he's not a Zionist, but "American through and through to my core." Israelis are foreign, he said, with no understanding of what American Jews are driven by or why.

"I was at a concert recently listening to Gershwin, Cole Porter. There were Israelis at the event," Hirsch sighed, "but they had no idea what that music meant to me."

Yet the most popular singers in Israel today, many of them second-generation survivors, are writing and singing songs about the Holocaust. Their performances are mobbed with teenagers as well as adults. "American Jews could never understand the appeal of a Holocaust revival in song," an Israeli commented, "But for us it's a national catharsis."

What's in the mind of Americans contemplating coming to Israel? "I really don't know," said former American Joseph Alpher. "I'm always surprised when I meet an American who gave up a good job, a good home, brought his family here, and is struggling economically. I wonder what made him come. What was so terrible there that prompted him to want a better life for his family?"

Known to his Israeli friends as Yossi, Alpher emigrated to Israel in his early twenties. Today he is executive director of the Jaffee Center for Strategic Studies at Tel Aviv University. The center is one of Israel's leading think tanks, and Alpher is highly respected by those who know him. He served in the IDF and also in the Mossad for a number of years.

Hardworking, open, straightforward, and not at all given to personal intrigue, Alpher has led a life that completely contradicts the notion that a get-the-job-done American can't get the job done in Israel.

"Israelis meet a lot of Americans who are running away from their personal problems," he explained. "Usually [those Americans are] single people, just divorced, or married people who think Israel will save their marriage.

"They are Jewish, so Israel seems like a solution. But they never make it. I shudder at the thought of tearing my wife and kids from their roots and starting something completely new when I wasn't forced to.

"If I were in America and a family like this came to talk to me, I would find it very difficult to smile and say, 'Sure, go ahead. You go live in Israel, and everything will be all right.' It won't be all right. It's a tremendous burden. It's a tremendous hardship, a tremendous change to make in life."

American *olim* may be the least assimilated of any group in Israel. Native-born Israelis question why Jews who "have it all" in the United States would choose to leave. ("There are Israelis who look you in the eyes and say, 'You're crazy. I'm going to go live in America. Why are you coming here?' " said an American immigrant.) The American accent and the coolly logical, efficient, and superior manner of behavior also grate on Israeli nerves.

Alpher, who has had twenty years of experience in watching fellow Americans fail, suggested the problem is typified by the impatient American—well educated, well off, with a technical or professional background: "He looks around him and is instantly convinced he can make things better, whatever his field. He probably can make things better, but he wants to skip all the stages of absorption, learning the language, the customs, until he finally reaches a point where people will accept him as an equal and listen to his advice.

"He wants to skip all that and just say, 'Look, I know better than you do. I do. Ask so and so. Here are my diplomas.' He probably does. 'So I don't know Hebrew. Bring a translator, and I'll explain to him what you guys have to do to make your sewage system work better.' He is absolutely right and will be totally frustrated. No one will want to listen to him."

Israel is a modern country, technically advanced. But there are immense cultural barriers for the *oleh* [immigrant] who thinks like an American. "Because he is Jewish," said Alpher, "because the guy talking to him looks like his Puerto Rican neighbor but is a Jew and is, in fact, his boss, he is going to have a rough time. There are huge cultural gaps between them."

"*Lama alita l'aretz?*" Why did you come here? The question is posed with subtle jealousy, meaning: "You had it so good in America. How could you leave what you had, when it's exactly what I want?" Israelis assume that all American Jews have it better in America. "I think people over fifty admire us for making aliyah. It's the people under fifty who wonder why we did it," complained a young American immigrant.

"It would be gratifying if at least a few Israelis said, 'Thank you for coming to help us,' " she sighed, cultural battle fatigue written all over her face. "But they don't see it that way. Some feel we are patronizing: 'I've got Western know-how. I have something to teach. Be grateful I am here.' Instead, we get 'Don't do us any favors. Why don't you go back to America? If you don't like it here, who asked you to come?' "

Several hundred thousand Israelis have fulfilled their dreams and gone to America. But they rarely acknowledge the likelihood that they're probably not coming back. Friends and family are reassured that they will be away for a short time, "a year at most." Everyone says a year. Belongings are usually left behind with parents and in-laws, because "why should we schlepp them to America, when we'll be back so soon?"

According to my own informal tally, the majority of Israelis residing in the United States are happy with the material side of life but never cease longing for their spiritual and cultural home. The ache to return is great. They live in Israeli neighborhoods or "shtetls," seldom socialize with American Jews, and rarely contribute money to American Jewish institutions or pro-Israel causes.

They might live in the United States for a decade, never read an American newspaper, and still listen to Israeli news on their shortwave radio every night. Some American Jews view Israeli immigration to the United States as the coming "earthquake" in the relationship.

According to the Israeli Association for the Prevention of Emigration, since the establishment of the state, the number of Israelis who have emigrated and live abroad, including their children born abroad, is 650,000 to 700,000. More than 600,000 of these live in North America.

"The biggest change that no one is dealing with is the gigantic emigration of Israelis getting out," explained one committed American Jew. "In the long run, it's going to lead to a major upheaval. All that will be left in Israel will be Orthodox Jews and Sephardic Jews, who will have no connectedness to western Judaism and the Diaspora. Then our kids will say, 'What's the connection? I don't have any relationship to them. My ancestors aren't there. They're living in L.A. They're living in Brooklyn.' "

Per capita, the contribution of leadership that Americans have made to Israel is high—including Golda Meir, Chief Justice Agranat, and Likud leader and Foreign Minister Moshe Arens—but too small a minority to stand out in the average Israeli's mind as, "This is American Jewry's contribution." Complained an American immigrant, "What the average Israeli sees as American Jewry's contribution is money, building edifices, putting plaques on them, writing your name on an ambulance, and so on. Which is true."

Ultra-Orthodox American Jews emigrate to Israel with entirely different motivations. They fear that their way of life is threatened in America. They also find kindred souls throughout Israel's Ultra-Orthodox religious community, which greatly softens the transition. From all evidence, the highly religious face significantly fewer problems in communication, understanding, and cultural adjustment.

Americans who have succeeded in Israel, who are happy and cannot imagine even entertaining thoughts of returning to the United States, provide the most interesting window into the cultural clash between American and Israeli societies. Because they have no ax to grind or excuses to make, their perceptions take on added validity.

Joanne Yaron is one such individual. She is a gregarious, successful writer, businesswoman, mother, and feminist. Yaron likes that last word. She is, in fact, considered one of the leaders of the Israeli feminist movement.

In her basement office in Tel Aviv, where she lives surrounded by paper and ringing telephones, she said, "I graduated from Syracuse University in 1956 with a degree in journalism and a very nice curriculum vitae. I had been assistant editor of the *Daily Orange*, but nobody would even talk to me about a job as a journalist. As a woman, editorial secretary was the most you could hope for, and they didn't deny it because that sort of sex discrimination was still allowed. We're talking 1956. Here I was this bright young thing thinking that she was going somewhere.

"Ever hear of Brenda Starr—lady reporter? That was a comic strip when I was a kid. That's why I became a journalist. Plus the fact that I noticed I could write.

"Things were really the pits for women in the United States, I mean all over, whether it was the Deep South or nice, modern New York City or God knows where. Maybe the Midwest was a little better in small-town papers. *Time* magazine, which always took the top journalism students, wouldn't hire girls.

"I found work and managed not to become an editorial secretary. But it was really difficult. And the pressures were terrible. I also got married. And then the pressures really started. I married an Israeli who I met at Columbia University, where I was studying for my master's degree.

"He was standing in front of me on line to register for classes. That's how I met him. In those days Israeli men were very exotic and very few. That's how I came to Israel. I don't know if I would have come otherwise. My mother's mother was born here, but I can't claim to have been a gung ho Zionist. My family was, so naturally I wasn't.

"But I certainly wasn't against it. It seemed like a great idea and a tremendous experience. Why not? Who changes countries except when you're twenty-one? It's a nice way to come to another country without too many expectations.

"I came and discovered to my great joy that this country was different. I thought—we didn't have the word *feminist* then—that Israel was light-years ahead.

"I was a professional with an M.A. Very few people had higher degrees in Israel at the time. To be an educated individual in Israel, you finished high school. If you arrived with a bachelor's and a master's, it was considered impressive.

"Nobody in their right mind expected me to stay home, even if I had fifteen children. On the contrary, it would be considered a waste. The support system was also tremendous.

"My mother-in-law, despite the fact that she's Sephardic

and therefore should be more traditional in what she expects of her daughter-in-law married to her only son, didn't expect me to stay home either. It would be a terrible waste of all that education.

"In America, we never looked at it that way. Education meant you got through school. I was very amused, very honored, and I worked on it. Why not?

"Socially speaking, here you're expected to send your child to kindergarten from the age of two. Contrary to the United States in the 1950s, early sixties, where you were a bad mother if you sent the kids out of the house, here you're a bad mother if you don't.

"And since Israelis like to interfere in each other's lives—and this I don't say as a criticism; it's one of the things I like—if you walk on a street with a child who's older than two, and it's the morning and he's with you, they'll ask, 'Why isn't he in *gan* [nursery school, kindergarten]'?

"So, in other words, the psychological support system for getting the kid out of the house and going to work is tremendous: 'Go, go to work. Use your education.'

"I'd be an idiot, mean to my parents, not contributing to society—all the things you dream of hearing and that you don't expect to hear. Things, of course, that men don't have to hear. So I found my paradise.

"I wrote my girlfriends, 'This is paradise. You won't believe it. Come!' It was nice to find my tribe. I thought that I had arrived in a feminist heaven. It took me a long while to realize this was far from the case. When I arrived, Israel was a society that considered me part of the elite, treated me as such, and who isn't happy to be treated as society's elite?

"I found a job which in the United States would be relatively very hard to find, which was as an assistant editor. One year later, I was appointed editor of the *Israel Export and Trade Journal*. Therefore, I began using my journalism training and background seriously.

"I was running a publication. They really appreciated me. They thought that I was terrific because of all those degrees and because I guess I did good work. And it was wonderful. It was like a dream. And I lived this dream for a long time.

"And probably if the feminist movement hadn't come around, I might not have noticed that things weren't as ideal as they were for me personally.

"One day in the *Jerusalem Post* I saw a tiny little ad for a meeting of a group of women who were getting together to discuss women's conditions. It started in Haifa and very quickly moved to Tel Aviv. I went to a meeting . . . and then I found my tribe.

"At that first meeting in 1971, I met women like myself, some of whom had degrees, careers, and were dropping dead from exhaustion—mentally, physically, or otherwise. Then there were other women there, ordinary, regular women who were not of the elite group.

"And through feminism I learned to understand that these were wonderful people. Because I, like many professional women, thought that women who were not professionals were not worth talking to, and certainly not worth sitting near in a social event.

"So through the feminist movement I learned a great deal about Israel that I hadn't known before. Because, like so many Americans, I accepted hook, line, and sinker the belief that I was living in a feminist paradise where women are drafted into the army, Golda Meir, and all the rest of it.

"There's no way, shape, or form that anyone can claim feminism was imported into this country. It may well be that this country was the first country that actually tried to apply what today we call feminism. They were not suffragettes. They were feminists. They didn't have the word. But that's what they were. They were far ahead of Susan Anthony.

"I began to reanalyze. Maybe personally Joanne is happy, but what about the rest of the women? What about the rest of the country? Why are only 28 percent of the women in Israel working? Now I think it's 43 to 47 percent, which still isn't much. But it was 33 percent in the early seventies, which was very low for a lady's paradise.

"I saw that Israel lives in a patriarchal society. If a female should want to get divorced here, for any legitimate reason, she can't unless her husband grants her the divorce. We live here under ancient Jewish law.

"A man can have a million girlfriends, mistresses, have children with them, and they're all legally his, unless the mistress is married to someone else. A woman can't even have coffee with a man. She can then be thrown out of her house by her husband and called a *zona* [prostitute].

"Of course, very few men will exercise this right unless they're trying to get rid of their wives. But if a man goes nuts, and he's incarcerated in an asylum, that's it. She's stuck for the rest of her life, because he has to grant her a divorce. She is his property.

"We're chattel. The only laws in Israel that have no secular backup, and therefore are fully controlled by the rabbinate, are the personal-status laws concerning marriage, divorce, and children. That is true for every community in every country in the Middle East. So I don't say it's only Israel.

"The Middle East is a religiously oriented region of the world, something that Anglo-Saxons find hard to comprehend. It will never be otherwise, I believe. We have religious wars every day. So stop thinking America when you come to the Middle East. This way of doing things has been in place, intact, since the beginning of time.

"Even when a Christian couple wish to marry in Israel, they must be from the same sect of Christianity. We have no 'intermarriage' in this country. A Catholic friend of mine met a Swiss gentleman, they fell in love, and came to live in Israel.

"They just adored it here and wanted to have a beautiful wedding in this lovely Scottish church in Jaffa. But they couldn't do it. He was Lutheran, and she Catholic, and they couldn't marry in Israel, because neither was ready to convert.

"When you learn the facts about Israel from that point of view, you can get very upset, coming from an American, Western background. On the other hand, you have to remember that, after all, this is not the United States.

"I don't believe there is official separation of church and state anywhere else in the world. We Americans think that what we have should be applied everywhere. But it won't work here. Nowhere in the Middle East. Ever.

"So, if you want to live here as a Westerner, and not always go around being angry and complaining as most Westerners do, you try to somehow apply your understanding—not only your heart and what you think is right. If you come to live in Israel, you can't expect it to look like Chicago.

"Since I became a feminist and started to read and understand what goes on in this country, I can no longer be complacent. I have to be angry. As soon as you have your awareness raised, that's the end of it.

"It's very difficult to change anything in this country. We fancy ourselves in Israel to be open-minded and modern. But we're not. We're very set in our ways.

"Every time you want to change something, they tell you—especially if you have an accent like I do—that it's American *meshugas* [craziness]. Or French *meshugas* or British *meshugas*, depending on who the speaker is.

"It cannot be that only native Israelis who don't have accents are allowed to come up with suggestions. But one gets that feeling. But somehow Israelis seem to go through a school system which doesn't teach them how to come up with suggestions or to care. And this is a problem.

"The national way of raising Israelis is '*Ma achpat lach?*' which means 'What do you care?' If you see someone smoking on a bus, and it's not allowed and you want to say something, the Israeli you're sitting with will say, '*Ma achpat lach?*' 'It bothers you, what do you care?' Now, you know Americans, we're taught that someday you will have to pay."

As is the case in the American Jewish community, there is no single Israeli view of American aliyah. The majority of Israelis perhaps still believe that American Jews should rightfully come, but have no real perception of the emotional trauma involved. A growing percentage of Israelis have concluded that it is either futile or unrealistic to pressure American Jews to emigrate. And then there are others who fully understand the difficulties but can't excuse the unwillingness to try to surmount them.

"Why are American Jews in professions that deal with our problems?" asked Hirsch Goodman. "Why are they doing those kinds of things? Why are they raising money for UJA? Why don't they just come here? Isn't there a sense that this is absurd?

"Is there a resentment against American Jews? No. There is a resentment on issues, like where in the hell are you guys on 'who is a Jew?' or why don't you come on aliyah, or stop stealing the Soviet Jews, or give us more money, or keep your bloody money. That sort of thing.

"It's pretty absurd, and I think that most realistic people recognize the absurdity. There are six million Jews who live in the United States. There are four million Jews who live in Israel. There is not going to be a Holocaust in America. I don't see the Jewish community in America being threatened by anything other than cholesterol.

"I don't think that we are ever going to be able to say to you, 'Listen, fellows, remember people like A. D. Gordon? Let's go out and build the Negev. Let's go whistle up a few roads. I know you have your Ph.D., but let's build this road to Metula because it's important.' That isn't going to happen.

"The fact is that Israel has no water, no land, no gold, no diamonds, no plutonium, no uranium, no oil, no nothing. It only has brainpower. If we can retain that brainpower, and if we can maintain our educational systems, we will produce very brilliant materials that will be marketed to the United States. That is a technocratic, not an emotional, relationship.

"I am not saying this to be negative. I am saying it very positively. I think it is far better to have mutuality of needs than to just feel that you are being supported with a handout.

"I recently attended a major Jewish convention with nearly twelve hundred people. They did an 'Exodus' celebration. The Baltimore Jewish community purchased the original *Exodus* ship. Leon Uris came from Baltimore, and he

wrote the book *Exodus*, and boys from Baltimore crewed the
Exodus from Europe to Palestine.

"For this very emotional evening, they had people who
went to Palestine as refugees on the *Exodus*, several members of the crew, and Leon Uris. They all gave each other
awards.

"Then came Rabbi Feldman from Russia who gave a
speech on what *Exodus* means to him. This guy has the gift of
gab, and he is really going at it. He tells the story of how he
didn't even know he was Jewish until somebody called him a
kike in school. He went back home and said, 'Papa, what's a
kike?'

"He was fourteen when he heard about refuseniks for the
first time; at sixteen he joined them, and after gaining their
trust, he became a big Zionist. One day they gave him 'the
book' in a brown paper bag, which he read under the blankets
at night with a lantern. The book was *Exodus*. It changed his
life, he became Jewish, he felt proud and wonderful.

"Then the rabbi comes to the culmination of his speech
and his life. Looking out at the crowd, he cries, 'God willing,
tomorrow morning at eight-thirty, American citizenship is
going to be granted to me.'

"Everybody in the audience gave him a standing ovation!
I almost fainted. Here's this rabbi, coming out of the Soviet
Union; his Zionist instincts were aroused by a purely Zionist
book that speaks about the creation of the Jewish state. And
for him, the culmination of freedom is getting American
citizenship!

"The audience loved the whole show. They were very
emotionally involved with it. American citizenship! They don't
understand that this is not what Zionism is about, that this
cannot be the message of *Exodus*.

"If twelve hundred people in a room didn't understand
that, if rabbis and Zionist émigrés from Russia are getting
across the message that what it means to them to be Jewish
and a Zionist is to be the rabbi in Palm Beach, then we are
lost."

"In graduate school in the U.S., I was encouraged to

attend a lecture by a particular Conservative rabbi," Dalia Shehori related. "The rabbi was saying, 'I come now from Israel. I met with the simple people. I also met with Begin and with members of Parliament from the Likud and from Labor.' He talked very warmly about Israel, how nice and beautiful it was, the sky and the landscape.

"Then he said, 'I want to tell you that each of you must try to make at least once a year a pilgrimage to Jerusalem.' For me, it was so obvious that he was going to say, 'You have to make aliyah.'

"Instead he said, 'You have to go at least once a year to do a pilgrimage.' It was such a blow. He goes to Israel, meets with Begin, and then he comes back to America, drops names, and says, 'Look, it is such a nice country. You have to go and visit.'

"When we met, I said to him, 'I listened to your lecture, and I was very disappointed.' I told him why. He said that he understood, and I was right, but he could not tell people that they should make aliyah.

"If he tells them that, then they will not come to the synagogue. He does not want to see them angry. He does not want to be excessive, you see, not to go to the extreme by saying, 'You have to make aliyah.' So this is what they are ready to take: 'Go to visit Israel.' "

"If I were an American Jew, if I were born in the States, I can hardly believe I would have made aliyah to Israel," said an Israeli senior official. "No way. It would have been too alien to me. I think it is unfair to come to an American Jew and to ask him that stupid question: Why don't you go to Israel? What kind of a question is that? The person was born here, was raised here, his friends are here, his family is here. What does he have to do in Israel?

"Many American Jews who went to Israel did not go there to fulfill a Zionist dream. They went either for economic reasons sometimes, or in most of the cases, for personal problems. They couldn't adjust here and so on.

"Not too many Americans actually made it in Israel. Some of them who have gone recently are the nuts, those who settle the West Bank. Of all the Jews in America, you managed to export us the nuts. It is really unfair.

"This is my feeling, and I strongly believe this is the feeling that many of us share about American Jews. I do not think it is relevant to criticize American Jewry for taking positions on that issue alone."

Uri Gordon, head of the aliyah department of the Jewish Agency in Israel, feels uncomfortable "being an Israeli among the Jews. I don't want to talk about Zionism, but 'Israelism' for the Jewish people. American parents are afraid their children will come to Israel and be brainwashed, will be kidnapped.

"In twenty years, there will be a new structure in Jewish life and new relationships between the Diaspora and Israel. Some of our friends in Chicago think they can sit there and tell us how to absorb immigrants.

"It is our mistake. We don't know the meaning of being a Jew in the Diaspora, and American Jews don't understand what it means to be an Israeli. We are two separate cultures. In the last year, something bad happened between us.

"For the last ten years, American Jews have called for 'freedom of choice'—freedom of choice for Soviet Jews in making aliyah to Israel or the United States. This drives me crazy. What is the meaning of freedom of choice? Why, when American Jews go to Russia, do they talk about freedom of choice, but when they go to Addis Ababa to see the Ethiopian Jews, they don't talk freedom of choice? They assume these Jews are our responsibility.

"Israel is the backyard of the Jewish people. The good people go to the U.S., the not-so-good to Israel. Twenty percent of Israeli professionals come from the Soviet Union. But instead of helping us, Jews in Berkeley and Chicago talk to me about freedom of choice.

"Israel does not exist to allow Jews to go from one Diaspora to another. We cried to Gorbachev to let the Jewish people go—not to Brighton Beach or to Chicago, but to Jerusalem."

Mikhail Gorbachev's *glasnost* policy opened the floodgates for Soviet Jews wishing to emigrate from the Soviet Union. The irony of this exodus was that the vast majority initially sought refuge, not in Israel, but in the United States.

Soviet Jews believe there are golden professional opportunities in America, if not gold on the streets. They typically have almost no contact with Israelis, have long been brainwashed against the Israeli state by the hostile Soviet press and government, and hear only horror stories about Israeli bureaucracy.

Unrest in the West Bank and Gaza and overall political uncertainties have made the United States a more attractive place to settle. Many refugees also have relatives in America and are drawn to large Soviet Jewish communities in such major cities as New York and Boston.

Thus, only 10 percent of the 1,169 Jews freed in 1988 went to Israel. Fifty percent fled to the United States, with the remainder traveling to other Western destinations. Israelis generally blamed the United States for luring these Jews away.

"American Jews are hijacking Soviet Jews coming out of the Soviet Union. These people only know about Israel what they read in *Pravda*," an irate Israeli complained before the new restrictions were put in place. "They land in Vienna, and American Jews say, 'OK, guys. If you want, you can come to America and get American citizenship. If you go to Israel, you lose your refugee status. And here is $7,000, which is what it costs to keep it.'"

Israelis have harbored deep resentment against Soviet Jews who exited the Soviet Union on Israeli visas, took advantage of Israeli assistance only long enough to get out of the country, and then headed westward. In the words of one Israeli government official at the time, "Israel is not a travel agent."

Further, U.S. settlement of Soviet Jewish refugees has cost both the American government and the Jewish community tens of millions of dollars each year—money that Israelis believe should have been earmarked for resettlement in Israel.

But in September 1989, the U.S. Immigration and Naturalization Service closed the doors to future Soviet Jewish immigration. Citing the financial burden created by the thousands of incoming refugees, the INS stipulated that henceforth only Soviets with relatives in the United States would be granted entry and citizenship.

Regardless of the motives, the prohibition has created a substantial increase in immigration to Israel—fulfilling Yitzhak Shamir's call to "end the American seduction of Soviet émigrés and let them come home."

"I understand how the Israelis felt about freedom of choice," declared an American Jewish leader. "But what were we supposed to do, send the Soviet Jews to Israel in a box?" The bruised feelings may linger, but the acrimony on this subject between U.S. Jewry and Israel has suddenly been defused by the actions of the U.S. government. "The chapter is already ended on this story," said Sylvia Hassenfeld, "and a new one is beginning," requiring the Jewish community in America to raise hundreds of millions of dollars for the resettlement of Soviet Jews in Israel.

Israeli officials talk about a flood of a million or more immigrants, a figure that American Jewish leaders term highly unrealistic. Regardless of the final numbers or the reasons behind the exodus, the mere vision sends a current of energy and excitement throughout Israeli society. "You cannot imagine what it meant to us these past years," said Zohar Carthy, "to know that Jews around the world did not want to come and live with us. We felt so isolated."

Carthy was appointed by the Israeli government in the summer of 1989 to head a Special Task Force on Women's Unemployment. She is more aware than most that finding work and housing for these immigrants will be an enormous struggle but maintains that the economy of the country will surge forward as a result.

"What we have witnessed," declared Simcha Dinitz, chairman of the executive board of governors of the Jewish Agency, "is nothing short of a miracle. It is difficult to overstate it. People eventually leave a country that nobody wants to come to. World Jewry must now understand that Israel has been put in the role of leading a mass exodus unparalleled in the history of the state.

"Give us an everyday operation, and we usually louse it up," Dinitz wryly noted. "This country is geared to do the impossible. Whenever we have to deal with a great influx of immigrants, it improves the whole environment of the country."

American Jewish leaders are more skeptical, charging that the Israeli leadership has done little real planning. Said one American critic, "The Israelis want immigrants until they're able to come." To which Dinitz responded, "The American Jews didn't believe the Soviets and Eastern European Jews would come here. The Americans think anybody denied the golden Mecca of the United States would prefer to stay in Mother Russia."

Sylvia Hassenfeld, president of the Joint Distribution Committee, which cares for Jews in distress all over the world, takes a cautious view: "The Israelis talk about the numbers streaming in, and it's true that fifteen hundred Soviet immigrants landed in Israel during the first week of this decade.

"If Israel handles the first 10,000 well, then perhaps there will be 70,000 by the end of the year, and 150,000 to 200,000 over the next couple of years. But let's face it, if the first 10,000 don't find jobs, they will be marching in the streets. These are not a docile people. They have high expectations."

18
THE WITHDRAWAL SYNDROME

FOR OVER THIRTY YEARS, THE AMERICAN JEWISH COM-
munity supported Israel's domestic and foreign decisions
almost unquestioningly. The unwritten pact or understanding was that the American Jewish community would provide
financial assistance, and Israel would determine policy. The
mere thought of second-guessing the Israeli government, or
attempting to intervene in Israeli internal affairs, was nigh
on perfidy.

American Jewry's unconditional support has withered
over the last decade—with Israel's image tarnished by the
Lebanon War, Sabra and Shattila, the Pollard case, the
stalled peace process, the "who is a Jew?" controversy, and,
not least of all, the *intifada*.

The taboo against washing dirty laundry in public has
been broken, and there is no turning back. The American
Jewish community, which once spoke in unanimity, has splin-
tered. American Jews are expressing their disagreements
with Israeli actions and policy with increasing frequency.

"I think the Jews in this country are moving into some
new phase of Judaism. I am not sure what it is or where it's
going," one activist said. "I'm talking about people who say

unabashedly, 'I am Jewish, but my connectedness to Israel is, well . . .' The focus is off. It's not on Israel. It's not like it was twenty years ago."

Some reflect the attitude "I give; therefore I have say over what occurs there." Others are more paternalistic: "I show my continued love for Israel through my criticism, as I would with my own child."

The parent-child metaphor is often applied by critics and sympathizers alike. "I have a much lower level of frustration about these issues than a lot of other Jewish volunteers because a lot of Americans don't view Israel realistically," said Eric Zahler, chairman of the UJA Young Leadership Cabinet. "They really want Israel to be on a pedestal, perfect. I'm much more tolerant and willing to say, 'Look, Israel is a living society; they do good things, they do bad things, and they make mistakes.'

"I would be very concerned if they couldn't make mistakes. Now, I'd be enormously distressed if they change the Law of Return. But it's like a parent and a child. If you have a dream that Israel is a state that's going to grow, you have to give it the freedom to do what it wants. Americans who haven't spent a lot of time dealing with Israelis as people don't see that."

For those Jews who support Israel right or wrong, dissent rings as Jewish anti-Semitism, self-hatred, bleeding-heart liberalism, arrogance, and a threat to the solidarity of the global Jewish community. Yet, for the majority, the very need to vent hurt feelings is extraordinarily painful.

Ed Robin, Larry Rubenstein, and Naomi Patz of the North American Forum, and Shmuel Ben-Tovim of the Israel Forum, generously allowed me to monitor and tape over ninety hours of debate and dialogue between American Jews and Israelis on two continents. As one participant so aptly phrased the process, "We should call this the 'What Hurts Me Forum.' "

The litany of hurts includes aliyah, the "who is a Jew?" question, the centrality of Israel in the lives of American Jews versus the centrality of Jewish life in the United States, freedom of choice for Soviet Jews, Israel's handling of the *intifada*, religious pluralism versus religious domination in Israel, the way American Jews should voice their criticism of Israeli policies (also known as intervention in internal affairs), the future of the peace process, the paucity of joint business initiatives—and the list goes on.

But what was most remarkable about these endless hours of soul-searching—which was also reflected in the dozens of interviews I conducted—was that the *intifada* was hardly mentioned. Not because American Jews don't care, but perhaps because they care so much. Sara Tobin pointed out that at the largest annual meeting of American Jews, the General Assembly of the Council of Jewish Federations, which took place in November 1988, the *intifada* was scarcely more than a side issue on the agenda.

"I was baffled by the level of intensity that was put forward on the 'who is a Jew?' issue," she said. "I was particularly disturbed afterward when it became a nonissue.

"Here was one of the biggest assemblies of the most influential Jewish leaders from all over North America, and all their frustration against Israel was legitimized in this one issue. I thought that it showed the tremendous paralysis. Of course, the *intifada* was not addressed at all. There was only one session that dealt with the Arab world, and the people presenting it had to do it very quickly, very briefly."

American Jews have been deeply affected by the televised pictures of the Israeli-Palestinian conflict, but they feel helpless. Who is right? Who is wrong? Would they behave differently if they were in Israeli military and political boots? Do they have all the facts? The only certainty is that the absolute answers are nowhere to be found.

"Look, we're Jews. We're all at fault. I would not be so bold as to point fingers," argued one participant in the American Forum. "We are all part of the problem. That's why we are here, because we don't want to avoid it. But it's a question of where we focus. Do we focus on the *intifada*? Do we focus on what we've felt, for example, following the massacres at

Sabra and Shattila? Do we focus on whatever might be the explosion at that point of time, or do we look at the bigger picture?"

Yet, if their public voices are low, American Jews have been expressing their emotions concerning the *intifada* with their feet and funds. Fewer and fewer are traveling to Israel. Some are withholding philanthropic pledges that would otherwise be channeled to Israeli needs.

And so the wrenching question for so many American Jews today is no longer to criticize or not to criticize—but whether it is justified, or moral, to distance themselves from Israel during its darkest hours.

As a window into this internal debate, here are the views of an anonymous Jewish leader: "How do we affect their destiny? We get angry at them; the money stops, and the tourism stops. Americans say, 'Look, we don't like that 'who is a Jew?' issue. We don't like what's going on with the occupation and so on. We're not coming this year. The King David is going to be empty for Passover because we're angry with you.'

"It's as if we have taken a child, and we've said, 'This child has disappointed us. It is no longer David overcoming Goliath. It's a child, he's on drugs, he's not getting good marks, and he's not shiny and clean and precious and wonderful. He is no longer a star. We're upset. Straighten up your act,' we say, 'and then call us.'

"Where is the tie to Israel's destiny? Either we're in or we're out. Either we're with them or we're not with them. Not this 'We don't like the politics. We're unhappy.' If that's the case, let's go over there and vote.

"I get very upset when I hear committed Jews who say, 'This year the gift is cut. This year I'm not going for Passover because I don't like what's going on,' and, 'Until they do this,' and 'Until they do that.' You sit and you listen and you think, 'You're this strongly committed to what is going on over there? They would love to have your vote.' But from this end, it's not a partnership."

There are many Israelis who welcome the financial support and pressure that can be exerted by American Jews for preferred causes. But others are simply wary or, worse, cynical. "Actually, we have become pretty outraged with the sanctimoniousness, the constant criticism, and the lack of understanding at the grassroots level for what Israel should be all about," said Hirsch Goodman. "Relations between Israel and American Jewish institutions have become cold. That emotional, wonderful, warm link that existed between Israel and American Jewry—our generation was probably the last to have that."

Batya Keinan, the Zionist socialist, was addressing a peace group in New York, when a young woman, about thirty, walked up to her and said, "I wish I had gone to Israel when I was fifteen, because today I know the reality. You Israelis failed to fulfill the Jewish dream."

Keinan shot back, "How dare you ask me to fulfill your dreams?! You are living a good life in America, and we are paying with our blood and our soul. Is it my duty to fulfill your dreams?"

Israeli writer Amos Oz declared sardonically in a BBC interview, "Since the Yom Kippur War, the Jews of the Diaspora want their money back." To American Jews who fight for Israel with their dollars and then demand an accounting, Keinan has one message: "Money is not blood. Don't do us any favors. You can exist in America as a proud Jew because we're paying the price here.

"There would be no Jewish pride in the Diaspora if there were not a Jewish state. We pay the price for your existence. Money is nothing compared with what we give for Jewish pride. We give our blood."

Similarly, Motta Gur suggested that it's easy to identify with Israel in time of victory or when Israel is in trouble, as in the Yom Kippur War. "It's much more complicated when American Jews watch television news and see pictures they don't like. But this is the time to identify, to give a sense of strength, and *then* to participate in open debate."

An Israeli expert on U.S. policy, Shai Feldman, a senior research associate at the Jaffee Center for Strategic Studies in Tel Aviv, was even more direct. "Get off our backs," was the first phrase that leapt from his lips when he was asked what American Jewry could do to help. Feldman is hardly right-wing. A Labor party member, he has impeccable liberal credentials and a clear understanding of the American scene.

Feldman is a man of intellectual depth. Many in Washington describe Shai Feldman as perhaps the Israeli most knowledgeable about the dynamics of the American political process. In his view, Israelis have problems when leaders of the American Jewish community intervene too often on issues that only indirectly impinge on the future of Israeli-U.S. relations—for example, certain diplomatic avenues taken by the government on the peace process and the future of the West Bank and Gaza.

"These are issues that Israelis feel are up to them to decide," said Feldman, "[that] Israelis who have served at least three years in the army and forty years in reserve service should have the exclusive right to decide.

"To maintain the cooperative atmosphere between the American Jewish community and Israel, the leaders of the American Jewish community should exercise their influence with the leaders of the State of Israel very selectively—on issues where they have a perfectly legitimate right to intervene.

"As a liberal, I would love American Jewish liberals to come and settle in Israel and join our forces here. But as things are now, the gut reaction of the Israeli would be to say, 'Look, he's pushing me in this direction. What if he's wrong? I'm the one who is living here. I'm the one who's going to be in the army unit that will have to bear the burden of the negative consequences of this decision.' As a general rule, that's the kind of reaction you will get.

"Therefore, I think that it's much wiser for American Jews not to engage in the internal Israeli debate on these issues. And it's an even greater mistake for Israelis to try to mobilize American Jews, or other people who do not live here, to support their causes.

"People of different viewpoints should do everything they can internally to win the debate. But any effort to solicit external allies in Israeli domestic affairs will be interpreted as a sign of weakness."

Shmuel Ben-Tovim, head of a public relations firm in Israel and chairman of the Israel Forum, believes the problem is not so much whether American Jews understand what is happening in Israel, but "the way American Jews identify with us on what we are going through.

"Because Israelis are also not happy with what's going on here. When something bad happens in your family—for example, your brother was arrested because he was accused of robbery—what would you do? How would you react? Would you say, 'He's not my brother, and I don't want to know about him anymore?'

"Or would you say, 'Perhaps he's not guilty. Even if he's done something wrong, why did he go wrong? Let me visit him and see what happened to him—why such a good guy would go wrong.'

"You would sympathize with him. You'd try to help him. Perhaps he can't justify what he's done. But you would be in true pain, and you would try to do something for him. You wouldn't reject him by saying, 'OK, I thought I was dealing with an honest man, but it becomes clear that he is a criminal, so bye-bye to our relationship.'

"Now what frustrates Israelis is that the reaction they are getting from most American Jews is not like family. Let's say that we are treating the situation very badly, hitting Arabs, making the wrong decisions, following the wrong policies. OK? If you are really our *mishpacha* [family], you should come and help us out of this situation.

"But the reaction is quite the opposite: fewer American Jews are coming here. Some say they are afraid. Some say they are not coming because of the *intifada* or they think we are wrong. OK. So we think *you* are wrong.

"But come here and say that you think that we are wrong. You will have a much better audience and much more clout saying it here and not just getting all upset when the 'who is a Jew?' issue comes out, which affects you there.

"Show some concern. Show some care. But what's happened is just the opposite. Of course, there are many exceptions—Jews who are coming ten times a year just to show that they are not deserting us.

"But if you look at statistics about what happened to tourism, Christian Germans keep coming to Israel at the same level or even more than before the *intifada*. Tourism from all over the world has been only very slightly affected, and it's picking up again. The only major section in tourism that went down dramatically is Jews from America. And there's no doubt that it created some kind of bad feeling."

How do Shmuel Ben-Tovim and other Israelis relate these feelings to the decades of financial support from American Jewry? "Whenever we serve the role that American Jews want us to serve—being the heroes, being something that you can walk in the streets in New York and identify and be proud that it's our family—then we are a family," said Ben-Tovim. "When we do something shameful, when they can't be very proud of us, they forget about us. And that's not the way a family, a good family, a close family behaves.

"We are not here only to play the role of the heroes and to fight and to get our children killed just so someone can walk in Independence Day in New York with his chest full of air. This is not what we see as our role in this relationship.

"What is our role? Our role is to keep and build and develop the only Jewish state in the world, hoping that some day all Jews will want to live here."

Is there a basic asymmetry to the relationship? "Well, maybe something false in terms of real sympathy or care for Israel," said Ben-Tovim. In response to the idea that Israelis do not really know or seem to care about the lives of American Jews, Ben Tovim added, "This is true, but American Jews don't care that Israelis will care.

"After being in the Forum, one of the things that I've

realized is that Israelis know so little about Jewish communities in the world. And when I personally educated myself like many Forum members, I said, 'Why shouldn't other Israelis learn it?'

"And I went to some major Jewish organizations and suggested that they need a good campaign in Israel explaining the different organizations. 'What are you doing for the future of the Jewish people? What are you doing for Jewish education? Show the Israelis that you are doing something good.' And all of them, without exception, would not spend one penny for that because they don't think it's important.

"They think it's important for the Americans because it helps them fund-raise. But why is it important for Israelis to know what they are doing here?

"Israelis are interested. And the Forum shows that when you find a way to reach them, they want to know. They want to become more acquainted with other communities, what they do, how they operate, how much they are involved in everyone's life. It's very interesting for Israelis.

"But no one makes the effort to educate them."

19
WHO IS A JEW?

No issue has proved more divisive between Israel and the American Jewish community than the "who is a Jew?" question. The Orthodox concern over whether immigrants to Israel are Jewish by halakic (Jewish legal) standards has a long history. But in November 1988, a latent concern became a full-fledged crisis. Israel's religious parties won 18 of a possible 120 seats in the Knesset, emerging as the decisive swing vote in a new government coalition. With only 40 seats going to Likud and 39 to Labor, both parties depended on the religious block to form a government.

"Who is a Jew?" concerns the nature of the Law of Return—the very heart of Zionism. The law states that all Jews may be granted immediate citizenship upon arrival in Israel, assuming the immigrant is not fleeing justice in another country. The Orthodox religious parties sought to amend the law to define a Jew as someone either born of a Jewish mother or converted by an Orthodox rabbi.

The Israelis' misreading of American Jewry was profound. Many Israelis, unschooled in the sensitivities of the American Jewish community, could not comprehend the outrage over what, in fact, might affect only a handful of potential *olim* who lacked Orthodox conversion papers.

What the Israelis failed to realize was just how many American Jews are indirectly affected by such a ruling: close to 40 percent have intermarried with non-Jews. The proposed amendment, in effect, questions the Jewishness, if not of oneself, then of one's child, spouse, friend, or other relative.

It also denigrates the legitimacy of Reform, Reconstructionist, and Conservative movements in the United States, by disempowering their rabbis to make conversions that would be honored in Israel. Yet 90 percent of American Jews belong to these three movements.

Anita Gray, a full-time volunteer on behalf of Jewish causes, is a national vice chair of the United Jewish Appeal, a board member of the Council of Jewish Federations, a leader in the Cleveland Jewish community, and an active participant in the North American Jewish Forum. She once was an Italian Catholic but converted to Judaism in her twenties, before she met her husband and long before she gave much thought to the centrality of Israel in Jewish life.

At the second meeting of the American/Israel Forum, the 1985 Moriah Conference in Israel, Anita attended a workshop on the "who is a Jew?" debate. It was attended by about forty Americans and Israelis of all religious persuasions. A heated discussion was under way for some time when Anita volunteered that she was a convert. "The Israelis were shocked," she said. "They had not met people like me—converts. It was as if I had two heads.

"An Israeli Lubavitcher [Hasidic] rebbe jumps up yelling, 'A Jew knows a Jew through the eye.' Then an aide to Begin stands up, points a finger at me, and declares, 'You're a tainted woman. Your children will not be able to play with my children.' I was devastated," Anita Gray confided. The tears were pouring down.

"The workshop ended on that note, but the pain of the sacrificial lamb was felt by American and Israeli alike. They all bore witness to the pain this issue brings to the Diaspora. When I converted, I had no knowledge of the significance of an Orthodox conversion.

"I keep the Shabbat, my house is kosher, my kids go to an Orthodox day school. But a quickie Orthodox conversion to satisfy the 'who is a Jew?' proponents in Israel would trash my Judaism. I'm not going to compromise that," she stated, "and yet I do believe that the problem is eminently solvable through a unified conversion that will not compromise either side."

Anita Gray's experience at that Forum session four years ago sensitized her to the feelings of Orthodox Jews on the opposing side of the issue, and also to the role of mysticism in Israeli daily life.

A young man stepped forward at the workshop to tell his personal story. As a commanding officer during the Lebanon War, he had orders to hold the line. Suddenly six Lubavitcher Mitzvah Mobiles (bringing religion to the soldiers) appeared from nowhere. He ordered them to stop, they refused, so he took out a gun and shot at their tires.

He missed. "I'm a general, an army man, and a great shot," he told the group, "but this changed my life. I chose from that day onward to follow the Orthodox path."

Gordon Zacks served as President George Bush's Campaign Chairman for the Jewish community. A successful businessman by profession, and an ardent supporter of Israel by avocation, Zacks devotes at least as many hours to pro-Israel causes as to his company. Six feet plus, sporting a crew cut and handsomely tailored suit, he is like a racehorse at the gate for any task that might help the Jewish state. Forty-one years ago, Zacks was campaign chairman of his high school effort to raise funds for Israel. Since then, he's been campaign chairman for the United Jewish Appeal and a host of similar efforts.

Yet even Gordon Zacks describes "who is a Jew?" as a potential breaking point between American and Israeli Jews: "In the forty years of my involvement, the most threatening and divisive issue we have faced is the encounter on the 'who is a Jew?' issue. If the definition is determined by the Ultra-Orthodox, the narrowness of the definition, the intolerance and insensitivity will rupture the support of the great majority of Jews in the Diaspora.

"It will destroy the liberal, democratic political freedom in Israel. Israel will become an unattractive nation to most Jews living in the U.S. I know the Israelis don't understand that, and it will come up again.

"I have always believed that, unless we were all willing to live in Israel and to live with the consequences of our decisions, we have no right morally to criticize those who make the decisions. But on the issue of 'who is a Jew?' and electoral reform, I feel that Diaspora Jews have a vital stake in the outcome and have a responsibility to mobilize—to insist publicly on electoral reform and to prevent the majority of Jewish people from being held hostage by the minority of the Ultra-Orthodox religious community.

"Never again should we be in this position. The outcome of the debate between Israeli Jews and Jewish religious nationalists will determine the future of American Jewry's relationship with Israel."

The wider American Jewish reaction to the proposed amendment was swift and angry. A delegation of American Jews warned Yitzhak Shamir against conceding to religious party demands in order to form a coalition.

Their message was clear: Make no mistake about it, we will not accept an amendment that effectively questions the legitimacy of the majority of American Jewry. The delegation's wrath caught Israelis off-guard. When the Council of Jewish Federations threatened to withhold philanthropic funds to Israel, pending the outcome of "who is a Jew?," many Israelis were left dumbfounded.

As Gordon Zacks put it, the "who is a Jew?" issue not only shook the entire Jewish community, but unified American Jewry against the Israeli policy establishment as no prior issue ever had.

"From the Israeli point of view," declared a Washington expert on the Middle East, "I don't think they had any notion that what they were doing was going to affect American Jews or that American Jews would care about it. I was shocked. I couldn't believe it." Becoming visibly agitated, a muscle in his jaw pulsating like a heartbeat, he went on: "You look for leadership. You look for the Israelis to do something. There is this real visceral need on the part of Jews here to be able to find a way to defend Israel. And how do they reward you? They come up with 'who is a Jew?' and say, basically, 'You're not a Jew.'

"Nothing could better explain the differences between American Jews and Israel and the lack of communication than the failure of the Israelis to understand this.

"Every Jewish family in the United States is affected by the notion that their child who married out, or their grandchildren who are the product of a mixed marriage, or their nephew or niece or whatever, is going to be denied legitimacy as a Jew as a result of some internal political machinations in Israel designed to enable people to gain power. It is absolutely outrageous.

"I had people screaming hysterically at me on the phone, saying, 'How can they do this? Give me a way. I am ready to give a million dollars now to stop this.'"

This man's next declaration, referring to his own fulfillment of his Zionist dream by moving to Washington, captured the full irony of the Zionism debate between Israelis and the Diaspora: "It was personal for me. I uproot my family to come to Washington. My wife is a convert. So, here, I devote my life to Israel. My whole life has been devoted to Zionism, and these people are going to tell me that my family is not Jewish?"

Many Israelis welcomed the American Jewish intervention and even tried to stimulate it. But others who concurred that the amendment should be prevented at all costs still voiced ire at the way the American Jewish community presented its case.

One well-known Israeli countered, "People are not giving to the UJA this year because of Israel and 'who is a Jew?' It doesn't mean anything to them, but we came within an inch of Shamir forming a government with the Orthodox parties.

"Our Minister of Education could have been a non-Zionist

Orthodox Jew, who would have decided how to appropriate money, what the syllabus would be, what books should be published, and what theaters should be subsidized.

"For me, it is an existential issue, and for them, it is an esoteric issue. American Jews get so uppity about 'who is a Jew?' when the idea for the whole bloody thing started here to begin with."

"It's the same thing as Kahane," said Hirsch Goodman. "American Jews find it disgusting that Meir Kahane can be elected to our parliament. Well, Kahane came from America. All his supporters are from America. All his money comes from America. I was in Cleveland one day, and I heard some guy announce that he had 500,000 bucks to send to Kahane. It was amazing.

"And then American Jews say they don't like what is happening to our country. Seventy-four percent of the aliyah from America to Israel is Orthodox, and 54 percent of them have settled on the West Bank and in Gaza. Then they say they don't like what's happening in my country.

"You have all these Hasidim in Israel taking their orders from a rebbe in Brooklyn. Do you see American Jews holding a protest march around his house?"

The American Jewish community could have taken a different approach, according to Shmuel Ben-Tovim, by explaining their case to the Israeli public, rather than to the leadership: "They chose to go to the Knesset members, to Shamir, and to Peres.

"Many people told them, 'Look, you have Project Renewal, developing cultural and financial links between cities in the U.S. like Los Angeles with Qiryat Shemona in Israel. Take a mission from Los Angeles, go to Qiryat Shemona, tell the people in Qiryat Shemona why "who is a Jew?" is so painful. Tell them, 'Look at the way we've helped you, poured money, and did everything for Qiryat Shemona. Now we need your help. Please go to the Knesset. Lobby your Knesset members. Explain that they are about to take an action that will affect Jews in Los Angeles very badly.'

"They didn't do that. Why? Instead they went only to the political power. They didn't go to the public in Israel and try to educate them as to why is it so painful, why is it so important to Americans. When the issue comes up again, if American Jews don't have any public support for their viewpoint in Israel, I'm not sure they will be able to prevent 'who is a Jew?' from passing."

An international accountant, author, and political analyst rolled into one, Dan Bavli contends that "who is a Jew?" was in the offing for many years, and it was quite clear that the majority of the American Jewish community would find it unacceptable. "Yet they never made that point clear. They never really felt threatened until that first of November 1988. And then they started screaming. They stopped it—but only after very heavy damage, damage that hasn't yet fully ended. There is still a lot of bitter feeling about it.

"All that could have been avoided if communications had been working properly. Part of communication is anticipation of what's going to happen and what the other side is capable of. It was quite clear that scenarios could arise where such legislation would become an actual threat. And yet nothing was done about it."

Criticism and debate are welcome, Simcha Dinitz stressed. "Unfortunately American Jews like to state their case in New York or through big delegations or public statements. Israel is not exactly closed to them. But when American Jews come here, they act like pussycats. I understand this awe, but they have to state their case."

PART IV

IS IT A LOVE AFFAIR?

The only focus of Israeli sentiment that is positive, in this entire globe today, is the United States. Yes, it sounds like a strong statement. It's nevertheless true.

—Israeli cabinet official

20
A CLUB OF ONE

FOR ALL OF THEIR SHARP-EDGED EXPERIENCES AND toughened view of reality, the men who constitute Israel's present generation of leaders are more sentimental and emotional about their relationship with the United States than with any other nation. Is it a love affair? Not exactly. The United States seems to represent, at least for these men, an elusive attachment that both heals and hurts but can never reach the plateau of unconditional commitment.

It is one of the disquieting lessons of adulthood that nations are united by interests, rarely by ideals or emotions. Even so, nations are led by men and women, who do feel, even if they carefully, diplomatically conceal their innermost thoughts concerning another culture. And it may be more difficult for Israelis than for any other people in the world to relate to their international friends—much less their enemies—purely on the basis of interests.

The loneliness of the siege mentality—you are either with us or against us—means that foreign political figures are typically evaluated in highly personalized terms. When Israeli leaders speak about a Carter, Reagan, Shultz, or Baker, they do so in the language of feelings ("warm" or "cold," "a friend," "the best friend," "cared about us," or "understood" or "didn't understand us"). When Israeli leaders reflect on the American-Israeli relationship, they tend to use images of family ties or friendship, rather than the cool rhetoric of political science. Yet, ironically, for most Americans, Israeli leaders have turned into "sound bite" figures, ten-second television personas who evoke no emotional response.

"There is a sense of closeness, of family, that we don't have with anybody else in the world," declared Avi Pazner, a universally respected foreign service professional, spokesman for Yitzhak Shamir, and press counselor at the Israeli embassy in Washington during the entire Camp David process. "There is a sense of knowing each other, of intimacy, of really leveling. The symbiosis is so strong, the chemistry is so good. We don't have a dialogue like that, I tell you, with anybody else. Not on a personal level or a business level."

As Director General of the Prime Minister's Bureau, Yossi Ben-Aharon fiercely shields Yitzhak Shamir from political harm, and he is well known for tough views on the peace process that rankle the nerves of U.S. officials. Said Ben-Aharon, "If you were to ask the same questions with regard to our relationship with other countries, you would find a much cooler, more down to earth, not exactly cynical, but let us say a more detached kind of analysis. With the United States, you cannot disengage the personal dimension from the political institutions."

Ben-Aharon has worked with a number of Israeli prime ministers. He contends that, by and large, the people who make decisions at the top level of Israeli society hold a very sentimental attachment to the United States. This feeling has been accentuated in the last decade by the sharpening contrast between the United States and other countries that, in Israeli eyes, were supposedly friends of the Jewish people in the past but have betrayed them in the present.

Ben-Aharon, soft-spoken but direct, acknowledged that "the feeling of a siege mentality in Israel is pervasive. It applies to most of Europe—even Holland and Denmark—countries that did so much for Jews in the Holocaust. All of this went down the drain to a very large extent in the last ten, twenty years because of the shift against Israel and in favor of the PLO, the unfair European treatment of what they consider to be Israeli occupation practices, and the rise of anti-Semitism in all of these countries."

The United States belongs to a club of one that is perceived as vital to Israel's survival, to its capacity to hold its own in many respects. Therefore, any action or statement that is viewed as a shift toward the negative is not only immediately perceived as a blow, but is generally inflated and interpreted as a personal affront. Said Prime Minister Shamir, "When you receive a blow from a friend, it hurts more."

Irish playwright Oscar Wilde wrote, "We and the Americans have so much in common, but there is always the language barrier." Between Israelis and Americans, there is often, if not always, a "feelings barrier." Angry or tough American words can literally cause personal depression among Israel's ruling stars.

"When the U.S. makes some kind of a decision that is perceived by Israelis as a blow, it is definitely taken very personally," said one official. "It's a shock. I've seen the shock, literally, on a good number of Israeli leaders when the U.S. came up with some statement, or some plan or proposal."

By the same token, the civilities that Americans excel at, and so take for granted, apparently have profoundly touched the hearts of Israel's current generation of leaders. Yitzhak Shamir, for example, has expressed the belief that Americans are the politest and warmest people he's ever dealt with.

Looking dapper in a new, European-cut gray-blue suit, Prime Minister Shamir was in high spirits as he bounded forward, hand extended in greeting, a wide smile reaching the corners of his eyes. This meeting was at ten o'clock on the morning of June 20, 1989. Less than four hours later, as Shamir attempted to preside over the burial of an American expatriate who had been knifed to death by two self-proclaimed members of the PLO, several hundred West Bank settlers cruelly shouted him down as a Nazi and a traitor. The unprecedented display of disrespect for an Israeli Prime Minister provoked all corners of the Israeli press to condemn the settlers' behavior as creating a black day in Israeli history.

But in his interview, I was caught off guard when Shamir surprisingly remarked, "It's easier to negotiate with Americans than with members of any other nation. It is a very agreeable experience, a very encouraging experience to negotiate with Americans, because on the human ground I think we are very near to each other. In Europe you can face superficial politeness, but the Americans are more polite basically. Not only the politicians and the statesmen, but also the media."

These were unexpected sentiments from the taciturn Prime Minister, a man who had spent so much of his life in the shadows of international intrigue, as a leader of the Stern Group and a member of the Mossad. Here was a man whom the Washington establishment had hardly embraced. His political stands are anathema to much of Washington's political elite, and friction has frequently developed during his two tenures as Prime Minister.

What was the explanation? Ben-Aharon noted that Yitzhak Shamir had only dealt with Europeans until he became Foreign Minister in 1980. When Shamir shifted his focus to the United States and started visiting America regularly, the change in atmosphere "took time to sink in because it was such a welcome and positive breath of fresh air."

In Ben-Aharon's words, Shamir was "completely mind-boggled" at the reception, the warmth, directness, informality, and friendship (remember George Shultz and the blueberry pancakes): "For Yitzhak Shamir, this was a phenomenon. It took some time for him to get used to it because he had been accustomed to a very reserved, cool attitude."

Americans' image of Israel's leaders is so often larger than life that it is difficult for us to appreciate just how overwhelmed they can be by the hallowed halls of U.S. power, or how awed by its effusion of goodwill, which is hardly a mainstay of Israeli political life. This is especially true for men like Shamir and Begin, who viewed the world as their enemy until they met the United States.

Ambassador Max Kampelman recalled a discussion with Menachem Begin at the Waldorf Astoria during Begin's first trip to the United States in 1977: "He was speaking about Carter as the greatest figure of the twentieth century, next to Churchill. Begin was just filled with praise for Carter.

"My only explanation was, here was this small Polish lawyer meeting the President of the United States. The President was gracious, kind, and expressed his love for the State of Israel. So he not only met the President of the United States, but he must be the greatest man who ever lived."

Men like Begin and Shamir were raised in a Polish environment of discrimination, prejudice, and hostility. All of their neighbors felt and acted superior. Both men lost family in the Holocaust. The sabra may feel more independent, stronger, and less subservient, but the self-identification of being from a small, unwanted, and embattled country is nevertheless an ever-present echo in his or her daily consciousness.

To be an American means one assumes, expects a certain level of respect. Americans abroad often cloak themselves in the power of their country (as in "You can't do this to me, I'm an American!"). Americans approach the world on the offensive, Israelis on the defensive.

Moreover, when Americans talk about loving Israel, they mean they love the image of Israel, an image that has been created over time. Scratch the surface, and most Israelis will acknowledge their fear that the American love affair with Israel is based on myths and expectations they cannot fulfill.

Israelis have difficulty expressing their feelings in shades of gray, and the typical Israeli undoubtedly tends to distrust verbal ebullience. Yet the same warmth of phrase that the top echelons would readily dismiss as insincere within their own society, is a comforting and welcome respite when it emanates from American leaders. Would Israelis be more "flexible" on the tough issues if we were more crass?

Probably just the opposite, since this type of behavior would only fulfill their worst expectations.

Shimon Peres, always the philosopher, observed that American culture has invented three great expressions: *human relations*, *public relations*, and *labor relations*. "Relations became a legitimate art," he pondered. "You will never find it in Heidelberg.

"Occasionally it is artificial. The level of compliments spread around in America is not exactly an example of understatement. Everything is brilliant and wonderful and great. Well, we know how to read this language by now. But occasionally you forget, and you take it at face value. Still, it helps, all in all.

"The Americans, when they speak about one another, they know how to mention the nice aspects of a person. Even when he's no longer needed, in old age, they are very sentimental. It's a joy. Yes, I like it. You have the feeling that you're appreciated."

As a result, Israeli leaders are more likely to downplay the long-term consequences of any occasional interpersonal frictions between themselves and American leaders (as opposed to sudden policy surprises, which they instantly inflate)—preferring to rely instead on the expressions of goodwill as a permanent glue.

"What hurt us more than anything in Secretary Baker's speech before AIPAC," declared a senior Israeli official, "was his reference to a 'Greater Israel.' Who talks about the concept of a 'Greater Israel'? Only the crazy fringes. Somebody advised him to say that. Why? It was a mistake. A big, deep mistake.

"But it's not the first time that our feelings have been hurt, and not the last. We had many troubles during Carter's time; even with Shultz we had some disagreements. With Kissinger we had disagreements.

"We are not going to mourn over that [the speech]. Maybe Secretary Baker will say something outrageous again next week, because he wants to achieve something. Because he doesn't know this is not the right way. He will learn. There is a lot to learn, and Mr. Baker is not yet dead with Israeli-American relations on a full, long bed."

Months later, Shamir provoked a major crisis with the Bush Administration when he referred to the need for a "big Israel" (*Yisrael gadol* in Hebrew), to accommodate the mass influx of Soviet Jews. Rightly or wrongly, the Americans immediately interpreted the statement as a reference to the Greater Israel concept.

Do Israel's present leaders trust Americans more because of the genteel way that we conduct negotiations? Not exactly. Pulitzer Prize–winning journalist David Shipler relates that during his tenure in Israel he asked all levels of Israeli officialdom, "If you were on the brink of a war, would the U.S. intervene to save you?" Everybody said no. Observed Shipler, "I hadn't expected so much anxiety about the American commitment."

An Israeli leader will rarely jeopardize perceived national interests because of his or her feelings for the United States or for American leaders. But the Israeli will go through intense soul-searching before taking a combative stance. "When it comes to the actual decision of whether to confront the United States, and to risk a head-on collision over an issue vital to our interests, I would hate to be in the shoes of the person who has to make that choice," Ben-Aharon stated.

Shimon Peres, currently Finance Minister of Israel and Deputy Prime Minister, previously Prime Minister, Foreign Minister, and Defense Minister, was dressed in a short-sleeved white shirt and casual slacks for an interview in the Tel Aviv annex of the Finance Ministry, an A-frame, Brooklyn-style brick bungalow that looks like every other bungalow on a narrow street of government houses.

One lonely Israeli guard in a khaki-colored Nehru jacket stood outside the doorway to Peres's office, with a small transistor military radio plugged into his ear.

Peres waved me in with the seemingly relaxed air of a man who isn't fazed a bit by working seventeen hours a day.

(When Peres took office as Prime Minister in 1984, his hand-picked cadre of thirtysomething "boys" soon discovered that none of them could match his pace or his ability to forgo sleep.) Still, Peres clearly seemed worn out from politics, not work. His speech was softer than ever, barely audible. His eyes showed fatigue.

He seemed almost relieved that this interview fell outside the boundaries of his daily battles. His mood became philosophical, dreamy, and he looked off into space. The poet in Shimon Peres rose to the surface. His recollections of books and specific lines from dusty works he'd read long ago brought to mind his Tel Aviv Labor Party office, which had been stacked with books. His desk, shelves along the walls, even the long conference table had been buried under recently published works.

"For many Americans," said Peres, "Israel represents the most solid thing in life: the past. Their own past and their forefathers' past. It rings a bell somewhere in the souls of Americans. A Bible Belt song like 'Let My People Go' stems really from those undecided and faraway times. Even black American people believe that Jerusalem is part of their own heaven.

"Israel represents the picture that Americans most admire: small and fighting, free and aggressive. The early Americans, battling the Indians, were a real mix of naïveté and cruelty. In this sense, perhaps Israel is a reminder of their history.

"And the Jewish people in America have a special place in the American mind. From time to time, it is hard to support them, but even more often, it is easy to rest back and admire them. I read a wonderful book, poorly written, detailing the creation of Hollywood by American Jews. The book claims that since the Jewish people were rejected from the American dream, they created an American dream of their own, which became the American dream in celluloid—more American, more dreamy, than the previous myth.

"I think about a man like Ronald Reagan, who acquired a love for Israel but has never been here. I once appeared with Governor Jerry Brown before the Union of Meat Cutters in San Diego. He made a wonderful speech. He said, 'Well, I live on my salary. I never invested in anything. The only thing I am going to invest in are the bonds of Israel, because I love Israel. If you would show me a map and ask me to identify Israel, I probably wouldn't find it. But Israel is in my heart.'

"Many Americans don't know where Israel is, but they know Israel is in their hearts. When Truman recognized Israel, it was more because of sentimental reasons than realistic ones."

Shimon Peres's personal relationship with the United States is perhaps unique among people of his generation, dating back to his young-adult years following the 1948 war. As the twenty-six-year-old head of the Israeli naval services, Peres arrived with his family at Ellis Island on Thanksgiving Day. Reminiscing about those days, his eyes began to sparkle; he suddenly looked younger.

"I shall never forget the time I first arrived in America," said Peres. "I had a normal passport with a diplomatic visa. The customs people looked at it, didn't understand what sort of passport it was, so they put us up overnight. I felt then the harshness of America.

"I didn't speak a word of English. I was there to represent the Ministry of Defense and to attend school. You see, I didn't have any formal education. But I had read a story that the New School for Social Research in New York would accept foreign students. I enrolled, went to the first lesson, and didn't understand a word.

"The teacher was talking about the psychology of economics. I didn't know what 'psychology' was. So I went back home, took the dictionary, went over all the *s*'s and all the *c*'s to discover there was not such a word. It took me quite a while to understand that psychology is what we call in Hebrew *psychologia*. But after a while, I started to get *A*'s in English.

"How could I get *A*'s? I asked the same question. The answer was the progress that I made. The professor was so kind, so encouraging. Ellis Island one night, and the university the next. Which demonstrates the distance one can make in the United States in such a short time.

"And then I became acquainted with the great American institutions: the *New York Times*, the educated *New Yorker*, the press, *Time*, Radio City Music Hall, the airports, the universities, the life—and finally the people. I enjoyed it tremendously. I learned the freedom of movement. I loved this period very much. For me it was meaningful.

"I like in America the tremendous curiosity. Israel is a nation of curiosity, but the people are more conservative. America is a conservative country, but the people are more curious. From the gossip columns to the scientific departments in the papers. For the marginal, for the unknown, for the rare, and for the unconventional. America is a people which is ready to try, to try and try again."

Yitzhak Rabin, Defense Minister and former Prime Minister, does not believe there are cultural or human differences between Americans and Israelis. Asked about this, Rabin at first responded angrily, his voice sharpening, and his cool, blue eyes turning to frost. "I'm not going to talk about the human dimensions," he snapped. "It's not a question of human research. It's a question of issues. I will not elaborate on personalities."

Few would characterize Rabin as a warm person, but he is always direct and cordial. Evidently the term *human dimension* carried an unintended and offensive meaning to Rabin. He listened to the words but heard "gossip." It was a good thing I didn't open with references to the "love affair" between the United States and Israel; he might have thrown me out of the room.

When the question was rephrased to ask for his perspective on the contrasting approaches to basic issues, Rabin visibly softened. "Oh, that's different."

He then launched into a forty-minute emotive exposition on the characteristic American inability to understand the sensitivities of Israeli security concerns, "which can be acute for the Israeli public but look almost minor to the Americans"; the dangers inherent in any U.S. effort to impose a final peace settlement on Israel ("I can tell you that any attempt by the United States to link the Israeli peace initiative to a permanent solution will lead nowhere"); and the naïveté of American policymakers in upgrading the dialogue with the PLO ("If I were an American, I would ask the administration, 'Have you got anything in return?' ").

Yitzhak Rabin doesn't mince words. His Spartan nature and raw turn of phrase—qualities that unnerve Americans—are the very characteristics that make him perhaps the most trusted political figure in Israel. An Israeli admirer of Rabin once confided, "Everyone says that Rabin has an analytical mind; I say he has an analytical mouth—very little emotion."

In April 1986 Rabin's directness shocked an American corporate delegation of aerospace officials. President Reagan and Defense Secretary Caspar Weinberger had invited Israel to join the Strategic Defense Initiative. This delegation of aerospace engineers was visiting Israel to examine the potential for joint cooperation on space-related technology.

Rabin had agreed to serve as the official host during their stay in Israel and to provide the good offices of the Defense Ministry in organizing their agenda. Ironically, it took months of negotiations, as well as the personal intervention of both Yitzhak Rabin and then–Prime Minister Shimon Peres to convince the Israeli corporate and government bureaucracy that the Americans were not coming to steal their secrets.

Until that time, Israel's defense community had always dealt with its American counterparts company by company or one on one, and was leery of discussing its capabilities in a forum setting, even though no press was allowed and the deliberations were entirely off the record. (Two years later I learned that what they were most worried about was that the Americans might stumble on information concerning top-secret plans for the Amos satellite launch in 1989.)

Once the Americans finally arrived in Israel, however, the schedule proceeded like clockwork. The generous hospi-

tality featured a special dinner hosted by Rabin and a slew of
top military brass at a military base, with an after-dessert
concert by an ensemble of young cadets playing stunning
chamber music.

The Americans were purring, Rabin took the microphone, and that's when it happened. Rabin's opening statement was a compliment to President Reagan for bombing
Libya only forty-eight hours earlier. Rabin's second remark,
as he peered around the room, went something like this:
"Gentlemen, I'm very glad to receive you, but I don't know
what you're doing here, since your government has not yet
signed the Strategic Defense Initiative agreement with the
State of Israel." There was dead silence.

Without missing a beat, Rabin then launched into a
twenty-minute speech on mutual opportunities in the SDI
arena. Meanwhile, twenty-two confused U.S. defense types
were sneaking glances at each other, attempting to discern
whether they had heard what they thought they had heard, or
if what they all thought they had heard differed from what
Rabin had actually said.

Another classic example of Rabin's candor is his now-
infamous order, in response to mounting deaths during the
intifada, for his soldiers to "break their bones" instead of
killing Palestinian combatants in the West Bank and Gaza.
"He thought he was giving an order the U.S. government
would welcome," said a close aide. "The idea was to impose
punishment but to reduce the number of deaths. Unfortunately, it came out sounding worse."

Rabin's unfettered turn of phrase is even more evident
when he's the injured party, especially where the U.S. government is involved. The kidnapping of Sheik Obeid, for instance, was definitely a Rabin initiative, but his decision also
represented a consensus at the highest echelons of the Israeli
government. Israel had three hostages in Lebanon, and all
efforts to free them over the years had collapsed.

Although Americans clearly value human life, we do not
define inaction on behalf of our military or civilian hostages

as a national sacrilege. For Israelis, there are few priorities as urgent as the rescue of a soldier.

"The U.S. government's outraged reaction to the Obeid kidnapping and the so-called retribution against Colonel Higgins hurt Rabin," a senior adviser confided, "because both the American and Israeli governments knew that the Hezbollah had really killed Colonel Higgins eight months earlier. The Iranian Foreign Minister, Velayati, had told that to U.N. Secretary General Pérez de Cuéllar, who in turn informed the Americans."

According to this same high-level Israeli source, the Americans and the Israelis both knowingly "participated in a 'cover-up' out of fear that an acknowledgment would only further incite the Hezbollah, leading to more killings."

He continued, "But the Americans let everyone think that Higgins was murdered because of Israel's abduction of Obeid. The fact that Higgins was already dead came out very slowly, very vaguely. What was said behind closed Israeli doors? 'American bastards.'

"Rabin doesn't ever show his feelings. What he said was, 'We did it for our hostages, we're responsible, and I don't care what the world thinks.' He withdrew into his shell. That was his reaction."

"Hurt?" said a Rabin aide. "Let's say that if Rabin gets criticism from Thatcher or Mitterand, it's less than one sentence by Robert Dole. The remarks by Dole hurt him. But on the other hand, he immediately could recount Dole's entire past, all of his curriculum vitae, his entire relationship with the State of Israel. Rabin is like a walking archive, and he remembers everyone according to their relationship with Israel."

The Israeli assertion about Colonel Higgins is difficult to confirm with absolute certainty. But Rabin's perspective on the incident does touch the nerve center of the American-Israeli relationship. In the aftermath of the Obeid action, one of the most senior White House advisers to the President told an Israeli diplomat that Israel "should never have risked it, because the media value of a dead American is so much greater than a dead Israeli."

"I know he didn't mean to suggest that an Israeli life is worth less than an American life," said the Israeli, "but that's the way it sounded."

Yitzhak Rabin is often described as the most complex Israeli leader, and certainly the most guarded. His feelings about the United States are like an onion—many-layered, and sweet or severe depending on the way you approach him. If an outsider asks Rabin to talk about his views, he will frame his response almost entirely in political and strategic terms. But when several of Rabin's rare confidants described his views, the picture they painted of the man was much more emotional.

Chief of Staff during the Six-Day War, Rabin was sent to Washington in the euphoric atmosphere that followed. His memories of the United States from that period are "of flying colors." He was received by the White House and the public more as a head of state than an ambassador. "There is no doubt about it," said one friend, "for him, the United States is like a second home. Those were the nicest days in his life.

"They paid tribute to him everywhere. All his positive feedback from the war was in the States. Rabin was the guest of honor wherever he went."

Rabin's assignment to Washington in his late thirties was also the first time he left Israel, apart from his participation in a brief military course in England as a young soldier. The focus of his entire political career has been the United States. During his five-year stay as ambassador, Rabin became an expert on the American government and Congress, and two decades later believes he is the only one who really understands America.

"Until now," said a friend, "no one in the Israeli establishment would dare to teach him even a word. Every senator and congressman wants to see him because he knew them in their previous political lives. Shimon Peres was the Francophile who turned to the U.S. when de Gaulle deserted Israel. But Rabin was always there."

A former aide insisted that when Rabin travels to the States, he "acts like an American." As an example, the aide said, "Once he told us, 'Don't laugh too much—the Americans don't like it.'"

According to the same aide, Rabin is a first-class fundraiser for Jewish organizations: "For Rabin, it is part of his life. He would stand up at a microphone and say, 'Joe, how come only ten thousand dollars?!'" On a strategic basis, Rabin maintains that without the political, economic, and military support of the United States, "it would be very difficult to live here [in Israel]. He understands that we depend on the United States."

What about his statements or actions that strain the relationship? "Look, he does care," said a colleague, "but sometimes he feels he has no alternative."

Moshe Arens agreed to be interviewed at seven in the evening on July 9, 1989. Although the sky was still light, it might as well have been midnight, he appeared so weary and drained. Four days earlier, speaking before the Likud Central Committee, Prime Minister Shamir had agreed to several limiting conditions on his West Bank/Gaza election plan—demanded by political rivals Ariel Sharon, David Levi, and Yitzhak Modai. The resulting rash of cables and harsh words emanating from Washington were a particular blow for Arens, who had worked so hard to pump new life into the Washington-Likud relationship.

Under these circumstances, Arens's willingness to be interviewed seemed a perfect example of Israeli leaders' readiness to stretch their already debilitating schedules, irrespective of the daily crises, to fit in x number of Americans.

Despite his fatigue, Arens, no less than Rabin, was lucid and precise in defining the gaps between the United States and Israel. The Israeli-born Rabin, who rose to the top ranks of the military as Chief of Staff, and Arens, who settled in Israel in the 1950s after earning his aeronautical engineering degree in the United States and completing a two-year stint in the U.S. Army, responded almost identically, although interviewed separately. For both men, all the clashes in understanding could be reduced to one word: geography.

"I think the gaps are primarily geographic in nature," said Arens. "It is very difficult for people in the United States to share the feeling of anxiety that Israelis have living in the Middle East, and to fully understand the environmental conditions under which Israel has to exist and survive."

Arens admitted, "Compared to some in the United States, people in Israel seem paranoid about their security. I think this is the result of a perception gap and perhaps a natural tendency in the United States to look at the Middle East as if it was the Midwest. As if it was an area similar in nature to the United States and therefore amenable to analysis that you would apply to the United States.

"I don't think that the gap is really one of culture. There are quite a few Americans in Israel, even if I'm the only American in the Israeli Cabinet. We've had a Prime Minister from the United States, Mrs. Meir, and a Deputy Foreign Minister, Yehuda Ben-Meir. There are many Americans in Israel in key positions. And there's probably no key Israeli who hasn't spent a great deal of time in the United States. It's simply the Middle Eastern environment that is very strange to people in the United States."

Rabin had put it more bluntly: "The basic difference is that we are here and the United States is there—which means we experience and perceive reality differently. Israel's independence was gained at war. Israel's existence and security have to be based on our capacity to defend ourselves by ourselves. Therefore, it's only natural that the danger for Israel, the way that we see it, is much more acute than the way that the United States perceives the danger for Israel.

"We cannot rely on guarantees given from the outside. Even a peace treaty with an Arab country depends on the stability of the regime. An international treaty is not like the Bible and not like the Koran in the Middle East.

"Then comes the question of what is needed for Israel's defense. By no means can any Israeli government, or any

Israeli Minister of Defense, aspire to parity in numbers of planes, tanks, divisions, et cetera."

Arens, as well as Rabin, expressed frustration that Americans are always seeking a quick American solution on Middle East terrain. "Americans rarely understand just how difficult and intractable the problems of the Middle East are," said Arens. "I think that the desire to solve problems is characteristic of the Western mind, including the Israeli mind. We are confident of our ability to analyze a situation, to identify the problem, and to find solutions to the problem.

"But it is only by living in a Middle Eastern environment that you can fully realize that we're dealing with a problem that really does not have an easy solution and maybe not any solution in the near term. Frequently I feel the people in the United States are dealing with an idealized picture of the Middle East.

"But it takes a lot more than faxes, television, and even ambassadors and their staffs in the resident embassies to give you a full understanding. There's really no substitute for living there. Feeling it. Feeling the risks and the dangers involved."

Rabin and Arens also echoed each other on the point that it is typical to the American approach that everything has to be solved yesterday.

Rabin wryly noted, "I thought that after certain experiences—Vietnam, some problems in Latin America, the U.S. Marine peacekeeping force in Beirut—there would be—how can I say it without being insulting?—more maturity, a more realistic, pragmatic approach toward the idea of solving everything yesterday. Sometimes 'open sesame' solutions, shortcuts lead to the exact opposite—not bringing peace or even tranquility closer, but bringing a deadlock and even an explosion."

Nevertheless, Rabin and Arens both insisted that the United States has a paramount role to play in any future peace process, that without American leadership, all efforts will be doomed to failure. "The fact remains," said Rabin, "that without the United States leading the peace process, it would cease to be viewed as a major issue throughout the rest of the world. The Palestinians also carry a tremendous burden of suffering. And they too would like to see the light at the end of the tunnel."

Ironically, it was the soft-spoken Arens who talked in starker terms about whether or not the United States would always be there for Israel in the future: "Have I been touched by the warmth and the human relations between the United States and Israel? There is no doubt about it. There's no precedent for the special relationship we share, I believe, in the spectrum of the relationships the United States has with other countries and possibly not even in the history of relationships between countries.

"And it's certainly very touching that, despite the differences in perception that we just talked about, and despite the tremendous geographic distances, such a close relationship has been built up between two countries that in many ways are so different.

"But I don't think it would be correct to say that the United States has always been there for Israel. The United States was not always there for Israel. Not in 1948, when Israel's fate hung in the balance. Not in 1956, when Israel was fighting a crucial battle against terrorism that came out of the Sinai at the time, and out of the Gaza strip. The United States was not there for Israel in June of 1967. In sympathy it may have been there, but Israel stood all alone in 1967, beleaguered and threatened by the surrounding Arab world.

"In 1948 there were many people in the State Department who didn't think that a Jewish state should be salvaged, and believed that U.S. interests dictated a close relationship with the Arab world. The United States embargoed a shipment of arms to Israel in 1948," said Arens, recalling these events from forty years ago as if they had just occurred.

"The government prohibited arms shipments to Israel, including rifles. I'm not talking about tanks or airplanes. We were facing regular Arab armies with small militias and no arms to speak of. The Egyptians, Syrians, and Jordanians had tanks, aircraft. The Egyptians had a navy. And Israel was embargoed.

"In 1956, President Eisenhower was very upset at what he considered collusion among Israel, France, and the United Kingdom. He thought it was essential to restore the situation to what it was before the Sinai Campaign. He didn't have any understanding of Israel's problems and the dangers we faced.

"And in 1967 there simply was not the readiness to take the risks, as they were perceived, in coming to Israel's aid by running the blockade Egypt had imposed on the port at Eilat. The sympathy was there, but that was it. It wasn't enough."

Arens stressed that the United States *was* "there" during the Yom Kippur War. "But again," he said, "it was Israel that withstood the onslaught, and it was Israel that beat the onslaught back. The United States did what it was capable of doing, which of course was very important.

"Living in the Middle East is hard times. It isn't just a question of the U.S.-Israeli relationship. It's a very difficult part of the world, maybe *the* most difficult. And it may very well be that in years to come we will not find full agreement between Israel and the United States in how we should advance toward peace in the Middle East. The fabric that binds us has considerable strength, and I do not think disagreements will lead to an unraveling. But we'll have to contend with that reality if that turns out to be the case."

Chaim Herzog, President of Israel, believes that the United States and Israel are "good friends." As Ambassador to the United Nations during the mid-1970s, he may have been one of the few Israelis who dealt with the U.S. government during a brief moment in history when the two countries enjoyed a mutual understanding on important issues.

Senator Patrick Moynihan was then U.S. Ambassador to the United Nations, and Henry Kissinger was Secretary of State. "Kissinger, Moynihan, and I would meet at the beginning of each General Assembly to go over the entire agenda,"

Herzog reminisced. "We knew in advance where we could hope for support and where we could not. We knew where we stood."

Herzog's tenure at the United Nations endured through three Presidents—Nixon, Ford, and Carter—and three ambassadors: Patrick Moynihan, William Scranton, and Andrew Young. He developed personal relationships with all three of his colleagues that reflected the strength of the American-Israeli bond.

Moynihan presided during the famous U.N. debate equating Zionism with racism, which went on for over six weeks and "brought us very close." It turned into a major battle and was finally brought to a vote in committee. "At the end, I raised my voice very loud indeed and called out that this will go down in history," Herzog said. "I said, 'We, the Jewish people who have been through so much, will never forget.' "

The most moving moment for Herzog came in the wake of defeat. A majority voted against Israel and for the resolution. Herzog instructed his delegation to be "utterly impassive, as if it didn't affect them at all." He recalls, "The Arabs began to cheer and mock. And you could see the blood going to Moynihan's head. He was on the other side of the room. I shall never forget it. Moynihan stood up, straightened his tie, and closed his jacket very deliberately—his face all red—and he walked right across the floor.

"I was standing on the other side of this big circle. Moynihan came over to me, took my arm, embraced me. In front of the whole bang lot. And then he uttered a pretty common four-letter word about what we could do to all those ———.

"The man who had spoken in that committee for us was the late Clarence Mitchell, the black civil rights leader. He supported us tremendously."

Scranton was U.S. Ambassador during the 1976 Entebbe debate following the daring Israeli mission. Said Herzog, "He departed from the text of the speech sent to him by the State Department, to support the Israeli operation. He said it [the mission] electrified the world in the most superlative way."

Were the Americans easy to get close to? "Yes, but the decision-making process took time. On many occasions it had to be approved by the President. But still they really were very easy to get to. The U.S. diplomats always upheld their own principles and their own policy."

Chaim Herzog views the gaps in understanding between the United States and Israel as largely tied to our different systems of government. Although both are democracies, "in general, we Israelis have a different approach. You have to remember, we have this rotten electoral system, which is a catastrophe, making our government dependent on minority groups and fractional groups.

"The President of the United States is elected, period. He therefore has all the authority in the world to represent the United States in talking to us. And, of course, his whole staff does. Israeli leaders are forever walking between the raindrops, walking on eggs, so as not to upset this or that minority group."

Ariel Sharon cannot understand why he has been described as an enemy of the United States, or why American officials have continuously boycotted him since 1982—in the wake of the Israeli invasion of Lebanon (the "Peace for Galilee Operation"), which he spearheaded as Defense Minister.

Sharon was forced to step down from his ministerial post by an Israeli investigatory commission, which held him accountable for the Lebanese Christian massacre of Palestinians in the Sabra and Shattila refugee camps in September 1982. Those were black days for the U.S. government, for Israel, and for the Jewish people. The massacre took place during the Jewish New Year celebrations.

When he was Minister of Trade and Industry, Sharon gave an interview at his office in the converted Palace Hotel Jerusalem, with its high ceilings, winding staircases, and palatial echoes of a distant Turkish past. There were few such buildings in all of Israel; it was virtually rebuilt from the ground up since 1948 with efficient, low-cost materials and serviceable architectural design.

Even in Jerusalem, where it is mandated by law that all new buildings be constructed with the famous soft-beige-and-pink Jerusalem stone—reflecting the sunlight with hues of golden red—home and office interiors are typically designed to be serviceable, not romantic.

Sharon's outer office was full of tall, green plants, and colorful Israeli posters hugged the walls. His team of young female secretaries, all wearing blue jeans, with gold rings covering their childlike hands, rushed to offer the visitor a chair and coffee.

At exactly the stroke of 5 P.M., a senior aide appeared in the doorway of Sharon's inner office to apologize. "The Minister asked me to say how sorry he is that he will be delayed by several more minutes." Six minutes passed, eight people filed out of Sharon's quarters, and I was asked to enter.

Ariel Sharon was wearing a navy blue summer suit, a light blue shirt, and a blue tie with red stripes. Closely cropped white hair framed green eyes. The man resembles a cross between a racehorse and a bear, a human energy field lumbering forward. Heavyset and of medium height, Sharon radiates raw power even before he utters a single word.

"I've been described as an enemy of the United States," Sharon complained. "This is how my own people color me, how they try to create my image. But it's not true.

"I feel great friendship toward the United States. My differences with them are not personal. I know how it developed. They were not used to the way I talk. I believe things should be put on the table when it comes to Israel and Jewish life.

"I remember one day a certain U.S. ambassador came and raised his voice. I said, 'I don't know how you talked to my predecessor, but as long as I'm here, you will never dare to raise your voice.' Now, Dick Fairbanks wasn't like that—he was nice." As noted earlier, the whole matter of raised voices is one of the ironies of cross-cultural perceptions.

Regardless of what I asked Sharon on this occasion, he returned to the same theme: Why was the U.S. government ignoring him? He had had little contact with Ambassador

William Brown even though Sharon had launched an ultimately successful campaign to dilute Shamir's proposed election plan for the West Bank and Gaza at the July meeting of
the Likud Central Committee.

"The American government did not understand how we
could succeed," Sharon commented. "They were caught by
surprise when Shamir agreed to our terms. Yet I have not
seen the ambassador for at least two months. He came to see
me this week with Senator Hatch, twenty-four hours before
the Likud meeting. It was very friendly, but there was no
time to discuss the issues. There has been no deep contact
with your government.

"They believed Shamir was going to win. But they never
came to discuss the problem. It's important for the U.S. and
for Israel that the parameters be made clear—what Israel
can do and what Israel can never do."

Speaking about miscommunications, Sharon recalled a
"rare" tense exchange with Ambassador Richard Fairbanks
in 1979 concerning Jewish settlements in the West Bank when
Sharon was Minister of Agriculture: "We were sitting with a
group of Americans and Egyptians in a beautiful old palace
in Alexandria. I was asked whether I planned to establish
new settlements. I said, as a joke, 'If you ask me about sites,
the answer is no—but about size, they will be bigger, and in
the future perhaps they will all be one.' It was a joke, a thing
to say on a long, beautiful afternoon.

"Coming home to Israel, I announced that there would be
new settlements. Fairbanks called, very upset. He said, 'But
you promised to limit the settlements to an increase in size.'
That's when I understood that you have to be very careful not
to joke with Americans."

Sharon insisted that his fight with the U.S. government
was emanating from Israel, instigated by his opponents
within. Even some of his closest advisers told me that Sharon
cannot grasp that the U.S. failure in the Lebanon War still
hovers like a permanent cloud over the U.S. Departments of
State and Defense, nor does he understand he remains the
target for these frustrated memories.

"The Bush Administration believes they can start a peace process without ending the *intifada*. It's a mistake. If I could talk to them, it would be different," Sharon insisted.

Surprisingly, the Israeli cabinet had thus far never discussed possible solutions to the political impasse with the Palestinians in the West Bank and Gaza. "If, instead of the hundreds or thousands of hours we spent debating this plan with members of the Likud Central Committee, we had allocated just three hours to one cabinet meeting, perhaps the situation would be different," he said.

"But we have never had a single discussion of possible solutions, even though our inner cabinet is composed of the best people to do so, including two former Prime Ministers. I suggested that Rabin and I prepare a range of scenarios. It was never accepted."

Ariel Sharon, the most feared Israeli in U.S. government circles, concluded the meeting with a "Sharonic" two-pronged message: "We understand the meaning of peace, and I believe we can arrive at peace. It is a pity the Americans don't keep contact or discuss it with me.

"But no one can preach to us about peace. American representatives, most of them, cannot accept that there can be a Jew from a small country in the Middle East who stands and talks as an equal. Unfortunately, this is not the way people here speak to them. As an Israeli and as a Jew, I don't feel I owe anything to anyone but God."

Sharon is both reviled and revered within Israeli society. But why do even his most strident opponents speak of him with awe and respect? "The legend is that he is very brave and ready to risk himself," said Batya Keinan, who represents the far left of the Israeli peace camp. "Sharon is ready to die, even if he makes you die in the process."

His relations with U.S. Ambassador Morris Draper have been notoriously difficult. One evening, Draper and Philip Habib were having a late-night heated session with Sharon, when Habib noticed that Sharon's staff was falling asleep. Habib quipped, "Look at all these young guys falling asleep, except for you, me, and Mr. Draper." Sharon didn't miss a beat. "A lot of Israelis are hoping that Mr. Draper will go to sleep for a long, long time," he said.

Draper emphasized that there was "incredible hostility between myself and Sharon, because I was at the forefront of trying to convince Haig to stop the Israelis from going into Lebanon." But underscoring the man's complexity, Draper recalled a private all-day visit to Sharon's home, when "he couldn't have been nicer."

Draper also recalled an incident involving Richard Vites, second in command at the U.S. embassy in Tel Aviv. Vites's wife had given him as a birthday gift a beautiful Arabian mare, which died only two weeks later. Vites was deeply upset. The next day, Vites received a surprise call from Minister Ariel Sharon. Also a horse lover with about twelve mares on his private farm, Sharon had heard about the loss.

"I never liked you," Sharon said, "but any man who loves horses as much as you can't be all bad. You're a supercilious American WASP, but please accept one of my mares as a gift. Come and choose any one that you want." Vites couldn't accept the gift, but he was moved.

"Did you know," Draper asked, "that Sharon has a law degree, and he also plays the violin?"

21
WILL YOU STILL LOVE ME WHEN I'M SIXTY-FOUR?

IT IS SAID THAT ONLY CHILDREN AND FOOLS PROPHESIZE about the future. Still, just as water carves its own pathway over time, the future of the American-Israeli relationship is already taking form.

A decade ago, Ehud Olmert was a young Likud member of the Knesset. Today he holds a ministerial portfolio and is touted as a major player in Israel's future. An interview in a popular Tel Aviv restaurant where Olmert, like many of his political colleagues, often holds court was his third or fourth restaurant meeting of the afternoon. Several more people were patiently waiting for him at different tables, and the waiter repeatedly brought over a cellular phone for incoming calls.

Olmert talked about the future of the American-Israeli love affair in almost a personal metaphor and with surprising candor. "The relationship which was shining and burning twenty years ago is changing," he said. "Israel is no longer a child, or an adolescent. Israel is a mature person that is growing a little bit fatter and losing some of its hair. It's baldish in some places. And the smile is not always very shiny. Some of the grace has been lost.

"We are not always in love with what we are or the image that we produce. But America is also changing in a slower but perhaps an equally significant, definite way. The America that we face today socially and politically is entirely different from the country that it was twenty years ago even. The role of the blacks, Hispanics, of the Japanese, Chinese, Koreans is changing the face of American business and politics.

"America, indeed, is no longer dominated by a WASP minority projecting emotions and memories of its own past. If I read America correctly, the values of European culture, the memories which were so influential in creating a framework for attitudes toward Israel, are not as central as they used to be.

"I'm afraid that America will change slowly, but in this direction. And therefore the sense of commitment, affiliation, what Israel represents—a sense of guilt to the Jewish people—will not be as it was. Israel in the future will be judged not so much by historical memories but by present performance.

"Who in America will have the time and the intellectual curiosity to study the historical framework, the larger picture? All they know is what they watch on TV. And that's not too inspiring these days, because the one missing element in television is the historical perspective.

"But whether we like or not, reality has its own reason. It forces itself on you. When Secretary Baker comes and says, 'You know it's time for you to set aside your visions, your dreams,' what he is reflecting first and foremost is that America has to set aside its visions and dreams about Israel." He paused.

"Perhaps I'm being too blunt. It is entirely immaterial whether Bush or Baker had visions about Israel in the past that they don't have today, although I believe Reagan and Shultz had such a vision. The new generation of leaders is reflecting a new emphasis in the perceptions of Israel in terms represented by Baker.

"I don't know Baker personally, but some of his friends,

people acquainted with him, told me he sees Israel as a partner for a deal. Israel is not a partner for a dream. Maybe Baker does not have dreams.

"Why should I neglect my dreams? Why should I set them aside? It gives me a historical sense of purpose. And that's what irritated me about Baker's view. I am perfectly ready to accept advice from a friend, and I'm sure that in his own way he considers himself a friend. Definitely those who wrote his speech were friends. Some of them are fellow Jews.

"I find that America is filled today with brilliant businesspeople making fascinating and exciting deals. But I fail to see the larger dream lying behind it. The warmth, the human touch, the vision are not there. The Bush Administration reflects this practical brilliance, but also the cool attitude. The world is changing, America is changing, and Israel no longer looks the way it did in the past. Does that make me feel bad? Not necessarily.

"The essence of life is continuous change. If you try to act like twenty when you're forty, you look ridiculous. I look at myself, for example.

"When old friends come to see me, I sometimes sense in their attitudes a kind of frustration or disappointment. They remember a very young person coming to the Knesset at the age of twenty-eight, with a head full of hair, always needing a haircut. He had great enthusiasm and was an outspoken crime buster. He was fighting everything, making waves every day.

"Now they say to me, 'You are different. You are dressed in tailor-made suits, and you are having a good time. And we heard that you are a successful attorney, making money. So where is the young, vibrant, ecstatic young man that you were?'

"And I say, 'I'm not that young man anymore because I'm not young anymore. I've matured. And what I'm interested in at the age of forty-three is not what I would have been interested in at the age of twenty-eight. If I were the same as I was, it would be a sign of weakness.'

"So perhaps the State of Israel is also passing through a

phase of maturity. We may wind up maturing the right way—
more balanced, less euphoric about what we are and what we
hope to be, more realistic, and confident about what we can
achieve and should achieve.

"In this sense, I believe we can be a great partner for the
United States. Some people tell me that sex at the age of
forty-five is different. I'm not yet forty-five, so of course I'm
not talking about myself. . . . But they say the emotions of
enthusiasm and the excitement from an early stage in a relationship can be replaced by a maturity which is rewarding
and satisfying. I think that we can have that kind of relationship with America. The novelty is not there anymore. We
know each other's weaknesses.

"We must get used to living with these weaknesses and
accept them with some compassion, some tolerance. American Jews also perceive Israel in a different way, relative to
the past. The unconditional enthusiasm and total acceptance
of everything that we represent is gone.

"The conflict with the Palestinians is not the only reason.
We are talking about an ongoing process that we have all
consistently denied over the years. Most American Jews do
not know Israel, have never been to Israel, never cared
enough to show more than general curiosity about Israel. The
Six-Day War was a dramatic turning point and a peak. There
will never be such a peak again, the same feeling of exultation.

"In a very naive and childish way, we really hoped that
forty years would be enough to solve all of Israel's problems.
This nation fought two thousand years for resurrection, and
we believed we could find solutions in forty years. It's not
serious. It's immature. The process takes time.

"We must find peace with the Arabs. I said to Geula
Cohen, Knesset member from the right wing Tehiya party,
'Sure, all of Eretz Israel is ours, but Begin apparently was
more sober than many of us when, having all the power to
integrate the West Bank into the State of Israel lock, stock,
and barrel in 1977, he refrained from doing it.'

"Why did he refrain from doing it? Was it because he didn't know that Judaea and Samaria were part of Israel? Was he not fighting for Eretz Israel long before such critics as Geula Cohen knew what Greater Israel was all about? Was he not the protector of this concept, perhaps more than any other person in Israel? And look what happened.

"When he assumed the position of Prime Minister, single-handedly controlling the entire government—able to call the day night and the night day—he refrained from doing just what he had been fighting for all his life. Because he understood that the reality of being Prime Minister is not the same as the desire of an opposition leader and that life is more complicated than rhetoric. I want a Greater Israel as much as Geula Cohen wants it. But perhaps it will take another two hundred years to achieve it, and in the meantime, we must have peace."

Israeli officials and Jewish-American officials specializing in the Middle East are sensitive about discussing their feelings toward one another as future partners in the peace process. Only in the last decade have American Jews been tapped for foreign policy positions concerning the Middle East and U.S.-Israeli relations. The sensitivities have been especially sharpened in the Bush Administration, in which most of the senior Middle East positions are held by American Jews—all of them dedicated and accomplished foreign policy professionals, deeply committed to a peaceful future for the State of Israel. Their views on the most effective path to peace, however, have been known to grate on the nerves of some Israeli officials, particularly in the Likud camp.

An American Jew "near the top" began expressing obvious pain when the subject arose—discomfort that was as evident in the hurt look in his eyes as in the emotional intensity of his words. "Israelis don't believe we can be accepted by the non-Jewish establishment," he said, "or that we can rise to the top in an open system and still retain our Jewishness.

"They may attack our views, but I believe they are really

jealous. We have defied every pronouncement of the last two thousand years that it is impossible to establish a normal life in the Diaspora.

"Initially they saw people like myself as a plus; now they see us as an obstacle. They're manic about our role, seeing us as either brothers in arms or enemies. They can't get it right."

On the Israeli side, the pain expressed was less personal, but no less acute. "Of course it is painful when American Jews are at the forefront of actions harmful to us," said an Israeli of stature, "especially when we see that the American Jew's entire judgment is colored by his predicament, and he therefore moves to the extremes in his analysis.

"I don't want extremes. I want a clear projection of American interests. But sometimes this kind of person unfortunately believes that he can put himself in our shoes and in the Arab shoes at the same time."

By way of explaining Israeli feelings about American Jewish "adversaries," both within the U.S. government and without, another Israeli related a story from the Bible. Twenty years after Jacob stole Esau's birthright, Jacob returned to the Land of Canaan. "It is said in the Bible that when a Jew faces an adversary, he should first try to bribe him, second pray to God, and third prepare for war. When Jacob sees his brother coming to meet him, he prays, prepares for war, and sends a present. Then Jacob bows to his brother seven times.

"The rabbis of the Bible criticized Jacob for bowing to his brother. The great sages said that, because [Jacob] bowed to his brother seven times, Esau was given the privilege of establishing a kingdom that would take seven successions before an independent kingdom of Jacob would be established.

"This story," the Israeli said, "should fully explain to you how we feel."

Americans root their visions of the future in the present, while Israelis project their future from the past. Continuing the parable about Jacob and Esau, a senior Israeli official

reached back almost four thousand years into history to portray the inevitable sensitivities of future relations with the
United States.

"Jacob also sent word to Esau, 'Tell my brother Esau, "So
says your brother and slave Jacob."' Twelve hundred years
later, the President of Judaea, Yehuda Hanasi, sent a letter to
the Roman Emperor using the same words, 'from your slave.'

"This shows you that the Jewish people never developed a
code of relationships with the outside world. The President of
Judaea saw himself as a supplicant, even though he was the
president of an independent country speaking to a peer, and
in spite of the fact that he, Yehuda Hanasi, was the great sage
who codified Jewish law.

"You see, this tale is registered in the Jewish Talmud as
a lesson for posterity. When our Prime Minister sends a
letter to the President of the United States, from what tradition does he draw? What is the point at which the Prime
Minister fails to project an independent view as the leader of
a sovereign state, but instead goes over into wording consis-
tent with a supplicant?

"Formulation has an impact. Even the way we Israelis
write a letter can determine our fate. Jews were never equal
at any time, in any place. Therefore we Israelis cannot break
away from looking back."

It is ironic that the lands of blackest memories for Jews in
the twentieth century—Eastern Europe and the Soviet
Union—are suddenly being described by Israelis as the light
to their future. Israel entered the 1990s on the wings of
revolutionary social change that could mean several hundred
thousand new Soviet and Eastern European immigrants ar-
riving in the next few years.

Yet, the repercussions go far beyond a population explosion or social upheaval. For Israelis of Ashkenazic descent, the
cultural doors opened to Eastern Europe and the Soviet
Union are also the doors to their past, to a heritage that for
centuries gave spiritual sustenance and comfort no less than
pain.

The prospects for political and business ties with these countries are like oxygen for so many Israelis, a return to familiar cultural manners and mores that even second- and third-generation Israelis have experienced in their homes. Several Israeli businesses have already established joint ventures in the Soviet Union, and the flights to Poland and Hungary are packed.

But "who will provide the capital?" asked Sylvia Hassenfeld. "Only the Americans." The Israelis want to barter, "but there is only so much you can barter."

"We belong to Europe," said Zohar Carthy, presaging an emerging internal Israeli debate of the 1990s. "The United States is too far away, and we are too Americanized. We must look to small European countries for our future and retake our place as part of the European culture."

"There is no turning back to European culture," countered Yehuda Amichai, Israeli poet extraordinaire. "Yes, America is without a culture of its own. But that's what I like about it. Americans are still naive, while the Europeans are terribly cynical."

Amichai has lived in Israel since 1939 and fought in five wars. If Israel were destroyed, "the only country I could live in is America," he said. "The United States is the only country where moral issues sometimes still dominate politics."

In 1963, the Los Angeles County Federation of Labor sent a delegation to Israel to celebrate the fifteenth anniversary of the state. The invitation was extended by the Israeli Labor Federation, the Histadrut. William Pollard, a leader of the Hotel and Restaurant Employees Union, was a member of that delegation.

"I shall never forget the most important figure I met and talked with—David Ben-Gurion, the father of that country," said Pollard, who has been a senior figure in the NAACP for the past two decades. "I was impressed with Israel's socioeconomic and educational concerns for its people, young and old, and with the special camaraderie.

"I did not see a perfect Israel then or on subsequent visits, but I certainly felt it was headed for a status of leadership that other countries could emulate."

William Pollard exudes an aura of gentle, grandfatherly wisdom. Of medium height, with open features and a hint of agelessness, Pollard is deputy director to the NAACP's executive director, Benjamin Hooks. He spoke on a personal basis about his admiration for Israel, echoing the perceptions and concerns of other lifelong American supporters.

During his many trips, Pollard met Meir, Rabin, Peres, Eban, and Allon, among others. "There was a kind of spirit that does not exist today," he said sadly. "I left elated over what I saw. I thought it was a great country. That is not to say I don't think it is great now, but a number of problems have arisen.

"Today my heart cries when I see Israelis beating on people, shooting those kids with what are reported to be rubber bullets. Knowing these people as I do, I can imagine what they would be saying if it was being done to them.

"I went through that Holocaust museum up to a point," he said, "and I had to come out because I just couldn't stomach what those Jews had to go through. To think that they would do that now to a bunch of children, I do not understand . . .

"I wonder what Golda Meir would say. I wonder what Ben-Gurion would say. Ben-Gurion told me, 'Bill, we don't have that stuff in Israel.' Today the leaders would say to me, 'Bill, if you're saying "Don't shoot them," what are you asking us to do? We are trying to get secure borders. That's our primary goal. What do you suggest?' "

Pollard wanted to make it clear that he doesn't care whether "they have a Palestinian state or not," but there has to be a "commitment to treat people humanely, as human beings." The attitude that prevailed at the founding of the country, he said, "was represented by people who have passed away or are in the sunset of their lives. The concern that was so beautiful during the days of Ben-Gurion and Golda Meir changed from one of softness to one of hardness and harshness. That is unfortunate, in my opinion."

American-watcher Shai Feldman mused, "Tell me about
the future of the peace process, and I can tell you about the
future of American-Israeli relations." Indeed, throughout all
of these interviews, not a single American or Israeli—from
the left or right—expressed a belief that the relationship
between the two countries would be unaffected by continuing
strife in the West Bank and Gaza. Some, however, were
simply more willing to pay the political price.

My own view, impossible to prove or defend, is that Israelis and Palestinians will find accommodation in the 1990s
through fits and starts. Oftentimes pedaling backward, with
tragic suffering and violence threatening the process, they
will inch forward toward a compromise formula for security
and dignity on both sides.

I happened to be in Israel in the days immediately following the U.S. invasion of Panama, dubbed Operation Just
Cause. To my amazement, this geographically distant event
and the reactions it triggered within Israeli society could
have greater consequence for the pace of the peace process
than any action by Yasir Arafat or other Palestinian leaders.
While the U.S. press and popular sentiment were supporting
the military operation, Israeli public opinion was starkly
negative.

Ze'ev Schiff, whose liberal credentials as a friend of the
United States are impeccable, was absolutely irate: "Even a
big power, which we look at with respect, can make a big
mistake. Size doesn't mean they are wiser or smarter or more
moral.

"For Israelis, the lesson of Panama, like Grenada, was
very simple. The United States made it clear to the world
that, when facing a conflict, they will be ready to use their
military might rather than compromise.

"In doing so, they strengthened the extremists in Israel,
who say, 'Look who is talking.' No one in Israel will ever
again accept American criticism. The Panama operation
could be used by the right as an argument against a peaceful
settlement of the Palestinian conflict.

"Add to this the ridiculous American performance. They

could have been more effective, more professional by taking
out only one man as we did with Sheik Obeid, rather than
launching an invasion that brings with it the death of so many
people and such terrible economic damage.

"There was no reason to admire the American operation,"
said Schiff. "The United States is not a light unto the nations."

Israel and the United States are both judged, rightly or
wrongly, by a higher order of commitment to serve as a light
to the world in our lives and in our judgments. The Hebrew
word for progress, *kidum*, comes from *kidima*, onward,
which derives from the word *kedem*, meaning ancient. "We
are in the middle of a circle, and by going onward, we shall
come back to the values we once had. A little light pushes
away a lot of darkness," declared Moshe Moshkovitz, a religious dove, behind-the-scenes adviser to ministers, and the
mastermind behind the creation of the world's largest biblical
theme park, to be located in Israel.

"This means that even a little country like Israel has the
power to push away the spiritual darkness of a big country
like the United States. American society is not a caring culture, but it is the most open and accepting to the light. It all
depends on us.

"In history there can be spiritual leaps. The Western
world is at the edge of a precipice, necessitating a giant jump
forward toward totally new thought. The United States is the
greatest, most powerful nation in the world, and thus more
able than any other to bring about this change."

The United States is a country on fire within; the nation
experiences a murder every twenty seconds and a rape every
four minutes, and parents live in fear of the molestation of
their children. The education provided our youth is one of the
poorest in the industrialized world, and our aged are cast
aside as refuse.

"That is different from what is happening in Israel,
where the issue is human rights," an American friend has

argued. But as an American, I too feel that my human rights are being violated by a culture so violent that the essence of "quality of life" has been reduced to financial gain.

The United States and Israel, Americans and Israelis, have each looked to the other as a reflection of the best of what each side wanted to be. As we enter the 1990s, moving toward a half-century of ties, the future of our relationship will be determined more by our internal social and spiritual progress than by strategic equations, the morality of the past, or even domestic politics.

Will we age gracefully, and together? In 1967, when Israel was young and heroic, when America was at the peak of its cultural optimism as a people having the power to challenge and right the wrongs of the past, a song came on the airwaves by the Beatles, a revolutionary young rock group capturing the hearts of the world with its universal message:

> When I get older losing my hair,
> Many years from now,
> Will you still be sending me a Valentine
> Birthday greetings bottle of wine.
>
> . . . When I'm sixty-four
> You'll be older too,
> And if you say the word,
> I could stay with you.